But Peter—kneeled down, and prayed;
and turning him to the body said, "Tabitha arise." Acts 9: 40.

# LETTERS FROM PETER

# BIBLE STUDY TEXTBOOK

# LETTERS FROM PETER

A NEW

- COMMENTARY
- WORKBOOK
- TEACHING MANUAL

Bruce Oberst

College Press, Joplin, Missouri

To My Father
HENRY W. OBERST
whose companionship I have
enjoyed, whose life for over forty
years has been that of a consistent Christian
and whose outstanding virtue
is generosity,
This Book is Lovingly
Dedicated.

# CONTENTS AND ANALYTICAL OUTLINE

## OUTLINE OF FIRST PETER

## OUTLINE OF SECOND PETER

(These various points are so interwoven throughout the chapter, that further outlining would be confusing rather than helpful.)

Suggested memory verses: 1:5-11, 19-21; 2:20-22; 3:8-13,18.

# PREFACE

The objective of *The Bible Study Textbook Series* is to improve the average Christian's knowledge and understanding of the Scriptures. I have tried to keep this objective in mind in the process of compiling this material. References are frequently made to Greek words (normally in their lexicon form), but these words are all anglicized and no knowledge of that language is necessary to understand these notes.

The *Expanded Translation* is as original as I could make it with my present knowledge and resources. It is best to consider this part of the work as an expression of the whole scope and meaning of the passage translated. For this reason, the Greek studnt will frequently notice words (and even phrases) not actually present in the original text. In those instances, the context and setting seemed to justify the insertion of such words or phrases. By this method of translation, it is hoped that misunderstandings and false ideas concerning the meaning of a passage will be kept to a minimum. But I have tried to be discreet and conservative in using words not found in the original, so that it may still be referred to as a translation and not a commentary. As a rule, words that fall within a parentheses indicate that the meaning of the previous word is being amplified; but this is not always true, and the reader may consider the decision of the translator to insert or omit these marks as purely arbitrary.

A Biographical list will be found in the closing pages. Authors and their works not mentioned in the footnotes are found there.

So many persons have assisted me in the compilation and arrangement of this volume that two or three pages would be necessary to record their names. However, a few acknowledgments are in order. To sister Eileen Crist, who has typed this entire work at least twice in the process of eliminating obscurities and errors, goes my heartfelt thanks. She has not only assisted me in this project, but in numerous others, and has never received a cent for her labors. Like Phoebe, "she hath been a helper of many, and of mine own self" (Rom. 16:2).

The encouragement of my wife has been a constant source of inspiration. She has gone out of her way to see to it that I had sufficient time to study and write. J. Charles Dailey has also provided much encouragement, with his appreciative remarks concerning the value of the book's contents. In addition, he gave many valuable suggestions concerning sentence structure and wording.

The original Scriptures were written by God through men

9

"moved by the Holy Spirit" (II Pet. 1:21). All other books were written by fallible man. This book is no exception. The author would sincerely appreciate letters pointing out ways in which the material might be improved, or his understanding of any passage made more accurate. Meanwhile, if these pages shall help some soul "grow in the grace and knowledge of Christ" (II Pet. 3:18). I shall feel genuinely rewarded.

—BRUCE OBERST

Suggested memory verses:

       1:3-5; 13-20.
       2:1-2; 10-11; 17.
       3:16 (women); 7-9 (men); 15-16; 21.
       4:15-16.
       5:5-9.

# INTRODUCTION

Commentaries on the Scriptures fall into two classes in my mind. Either they are of the "popular" variety that are superficial and often inaccurate, or they are so excessively technical that none but a reader trained in the Greek language can feel at home in them. Bruce Oberst has achieved a delicate balance between the extremes in this present volume.

As you read the expanded translation, you cannot help but feel familiar with the Holy Spirit's message through Peter. Then as you read the comments, there is enough of the technical language information to be useful for the trained reader, and yet not in a quantity discouraging to that one untrained in New Testament Greek.

Finally, there is the application of the text to contemporary life. Of what value is the Faith if it remains merely an academic profession? Our fellowship with Christ must change our conduct! Brother Oberst has splendidly applied the text to moral and ethical values and practices.

It has been my privilege to be associated with Bruce Oberst for the past seven years in the training of men to preach the unsearchable riches of Christ. The message of the Cross has deeply molded his own life and saturated his very being. The fruit of the Spirit are quickly discoverable in his everyday life. It is from this consistent Christian living that he brings forth this usable volume on the letters of Peter.

—CHARLES DAILEY, 1962

# I PETER

## A SHORT SKETCH OF THE HUMAN AUTHOR

1. Peter was a fisherman (Matt. 4:18). He continued in this trade for a while after he was led to Christ.

2. He was led to know Christ by his brother, Andrew (Jn. 1: 40-42).

3. His home-town was Bethsaida (Jn. 1:44). The location of this city is somewhat in doubt, but it was not far from Capernaum. (Compare Matt. 8:5 with verse 14 and Mk. 1:21 with verse 29.) Bethsaida means "house of fishing" or "fishery."* Most geographers locate the city on the north end of the Sea of Galilee and just to the east of the Jordan.

4. Peter was married and evidently had a family. Matt. 8:14 speaks of his wife's mother or mother-in-law being ill. The Romanists will have to admit it is rather difficult to have a mother-in-law without having a wife. Nor did he break his matrimonial ties when he was laboring so industriously as an Apostle, for he is specifically cited by Paul in I Cor. 9:5 as having a Christian wife. Furthermore, it is required of an Elder that he be married (I Tim. 3:2; Titus 1:6) and Peter was an Elder at the time he wrote the first epistle (I Pet. 5:1). "Marriage is honorable among ALL . . ." (Heb. 13:4). It is the false teacher who is "forbidding to marry" (I Tim. 4:3).

5. His father, whose name is *literally* rendered *ionas* (Jonas) has had his name variously translated as Jonas, John, Jonah, and Jona. However, all are translations of the same Greek word.

6. Being brought up in his father's occupation, he and Andrew "were fishers" (Matt. 4:18). Luke 5:1-10 reveals that Peter (and evidently Andrew) became partners (*koinonos*) with the sons of Zebedee in the fishing business. This seems, however, to be a later

---

*On the location of this city, and the possibility of two cities on the shores of Galilee with the same name, see the very informative discussion in the *International Standard Bible Encyclopedia*. On the whole, it seems best to locate it on the *west* side of Galilee, as a "fishing village suburb" of Capernaum. This, I think, beyond a doubt, to be the home of Peter. Whether there was another Bethsaida in the same area is another question. Some would explain the above Scriptures by saying that Peter later *moved* to Capernaum from Bethsaida. "Peter and Andrew had dwelt at Bethsaida (Jn. 1:44). They may have removed to Capernaum, or Bethsaida, being near by, may be here counted as a part, or suburb, of Capernaum."—McGarvey on Mark 1:29.

development, for in Matt. 4:18-22 Peter and Andrew are working together with their father and James and John are working together with theirs. After the Resurrection, Peter returned to his chosen trade with the words, "I go a fishing. (Jn. 21:3).*

7. If Peter had any formal education, other than that which was standard for a Jew of his day, we are not told of it in the Scriptures. In fact, the opposite seems to be true, according to the fourth chapter of Acts. The Sanhedrin, before whom Peter and John were arraigned for preaching of a resurrected Jesus, perceived that they were "unlearned" (agrammatos) men. The word is made up of two parts. The first "a" in the word deprives the rest of the word of its force, as in our prefix un-. The latter part of the word is from gramma (whence our word grammar)—literally, a letter, character in the alphabet. It also meant simply writing, or even a compilation of writings—a book. A grammareus was one skilled in writing, a scribe. The word came to be associated with one who was learned, especially in matters that pertained to reading and writing. Compare Jn. 7:15 where the Jews said of Jesus, "How knoweth this man letters (grammata) having never learned." Peter's background was not that of a "lettered" man.

The Sanhedrin also perceived Peter and John were "ignorant" men. The stigma now carried with this word is not in the original. Today if a man is termed "ignorant" he is usually thought of as a dull-witted or stupid individual. The word idiotes (whence our word idiot) cannot be so construed. It properly meant "one in private life" (Bagster) and, therefore, one who was devoid of special learning or gifts. We would say "just a plain person." In Greek writing it was used of a common soldier (as opposed to a military officer), a writer of prose (as opposed to a writer of poetry). Hence here "an unlearned, illiterate man, opposed to the

---

*This statement is not to be understood as a renouncing of his apostleship, much less of his faith. The apostles had to eat also. During their travels with Jesus, they were maintained by the kindness of the people and by what was placed in "the bag" (Jn. 12:6, 13:29). Perhaps there is a note of despair shown in his statement, but one must not be too quick to misrepresent his intentions. Remember, he had a wife (and probably children) to support.

learned, the educated"—Thayer.*

What an illustration we have here of God taking a humble, common, ordinary person who was willing to be used of Him, and turning his life into a spiritual dynamo! How far-reaching was his influence! There was Paul—learned, educated, and in many ways refined. God used him! There was Peter—rough, uneducated, unlettered. God used him. Peter could say to those who needed help "What I have, that give I thee." Reader, are you giving what you *have* to God? Only the Lord Himself knows what He can do with *your life* if all is laid on the altar for Him!

8. Peter was among the "inner circle" apostles—a title given to Peter, James and John because of their intimacy with Christ during His ministry. It was these three apostles who witnessed:

    a. The raising of Jairus' daughter, Mk. 5:37.

    b. The Transfiguration, Matt. 17:1.

    c. The Lord's agony in Gethsemane, Matt. 26:37.

    d. These, along with Andrew, were the recipients of special instruction on future events, Mk. 13:3 ff.

9. His character and nature was enthusiastic and energetic, though sometimes impulsive and impetuous.

    a. When Jesus walked on the water, Mass. 14:22-33.

    b. His denial of Christ. Compare Lk. 22:31-34 with 22:54-62, or Matt. 26:31-34 with 26:69-75.

    c. His bold entrance into the empty tomb, in contrast to John's hesitance. Jn. 20:1-8.

    d. He was the first of the apostles to witness the Resurrection, I Cor. 15:5, Lk. 24:33-34.

10. His role as leader among the apostles and in the early church.

Even before Pentecost, his leadership ability is shown in that he was usually the spokesman for the apostles: Jn. 21:3, Matt. 16:13-16, 18:21, etc.

In every list of the apostles (Matt. 10:2-4, Mk. 3:16-19, Acts 1:13), Peter is mentioned first.

In the Book of Acts, he is by far the most prominent character next to the apostle Paul. This is especially seen in the early chapters. He was the first to preach the Gospel to the Jews (Chap. 2) and in his mission to Cornelius (Chapters 10 and 11), the first to

---

*A Greek-English Lexicon of the New Testament, by C. L. W. Grimm. Translated and enlarged by J. H. Thayer.

formally and officially preach the Gospel to the Gentiles. In this way he opened the doors of the Lord's church with the keys of the kingdom of heaven (Matt. 16:19).

With the exception of the "dissimulation" at Antioch (Gal. 2:11-14), where Peter "drew back and separated himself" from the Gentiles for fear of the Jews, the remainder of his life is commendable as far as the Scriptures describe it. Time and again he is mistreated, threatened, imprisoned and beaten, but never again does he deny his Lord. His zeal and fidelity is nowhere better evidenced than Acts 4:13-20. With John, the Sanhedrin forbade him to speak at all in the name of Jesus. He replied, "Whether it is right in the sight of God to hearken unto you rather than unto God, judge ye: for we cannot but speak the things which we saw and heard." Later, after being thrown into prison and miraculously delivered, they were again brought before the council. The high priest said, "We strictly charged you not to teach in this name: and behold, ye have filled Jerusalem with your teaching, and intend to bring this man's blood upon us." But Peter and the apostles answered, "We must obey God rather than men" (Acts 5:28-29).

## THE PLACE OF PETER'S EPISTLES IN THE NEW TESTAMENT

If the Apostle Paul has placed emphasis on faith in his epistles, James on works, and John on love, Peter has stressed the need of persevering and consistent *hope*—particularly in the midst of trial and difficulty. He is, therefore, frequently termed, "The Apostle of Hope." Note that the subject of suffering for Christ is treated in *every single chapter* of his first letter, encouraging the Christians not to succumb to it. In his second epistle, the false teacher and deceiver is warned against in every chapter. But in both epistles the warnings are intended to *encourage the Christians toward steadfastness*, in view of their coming reward. Note I Pet. 1:13, 4:19, 5:12; II Pet. 1:12-15, 3:11-14, and especially II Pet. 3:1-2, where Peter himself tells us he has a common objective for both epistles.

## INTRODUCTION TO I PETER
I. THE HUMAN AUTHOR.

Though some doubts and uncertainties were entertained in ancient times concerning the Petrine authorship of the second epistle, that Peter was the author of the first has never been seriously questioned. From the very beginning it was accepted as an inspired message from the Apostle whose name it bears (1:1, 5:

16

12-13). The historical attestation to its authority as an apostolic document is more than adequate. Polycarp, a disciple of the Apostle John, was martyred in 156 A.D. at about 90 years of age. He refers to the epistle in unmistakable terms as authentic. Irenaeus (A.D. 115-195, Polycarp's disciple, quotes it many times.* Clement of Alexandria (A.D. 150-216), cites it many times in his *Stromata*, one passage (4:8) being quoted five times by actual count. Eusebius, often called The Father of Church History (A.D. 260-340), said, "One epistle of Peter, called his first, is acknowledged. This the presbyters of ancient times have quoted in their writings, as undoubtedly genuine."**

## II. THE HUMAN WRITER.

In 5:12 we have the statement, "By Silvanus I have written unto you briefly . . ." (Silvanus is another name for Silas, the traveling companion of Paul.) Some have supposed that Silvanus was involved in the composition of the letter as the writer or secretary, rather than the messenger. This is the view of A. T. Robertson, who also infers that Silvanus was, on occasion, *Paul's* amanuensis. By comparing II Thes. 3:17 with 1:1-2, one sees this as a possibility but not a certainty. The word here rendered "by" (*dia*) it is true, was sometimes used anciently of one who wrote *for* another. It basically means "through" or "by means of." But most critics have simply understood by this that the epistle was being sent *by* this "faithful brother."

In 1:1-2 we have two facts about those to whom this epistle was addressed: (1) they lived in Asia Minor (Turkey) and (2) they were Christians.

Some have thought that Peter, like James (Jas. 1:1) was addressing Jews exclusively. This error, it seems, has arisen mainly because of confusion concerning the term "dispersion." See comments, 1:1. That Peter does address his letter to Hebrew Christians seems obvious, for throughout the epistle he assumes the

---

*This was a very natural development. Peter's epistles were addressed to churches of Asia Minor, and most of Ireneus' labors were in this area.
**Ecclesiastical History, III, 23:3.

reader is familiar with the Old Testament and its terminology: 1:10-12, 2:5-9, 3:6.*

But it is also very obvious from even a superficial reading of the book, that the apostle intended Gentile Christians to receive and study it. See such passages as 2:10 (compared with Eph. 2: 11-13) and 4:3. Peter's benediction is general; "unto you all that are in Christ" (5:4). True, the "Gentiles" are mentioned in the third person, 2:12, 4:3, but Peter consistently uses this term with reference to *wicked* Gentiles—heathens.

It seems best, therefore, to regard the epistle as being addressed to *all* Christians within the geographical boundaries specified.

IV. DATE OF WRITING.

Conjectured dates range from A.D. 58 to 64. We have one certain fact to guide us here: it was written before the destruction of Jerusalem, A.D. 70. There are several references to that history-making event within the epistle; 2:12, 4:7 (where see notes).

# CHAPTER ONE

## I.  INTRODUCTION AND GREETING
## 1:1,2

**1:1  Peter, an apostle of Jesus Christ, to the elect who are sojourners of the Dispersion in Pontus, Galatia, Cappadocia, Asia, and Bithynia,**

### Expanded Translation

Peter, a commissioned messenger of Jesus Christ sent forth with orders, to the selected and chosen ones who are journeying in a strange land to their heavenly home—those scattered throughout Pontus, Galatia, Cappadocia, Asia, and Bithynia,

---

**Peter**

A descriptive proper name, signifying a stone, or a rock. Its Aramaic equivalent was Cephas. This name was given to Simon by the Lord Himself, in anticipation of the hard, staunch, unyielding "rock-like" character Christ knew this man would come to possess (Jn. 1:42). See the sketch of his life in the introduction.

---

*The strength of this oft-mentioned point, however, is questioned. In Paul's epistles to churches of largely Gentile converts, the Scriptures and terminology of the Old Testament are freely employed.

### an apostle of Jesus Christ

An apostle is "a delegate, messenger, one sent forth with orders"—Thayer. The author immediately confirms his right to pen an authoritative epistle by stating that he was commissioned by Christ. Jesus had told His Apostles before His ascension, "These things have I spoken unto you, while yet abiding with you. But the Comforter, even the Holy Spirit, whom the Father will send in my name, he shall teach you all things, and bring to your remembrance all that I said unto you (Jn. 14:25-26). Hence the Holy Spirit was moving Peter, even as he later wrote concerning the prophets (II Pet. 1:20-21). See also 1:12.

### to the elect

The word "elect," *eklektos*, means picked out, chosen, selected, or, as we would say, "hand picked." The obvious reference here is to Christians, those whom God has chosen to obtain salvation through Christ and to be the special recipients of His favor, as in Col. 3:12 and Tit. 1:1. Note the same word in 2:9: ". . . ye are an elect race."

### who are sojourners

This phrase is simply another way to describe Christian people. Some have thought the reference was to literal sojourners journeying through these countries on foot, with pack, cane, tent, etc. But the obvious reference is to those who were on a *spiritual* journey! Hence, Thayer's complete definition of the word *parepidemos*: "Properly, one who comes from a foreign country into a city or land to reside there by the side of the natives; (hence) stranger; sojourning in a strange place, a foreigner; in the N. T. metaphorically in reference to heaven as the native country, one who sojourns on earth, so of Christians." The same word is used in 2:11 in the same sense, and also in Heb. 11:13, where it is rendered "strangers." Our home is not on this earth. We are on a journey—a "business trip" if you please! The song writer caught the idea in the words:

> I am a stranger here, within a foreign land;
> My home is far away, upon a golden strand;
> E. T. Cassel

### of the dispersion

This term is used in James 1:1 in obvious reference to the Jewish people. However, the wording of that passage is not precisely the same as the one before us. Notice at least two differences: (1) In James it is specifically mentioned that James is addressing his epistle to the "twelve tribes"—limiting and confining his recipients to the Hebrew people. (2) Here the term "of the dispersion" occurs without the article in the original. But in James it is *en tei diasporai,* "in *the* dispersion."

The Jewish dispersion generally has reference to those Jews living outside of Palestine, yet maintaining their religious observances and customs among the Gentile nations. See Jn. 7:34-35. This scattering of the Jews began during the times that they were carried away by the king of Assyria in the case of the Ten Tribes, and in the Babylonian captivity in the case of Judah. Many of those carried away never returned to their native country, but did maintain religious observances. These were termed "The Dispersion." But the mere word *diaspora* is not of itself so limited in its scope. The verb form occurs in Acts 8:1, where, concerning the Jerusalem church we are told, "And there arose on that day a great persecution against the church which was in Jerusalem; and they were all *scattered abroad* throughout the regions of Judaea and Samaria, except the apostles." Again in verse 5 of that chapter: "They therefore that were *scattered abroad* went about preaching the word." See also Acts 11:19.

It seems best here to also give the word a general sense. We have already seen that the epistles of Peter were certainly addressed to Gentile Christians as well as Jewish. (See the Introduction.) Macknight contributes this thought: ". . . the Gentile believers in Pontus, &c. might be called 'sojourners of the dispersion of Pontus,' although none of them were driven from their native countries. For *the dispersion* may signify, that they lived at a distance from each other in the widely extended regions mentioned in the inscription; and that they were few in number, compared with the idolators and unbelievers among whom they lived."

### in Pontus, Galatia, Cappadocia, Asia, and Bithynia

All kingdoms or provinces lying within the present borders of Turkey. They may be easily located on any good map depicting the Roman provinces in New Testament times. PONTUS—located near the Euxine or Black Sea, a sea often in ancient times simply termed "Pontus," and giving this country its name. Jews and proselytes were present from this country on the day of Pentecost (Acts 2:8), as they were also from Cappadocia and Asia—a fact which may at least partially account for the existence of Christians and churches in these countries. GALATIA—located in the north part of the central plateau of Asia Minor. Evidently there were quite a number of churches in this area, I Cor. 16:1, Gal. 1:2. It is specifically mentioned as being included in the labors of the Apostle Paul. See Acts 16:6 and 18:23, as well as his epistle to the Galatians. CAPPADOCIA—in east-central Asia Minor, bordering Armenia. ASIA—bordering the Aegean Sea. John wrote to "the seven churches that are in Asia" (Rev. 1:4). BITHYNIA— was also a coastal province, in the north of Asia Minor. Its northwest corner bordered the Propontis and also the famous Bosporus Strait. (The latter is usually considered the dividing line between Asia and Europe. It has been the scene of many wars.) Continuing east, the country follows the "hump" of Turkey's northern coastline. Paul and Silas had assayed to go into this country (Acts 16:6-7), but "the Spirit of Jesus suffered them not." Evidently other evangelists labored here soon afterward with the Lord's blessing.

**1:2 according to the foreknowledge of God the Father, in sanctification of the Spirit, unto obedience and sprinkling of the blood of Jesus Christ: Grace to you and peace be multiplied.**

## Expanded Translation

in accordance with the foreknowledge of God the Father, by the sanctifying influence of the Holy Spirit, into the realm of obedience and sprinkling of the blood of Jesus Christ. God's favour be upon you and peace be increased.

---

### according to the foreknowledge of God the Father

The words "according to," from the Greek word *kata*, may be taken in the sense of "in conformity with" or "in accordance with." The idea is that we are the elect of God *just as* He foreknew.

The word "foreknowledge" constitutes a very literal rendering. The Greek *prognosis* is compounded of *pro*, before (as our prefix *pre-*) and *gnosis*, knowledge. Hence our modern words of prognosis, prognosticate, etc. The lexicons give its meaning as foreknowledge, prescience; hence forethought, previous determination, pre-arrangement. purpose.

It is taught by some, here, that this pre-determination on the part of God has reference to an inflexible arrangement He has made from eternity that certain individuals shall be saved, and that others should just as irrevocably be condemned. "Has not God pre-planned it all?" is the thought—"Why try to change His plan?" The whole doctrine, however, supposes that when God foreknows a matter, the persons involved within the sphere of His foreknowledge necessarily lose their freedom of choice. It is helpful to notice the only other occurrence of this particular word in the New Testament. In Acts 2:23 we are told that God had "foreknowledge" of Christ's crucifixion. Surely our Heavenly Father *did* plan and will the death of His beloved Son ahead of time. But are we to conclude from this that our Saviour was a helpless victim of circumstance, carried by the irresistable current of Divine Providence? If so, it seems strange that He would speak thus: "Therefore doth the Father love me, because I lay down my life, that I may take it again. No one taketh it away from me, but I lay it down of myself. I have power to lay it down, and I have power to take it again. This commandment received I from my Father" (Jn. 10:17-18). Simply because God *knew what course of action would be taken* does *not* necessarily mean that He *forced the persons involved to take that course.* As Matthew Henry suggests: "Foreknowledge may be taken . . . for mere prescience, foresight, or understanding, that such a thing will be, before it comes to pass. Thus a mathematician certainly foreknows that at such a time there will be an eclipse. This sort of foreknowledge is in God, who at one commanding view sees all things [or at least *can* see all things] that ever were, or are, or ever will be. But such a prescience is not the cause why anything is so or so, though in the event it certainly will be so, as the mathematician who foresees an eclipse does not thereby cause that eclipse to be."*

It is also well to notice that in the second chapter of Acts, Peter was speaking of *one person* when he spoke of the Father having foreknowledge of His Son's violent death. But in *this* passage the reference is *not* to *individuals*, but a *class* or *group* of people—Christians. The Apostle has just spoken of "the elect" and "sojourners," both of which terms apply to the Christian society, the

---

*Matthew Henry's Commentary*, Vol. VI, P. 1003.

church. It therefore appears that though God *may* know ahead of time who will or will not accept Christ as their Lord, *this verse* only shows that God foreknew He would have a group who would be His "elect" and "sojourners" at this time in history. The church was no "after-thought" of God. He planned and arranged for it in advance, even "before times eternal" (Tit. 1:2).

Notice here the work of the Godhead in man's redemption. All three members are mentioned in this verse. God planned it, the Spirit worked it, and Christ sealed it.

## II. THE GREAT SALVATION
## 1:3-12

### 1. Thanksgiving For It 1:3-5

**1:3 Blessed be the God and Father of our Lord Jesus Christ, who according to his great mercy begat us again unto a living hope by the resurrection of Jesus Christ from the dead,**

### Expanded Translation

Let blessings and praise be to the God and Father of our Lord Jesus Christ, who, influenced by His great mercy and compassion, begat us a second time unto a living hope through the resurrection of Jesus Christ from among the dead,

**Blessed be**

The word is *eulogetos*, from the same root as our words "eulogize," eulogy," etc. It signifies: blessed, praised, worthy of praise or blessing.

**the God and Father of our Lord Jesus Christ**

Jehovah is not only Christ's father, but His God, ". . . I ascend unto my Father and your Father, and my God and your God" (Jn. 20:17). As our Lord hung on the cross He prayed, "Father, forgive them for they know not what they do" (Luke 23:34). But on the same cross his cry later was, "My God, my God, why hast Thou forsaken me" (Matt. 27:46). The Scripture plainly teaches that Christ is one with God—Jn. 1:1, 10:30, 14:7-11; I Jn. 5:20, etc. This thought must be harmonized with that which is here stated by Peter.

**who according to his great mercy**

On "according to," see v. 1. Our Father, dominated and influenced by this trait of mercy, provided for our redemption. It was not just mercy, but "great" mercy. (*Polus*—abundant, plenteous, much; hence: great, strong, intense, large.)

The word "his" is emphatic in the original: we were saved because of God's mercy, not because of our goodness. Compare Eph. 2:8-9. The prophet said, "It is of Jehovah's loving kindness that we are not consumed, because His compassions fail not" (Lam. 3:22).

What is *mercy?* The word *eleos* has special and immediate regard to the *misery* which is the consequence of our sins. God wants to assuage and entirely remove this misery and suffering.* Though punishment and *eternal* suffering is due us, He withholds our just desserts because He possesses this characteristic.

### begat us again

One word in the original, *anagennao: ana, again,* and *gennao,* to beget, generate. We were begotten the first time by our physical or human fathers (for so is *gennao* used in Matt. 1:2, 16, etc.). We were begotten the second time by our Spiritual Father. God is responsible for our *very existence* as spiritual creatures. When there is a new begetting, there is new life. This, above all, seems to be Peter's point of emphasis—*God* is to be praised for your new life! See further comments, verse 23.

### unto a living hope

The Christian's hope is not cold, dead, and lifeless. It has vital power within itself and exerts the same upon the soul—it is active, powerful, vibrant! Compare Rom. 8:24-25. "The hope of eternal life in a true Christian is a hope that keeps him alive, quickens him, supports him, and conducts him to heaven. Hope invigorates and spirits up the soul to action, to patience, to fortitude, and perseverance to the end."—*Matthew Henry.*

### by the resurrection of Jesus Christ from the dead

Here is the basis or foundation of our hope of salvation. It was actually necessary before our sins could be forgiven (I Cor. 15: 1-4, 16-17). Also, His Resurrection gives us assurance that *we* shall be raised. (I Cor. 15:12-22, I Thes. 4:13-18.) Christ kept His word relative to His own resurrection; He will keep it concerning ours in the last day!

### 1:4 unto an inheritance incorruptible, and undefiled, and that fadeth not away, reserved in heaven for you,

### Expanded Translation

unto an inheritance given to us by our Father, never perishing or decaying, unstained and unsoiled (that is, pure), never losing

---

*Trench, Synonyms of the New Testament, pp.169, 171.

its original lustre or beauty, guarded and kept in watchful custody for you.

---

**unto an inheritance**

The word *kleronomia* signifies an inheritance or patrimony, an estate inherited from one's father. Our heavenly Father has surely prepared for us an inheritance greater than all this world's wealth! We are citizens of that country (Philip. 3:20), and He has promised us a mansion there (Jn. 14:2).

**incorruptible**

*Aphthartos* refers to that which is uncorrupted, not liable to corruption or decay imperishable. See 1:23, 3:4, I Cor. 9:25. Here on earth, everything has within it the seeds of decay. Roofing materials, even pots and pans, are "guaranteed for life." Be not deceived, *they, too, shall some day rot!* Even our physical bodies are such, ". . . for dust thou art, and unto dust shalt thou return" (Gen. 3:19). "The things which are seen," Paul stated, "are temporal; but the things which are not seen are eternal." (See II Cor. 4:16-18). This is why the Lord exhorted us as He did in Matt. 6:19-21, and why the Apostle exhorted the Corinthians as he did in I Cor. 15:50-58.

Furthermore, on earth we will soon part with our mansions, however beautiful (or ugly) they might be. No so with our heavenly home!

**undefiled**

*Amiantos* is composed of the alpha privitive plus *miano*, a verb meaning to dye with another color, stain. Our eternal abode will not be defiled or soiled; it will be "free from that by which the nature of a thing is deformed and debased, or its force and vigor impaired"—Thayer. Thus a good synonym would be *pure*.

Again we find a contrast to earthly possessions and inheritances. Our future estate will not provide for temptations to the flesh, hatred, sensualities or crime—all of which so frequently accompany the acquisition of earthly estates. There will be no cigarette smoke to inhale, no alcohol breath to breathe, no filthy language or lying to hear, no indecency or immodesty—all will be perfectly pure and unsullied there! See also Rev. 21:27.

**and that fadeth not away**

The term "fadeth away" (compare *amarntinos*, its close relative), refers to that which not only lasts on and on for an indefinite period of time, but never loses its original beauty, lustre, and brightness. In sharp contrast to those mundane things with which we are familiar, the golden streets of heaven shall never tarnish. As Trench says of our heavenly inheritance, "Not merely decay and corruption cannot touch it; but it shall wear its freshness, brightness and beauty forever."*

### reserved in heaven for you

The word "reserved," *tereo*, indicates to keep, guard, preserve, to keep in watchful custody, to reserve with a happy issue. There will be no tickets sold to heaven at the gate. All mansions there will be "reserved" (Jn. 14:1-3). It is a prepared place *for those who have prepared on earth to go there!* See Tit. 1:2, Matt. 25:34, II Tim. 4:8.

**1:5 who by the power of God are guarded through faith unto a salvation ready to be revealed in the last time.**

### Expanded Translation

who by the power and might of God are being guarded through (or by means of) faith (or trust) unto a salvation prepared and ready for uncovering in the last time.

---

### power

*Dunamis*, whence our words dynamo, dynamite, etc.

### are guarded

*Phroureo* was commonly used of those who were guarding or watching with a military guard. (See II Cor. 11:32, compare Acts 9:24.) Here used, as in Phil. 4:7, to keep in a state of settlement or security. God's protective power is mightier and more to be trusted than any military force man might assemble! (Psa. 20:7).

### through faith

Here is *our* part. God has never promised to preserve the faithless and disobedient. So in Jn. 10:27-29, those sheep who *heard* the voice of Christ and *followed* Him were the recipients of God's protecting and shielding hand.

### ready to be revealed in the last time

The phrase "to be revealed" represents one word—*apokalupto*. It is composed of *apo*—from, of, away from, plus *kalupto*, to cover, hide, conceal. Here in the passive, it means literally to be uncovered, unveiled, or revealed.

---

*Synonyms of the N. T.*, p. 255.

The "last time" will be when our present Christian dispensation is over, i.e., when Christ returns to earth.

## 2. Worthy of Trials and An Afflication 1:6-9
**1:6 Wherein ye greatly rejoice, though now for a little while, if need be, ye have been put to grief in manifold trials.**

### Expanded Translation
In which salvation you rejoice exceedingly within yourselves, even though presently, if it be necessary (and in this case, since it *IS* needful), you have been grieved and pained by all sorts of trials and testings.

---

**Wherein ye greatly rejoice**
The phrase *could* be imperative—"wherein greatly rejoice!" The word *agalliao*, used here, is rendered in 4:13 "with exceeding joy."

**though now for a little while**
That is, a *short* while. Even several years of suffering here will seem as nothing in eternity!

**if need be**
The word "if" shows contingency. However, many here give the Greek word *ei* the meaning "since," rendering the clause "since it is necessary . . ."

**ye have been put to grief in manifold trials**
Contained in the word "manifold," (*poikilos*) according to Souter, is both the idea of many in *number* and diversity of *kind*. (Compare Jas. 1:2.)

"Trials" (*peirasmos*) originally had reference to an experiment, attempt, trial or experience. In the Scriptures it is often used of an enticement to sin, and is, in those passages, properly rendered "temptation." (Matt. 6:13, 26:41; Luke 8:13, etc.) Here the reference is to adversities, afflictions or trials which God allows to come upon us to test our faith, holiness, and character. It is His hope that they shall have a refining and purifying influence upon our Christian character.

**1:7 that the proof of your faith, being more precious than gold that perisheth though it is proved by fire, may be found unto praise and glory and honor at the revelation of Jesus Christ:**

### Expanded Translation
in order that your tested faith—the faith that has gone through the trial and emerged victorious—being of much more value and

worth than gold which is perishable though it is tested with fire, may be found, in the end, deserving of praise and glory and honor at the (second) coming of Jesus Christ.

---

**that the proof of your faith, being more precious than gold that perisheth**

In the noun "proof" (*dokimion*) lies the notion of proving a thing to see if it be worthy to be received or not. When the ancients "tried" metals, for example, they did not do so "except in the expectation and belief that, whatever of dross may be found mingled with it, yet it is not *all* dross, but that some good metal, and better now than before, will come forth from the fiery trial. It is ever so with the proof to which He who sits as a Refiner in His Church submits His own; His intention in these being ever, not indeed to find His saints pure gold (for this He knows they are not), but to make them such; to purge out their dross, never to make evident that they are all dross."* See Isa. 1:24-26 and especially Job 23:10.

That which is "more precious" (*polutimoteron*, comparative form of *polutinos*, literally, of great price, more costly) in God's sight is the faith which has been *proved* and, bearing up under the test, stands *a*-proved. It has shown itself to be that real, solid, genuine faith that does not succumb under adverse circumstances.

**may be found unto praise and glory and honor at the revelation of Jesus Christ**

all of which rewards which belong only to those who have such faith as overcomes the world (I Jn. 5:4). Here again we see Peter's ever-present purpose: to encourage those being persecuted and tried. It is the faith that is tested, tried, proven, and approved that shall receive such a reward. And when shall that reward be given? In the *end*, when Christ returns, *if He will find you true!*

The analogy of the refining process might be outlined as follows:

I. Refining process.
    1. Gold: proved by fire.
    2. Christian's faith: given trials and testings.
II. Product produced from process.
    Gold: pure gold remains after admixtures, alloys and dross removed.
    2. Christian's faith: "more precious than gold . . ."

---

*Trench, *Synonyms of the New Testament*, p. 279.

III. Time of existence.
    1. Gold: "perisheth."
    2. Christian's faith: abides "till the revelation of Jesus Christ"—when it will become sight!
IV. Reward.
    1. Gold: greatly admired by man because of its fine quality.
    2. Christian: receives praise, honor, and glory from God.

**1:8-9 whom not having seen ye love; on whom, though now ye see him not, yet believing, ye rejoice greatly with joy unspeakable and full of glory: receiving the end of your faith, even the salvation of your souls.**

## Expanded Translation

(Christ) whom having not seen you love, in which person, though at present you do not see Him, yet believing, you exult and rejoice exceedingly with a joy to which human words are inadequate and which is clothed with splendor, receiving for yourselves the final reward of a life of faith—the salvation of your souls.

---

**whom not having seen ye love**

They had not viewed the Saviour: (1) Because of the place in which they lived. (See 1:1-2.) (2) Because of the time in which they lived—though this might have been possible for some of the older ones. We see Christ, not with the physical or bodily eye, but the eye of faith. See Jn. 20:29, Rom. 8:24,25. Compare I Jn. 4:20. Some have said Paul's emphasis was upon faith versus works, James' was upon works versus faith alone, and Peter's was upon faith versus sight. Hence the title, "The Apostle of Hope."

How could they love such an One? Because of what He had done and was doing for them (Rom. 5:5-11, I Jn. 4:19), and for what He was and is.

**rejoice greatly**

*Agalliao.* See on V. 6 ("greatly rejoice").

**with joy unspeakable**

The latter word is an excellent representation of the original, for the word is composed of the alpha negative plus *ek*—out, out of, and *laleo*—to speak. Hence, that which cannot be spoken out, uttered, or divulged. Vine puts it, "unable to be told out."* Surely here the poet was right, "The heart has reasons which the tongue cannot express."

---

*W. E. Vine, *An Expository Dictionary of New Testament Words.*

**and full of glory**

It is made glorious, clothed with splendor and rendered excellent, because the heavenly joy surpasses all others! In the sight of the worldling, the joy of the Christian is an enigma. To us it is glorious, but not altogether capable of description.

**receiving the end of your faith**

The word "end," *telos*, is rendered "finally" in 3:8 and "end" in 4:7. It here refers to that by which a thing is finished, its close, issue (as in Matt. 26:58), hence final lot, culmination, outcome. In this present life, "we walk by faith, not by sight" (II Cor. 5:7), and eternal life will be ours, "if so be that ye continue in the faith, grounded and steadfast, and not moved away from the hope of the Gospel which ye heard . . ." (Col. 1:23). However, it is possible for us to lose or renounce our faith (I Tim. 1:18-20), and fall away from a state of trust and consecration (Gal. 5:4). Peter specifies here that our salvation shall come when our faith shall have gained its end result, that is, at the end of a life of faithfulness, salvation shall be our reward.

### 3. Deep Concern of Prophets and Angels 1:10-12

**1:10-11 Concerning which salvation the prophets sought and searched diligently, who prophesied of the grace that should come unto you: searching what time or what manner of time the Spirit of Christ was in them did point unto, when it testified beforehand the sufferings of Christ, and the glories that should follow them.**

### Expanded Translation

About this salvation the (Hebrew) prophets sought carefully and searched diligently to understand and comprehend—they who had prophesied concerning the grace which was to be bestowed upon you—investigating to find out to whom or what manner of time was signified by the Spirit of Christ which was in them, when it predicted the sufferings of Christ and the glories that were to follow such sufferings.

---

**Concerning which salvation**

That of Christians, just spoken of (v. 9).

**the prophets sought and searched diligently**

—a phrase which graphically describes the interest of the Old Testament prophets in the salvation through Christ made known in the Christian dispensation. They "sought" *ekzeteo*, literally, "sought out," hence to search for, investigate, scrutinize. They also "searched," *exereunao*, a word of very similar meaning: to search out, search anxiously and diligently. If there is any technical difference between the meaning of these two words, it is certainly very slight. The Apostle's intention in inserting this phrase is obviously to show that the prophets were deeply and sincerely interested in the salvation of which they prophesied, so much so that much energy and thought was put forth as they made inquiry and research *into their own prophecies!*

The most humble believer is now able to see very clearly what the most distinguished prophet only saw obscurely. Their revelations were real and inspired, but they were not clear in all details, *especially to those of that age.* Enough was understood by them to maintain the faith of God's people who looked for a coming Messiah. But these prophecies frequently troubled and perplexed the "seers" themselves, and they "searched" them out, as miners seek treasure (for so was *exereunao* used by the ancients). They were not only prophets, they were men! As such, they could not fathom their own words. Read Matt. 13:17. Compare such passages as Dan. 7:15.

**who prophesied of the grace that should come unto you**

"Grace," *charis*, here, has specific reference to our redemption, the epitome of God's expression of love, kindness, and favor toward us—a favor completely undeserved!

**searching what time or what manner of time**

The first word rendered "time" is absent in the best manuscripts. The first "what" in the phrase is an interrogative pronoun, *tina*, in the masculine singular. Hence we have, "searching (to find out) what person or what manner of time . . ."* Their attention was fixed upon both the *people* of which they prophesied and the *times* or dispensations to which their predictions pointed.

**the Spirit of Christ which was in them did point unto**

i.e., the *Holy Spirit* which was in them, the third person of the Godhead. (See II Pet. 1:21 and comments there.) Note that the same Holy Spirit influenced God's spokesmen in the Christian age also (v. 12).

**when it testified beforehand the sufferings of Christ, and the glories that should follow them**

---
*Compare Luke 24:25-27, Matt. 24:3, Acts 1:7.

Or, when *He* (the Holy Spirit, a Divine Personality) testified beforehand. See Jn. 16:13-15.

The "glories" after the predicted sufferings, were his personal triumphs: His resurrection, ascension, coronation, and reign at God's right hand. But these "glories" would also include the great plan of redemption and the establishment of the church —certainly glorious consequences of His coming to earth predicted by the prophets. On this last phrase, compare Dan. 9:24-27, Isa. 53:3-9, Acts 3:18 and 26:22-23, Luke 24:44-47.

**1:12 To whom it was revealed, that not unto themselves, but unto you, did they minister these things, which now have been announced unto you through them that preached the gospel unto you by the Holy Spirit sent forth from heaven; which things angels desire to look into.**

### Expanded Translation

To whom it (i.e., this great plan of redeeming mankind through Jesus Christ) was uncovered and made known, that not unto themselves but unto you were they performing this service concerning these things, and they have now been announced unto you by the Holy Spirit which was sent forth from heaven; into which things angels strongly desire to stoop down and peer carefully into.

---

**To whom it was revealed**

The word *apokalupto* ("was revealed") is compounded from *apo*—from, off, away from, and *kalupto*—to cover, hide, conceal, throw a veil over. (See 4:8, "covereth.") This plan of redemption through Christ was *uncovered* and that which was hidden was *brought to light*. Revealed to the prophets? No. The Apostle continues:

**that not unto themselves, but unto you, did they minister these things**

The word "minister," *diakoneo*, is the verb form of the noun, *diakonos*, deacon. It means to wait upon, attend upon, serve, and specifically to perform a service by commission. Little did those sages of old realize the significance of their words, or to what great extent they were attending to the needs of those who would be living *twenty-five hundred years later!* What a blessing to live in the Gospel age where many of our privileges are greater than those enjoyed by the prophets themselves!

**which now have been announced unto you through them that preached the Gospel unto you**

Compare Heb. 11:39-40. Peter here shows their own great value as Christians by emphasizing the fact that the concern was *unto you*. We enjoy to the fullest what they could not even comprehend!

This message was carried to the readers by "them that preached the gospel." Living in what is now Turkey (See 1:1, notes), they first had the Gospel preached to them by the Apostle Paul and his companions. But the truth here expressed would apply also to every true preacher of the Gospel.

**by the Holy Spirit sent forth from heaven**

See also v. 11. The Holy Spirit spoke through the prophets who *predicted* the message AND He also spoke through the Apostles and others who preached the *fulfillment* of their prophecies. God speaks of the Old Testament as the Holy Spirit's message (Heb. 3:7, II Pet. 1:21). And here the Gospel Message is shown to have the same source.

**which things angels desire to look into**

Note the Expanded Translation. Peter had said before that this great salvation we enjoy through Christ had gained the keenest scrutiny of the most holy men *on earth*—the prophets. Now he turns to the *heavens*—the inhabitants of the skies!

The "which things" refer to the matters of prophecy and their fulfillment in the Christian dispensation, mentioned in vss. 10-12. The verb "desire," *epithumeo*, is the same word so frequently rendered "lust" in our New Testament. It means to set one's heart upon, have a desire for, long for, etc., used here in a good sense.

Of particular interest in this phrase is the Greek word translated "look into" (*parakupto*). It is from *para*, beside, and *kupto*, to bend forwards, stoop down. Thus the meaning is, to stoop to a thing in order to look at it. Notice how the Apostle John employs it: "And they (Peter and John) ran both together: and the other disciple out-ran Peter, and came first to the tomb; and *stooping and looking in,* he seeth the linen cloths lying; yet entered not in . . . But Mary was standing without at the tomb weeping: so, as she wept, she *stooped and looked into* the tomb . . ." (Jn. 20:4-5, 11). This same word is employed by James to show how the "blessed man" reads his Bible! (Jas. 1:25, "looketh into.") In that passage as well as this, it implies interest and concern on the part of the observer or reader. Christian, read your New Testament as *the angels would like to! Look carefully into it!*

Why such interest on the part of angels? Perhaps Heb. 1:14 supplies a partial explanation. But even with their strong desire to understand our salvation, this longing goes on and on *unfulfilled* on the part of the angels. Is our desire to understand God's scheme of redemption as strong as theirs, *when we are capable of understanding it?*

The purpose of this latter statement was doubtless to show the greatness of our salvation through the Son of God, and the benefits we have therefrom—neither the prophets nor the angels being able to ascertain the real nature of this great plan of pardon.

## III.   CALL TO HOLINESS
## 1:13 — 2:12
### 1.   Sobriety and Spiritual Readiness 1:13,14

**1:13 Wherefore girding up the loins of your mind, be sober and set your hope perfectly on the grace that is to be brought unto you at the revelation of Jesus Christ;**

### Expanded Translation

Wherefore (on this account) girding up the loins of your mind (and thus preparing it for whatever difficulties you may encounter), be perfectly self-controlled and fix your hope unswervingly on the grace that is to be brought unto you at the time Jesus Christ comes again.

---

**Wherefore**

i.e., "Because of what I have just stated . . ."

**girding up the loins of your mind**

This phrase is a metaphor signifying *preparedness*. It is derived from a practice of the Orientals. In order to be unimpeded in their movements, they were accustomed, when about to start on a journey or engage in any work, to bind their long and flowing garments closely around their bodies and fasten them with a leathern girdle. The thought is that of mental and spiritual *preparedness* for the assignments and work of a Christian, being similar in meaning to our expression, "Roll up your sleeves."

Notice here that we are to gird up the loins of our *minds*. It is as if the Apostle pictured the minds of *some* as though they were a loose, hanging, flowing garment. His advice is, "pull it together." Thus Souter, in commenting on this phrase, says the opposite of *mental slackness* is referred to.* The word rendered "girding up" is here in the middle voice—the action being done to or for one's self.) Our minds must be braced and prepared for the vicissitudes of life and the trials that come our way.

**be sober**

*nepho*, literally meaning to "be sober" in the sense of being un-intoxicated. We must be free from every form of mental and spiritual drunkenness, from passion, rashness, etc. The word refers to one who is calm and collected in spirit, temperate, well-balanced and self-controlled. Living in this manner, we are better equipped to ward off Satan, as is shown also in 4:7 and 5:8.

**and set your hope perfectly**

That is, altogether or completely. Most critics connect the "perfectly," with the hope. However, some connect it with the "be sober," translating the phrase "with perfect soberness set your hope . . ." or "with the strictest self-control fix your hope . . ." etc.

**on the grace that is to be brought unto you at the revelation of Jesus Christ**

Obviously referring to our ultimate salvation which will be granted to us when Christ returns to earth. Compare the use of "grace" in v. 10.

On this whole passage, compare Luke 12:35-36.

**1:14 As children of obedience, not fashioning yourselves according to your former lusts in the time of your ignorance:**

## Expanded Translation

In the manner of children who practice obedience, not conforming yourself in mind, character, speech or action to the strong desires which formerly ruled you in the days in which you lacked knowledge:

---

**As children of obedience**

A Hebrew idiom referring to those whose obedience is their outstanding quality or characteristic; i.e., "as obedient ones . . ." Compare Eph. 2:2 and the term "sons of *dis*obedience."

---

*Souter's *Greek-English Lexicon of the New Testament*.

**not fashioning yourselves according to your former lusts**

The word *suschematidzo* ("fashioning yourselves") is derived from *sun*, with, and *schema*, figure, fashion, form. When used of people, *sun* indicated everything in a person which strikes the senses: the figure, bearing, discourse, actions, manner of life, etc. "Fashioning yourselves," then, is to fashion in accordance with, conform or assimilate one's self to, etc., and would include the whole "pattern" or "shape" of one's life. Please carefully notice the only other passage in the New Testament where this word occurs, Rom. 12:1-2. We must "fashion ourselves" after *Christ*, not after our former desires of the flesh.

**in the time of your ignorance**

*Agnoia* simply indicating lack of knowledge. See Acts 17:30, Eph. 4:18. We must not go back to those days before we were enlightened by the Gospel Message.

## 2.   Godliness 1:15,16

**1:15-16 but like as he who called you is holy, be ye yourselves also holy in all manner of living; because it is written, Ye shall be holy; for I am holy.**

### Expanded Translation

but (in contrast) according as he who called you is holy, you yourselves must also be holy in every phase of your behavior and conduct, inasmuch as it has been written (and still applies), you must be holy, for I am holy.

---

**but like as he who called you is holy,**

Christians must be "holy" (*hagios*). The word carries the basic thought of *separation*. When meat or other objects were to be given as a sacrifice to the gods, they were *hagios*—i.e., not to be employed in their common or ordinary usage, but dedicated to the idol(s). So God's children are *separated for a holy purpose*, set aside, as it were, exclusively for God's use! Note that our holiness is to extend to *every phase* of life and conduct—"in ALL manner of living."

**because it is written**

Literally, "it stands written"; i.e., "Here is a reason from the Scriptures which I am applying to the present case." The Scripture referred to is found in Lev. 11:44, 19:2, or 20:7.

## 3.  Fearing God 1:17

**1:17 And if ye call on Him as Father, who without respect of persons judgeth according to each man's work, pass the time of your sojourning in fear:**

### Expanded Translation

And in view of the fact you regard God as your Father and therefore call upon Him, who without respecting any man's person (race, color, status, wealth, etc.) judges according to the nature of every man's doings, you must live reverently all the time of your stay here on earth;

---

**without respect of persons**

This phrase is all one word in the original—an adverb describing the manner of God's judgment. His judgment will be *without partiality*. But man's judgment is often partial (Jas. 2:1-9), and Peter himself had been guilty of this sin at Antioch (Gal. 2:11-14).* The over-all meaning of the word before us is respect of persons in the sense of *partiality*. It is the fault of one who, when called upon to give judgment has respect to the outward circumstances of men and not their intrinsic merits. He therefore prefers, as the more worthy, one who is rich, high-born, influential, or powerful, to another who is destitute of such gifts.

God's judgment is complete, unbiased, thorough, exact, and honest — all of which traits are frequently lacking in earthly courts and judges. This truth about the character of God's judgment may either be a consoling and comforting *or* a fearful and horrifying realization. If our hearts are pure and undefiled, we will not fear the piercing and penetrating judgment of God as He lays bare "the thoughts and intents of the heart." But if we are harboring secret sins and hidden crimes of which we have never repented, these words of the Holy Spirit may turn into words of dread! Instead of "looking for and earnestly desiring the coming of the day of God" (II Pet. 3:12), there is only "a certain fearful expectation of judgment" (Heb. 10:27).

**according to each man's work**

Each man is held responsible for his own actions, thoughts, and words. Perhaps the thought of God's waiting *reward* is in the mind of the Apostle here—encouraging them to *personal fidelity*,

---

*On God's impartiality in judgment, see also Acts 10:34, Eph. 6:9, Col. 3:25, Rom. 2:11.

even in the midst of persecution and trial.

**pass the time of your sojourning in fear**

The word *paroikia* ("sojourning"), is not the same word as sojourners in 1:1. It is from *para*, beside, and *oikeo*, to dwell. Thus, literally, "to dwell by the side of," that is, by the side of *foreigners* or *strangers*. It was used of the stay which travelers made in a place, while finishing some business. Christians, then, are here pictured as *temporary residents* in this present world. Their home is not here—they are only here a short time to take care of some very specific business: preparing for their *eternal* home and urging others to do the same! See Heb. 11:13-16.

IN FEAR—i.e., of God. Our lives must be lived with a holy awe, reverence, and veneration toward our Heavenly Father (Acts 9:31). In its highest form, it comes to be *filial* fear of God Himself, and the fear of the day of judgment is cast out (I Jn. 4:17-18). Did you hear about the two boys who were about to commit some crime? One said, "I'm not going to do it because of what Dad would do to me." But his brother said, "I'm not going to do it *because of what it would do to Dad.*"

### 4.  The Christian's Ransom 1:18-21

**1:18-19 knowing that ye were redeemed, not with corruptible things, with silver or gold, from your vain manner of life handed down from your fathers; but with precious blood, as of a lamb without blemish and without spot, even the blood of Christ:**

### Expanded Translation

realizing that you were freed by ransom, not with perishable things such as silver and gold, from the hollow and useless life handed down from your ancestors; but rather with the precious blood of Christ, like that of a lamb without blemish and without spot.

---

**knowing that ye were redeemed**

That is, were liberated by payment of ransom. The word *lutroo*, according to Vine, signifies the actual deliverance, the setting at liberty. It was frequently used by the ancients when slaves were brought out of captivity. The slave was evaluated by the amount of money paid.* Living in the confines of sin, we were captives of Satan (II Tim. 2:26). But our Saviour tells us, "He hath sent me to proclaim release to the captives" (Luke 4:18). And what was the price the Father paid that He might have us back in His

---

*See the use of *Lurron*, the noun form, Lev. 19:20, Isa. 45:13 (Septuagint).

good graces? $100,000? No! Something far more valuable was paid!

**not with corruptible things, with silver or gold**

"Corruptible" being used here in the sense of "perishable"—i.e., liable to decay and ruin. The word *phthartos*, used here, stands opposed to *aphthartos* ("incorruptible") which occurs in 1:4. The two words are vividly contrasted in I Cor. 9:25: "And every man that striveth in the games exerciseth self-control in all things. Now they do it to receive a corruptible (*phthartos*) crown; but we an incorruptible (*aphthartos*)."

**from your vain manner of life handed down from your fathers**

Their previous life was "vain," devoid of success, useless, to no purpose, hence, corrupt, perverted—for so the word *mataios* signifies. Surely several of them had been relatively successful in realms of *business, politics, music,* or *farming.* But until a man hands his life over to the Master, unconditionally surrendering his whole being to Him, *his life is only a hollow void!*

Their previous way of living had been passed down to them by their forefathers and ancestors. In the case of the Jews, it meant holding to the Law of Moses, along with all the accompanying traditions of the family's particular sect. In the case of the Gentile, it meant the perpetuation of Idolatry and often some heretical philosophy. It is human nature to want to preserve the *status quo* in the realm of religion. Ancestor worship is still extant and not only in China!

**but with precious blood**

Much more precious, costly, and dear in the mind of God than all the gold of Croesus! Here is the "ransom money," and only Christ could pay it.

**as of a lamb without blemish and without spot**

The picture of the sacrificial lamb was familiar to all Peter's readers, but especially to the Hebrews, and the latter well knew the requirements of perfection God demanded (Lev. 22:21-22). Christ is frequently referred to as such a lamb, sacrificed once and for all (Jn. 1:29, 36; Acts 20:28; Rev. 13:8, 5:6).

The contrast of these verses is one of *values.* The blood of our Saviour is far more valuable than *any amount* of money ("silver and gold").

**1:20 Who was foreknown indeed before the foundation of the world, but was manifested at the end of the times for your sake,**

### Expanded Translation

This sacrifice of Christ and the work it would accomplish was known by and provided for ahead of time by God; indeed, even before the world was cast into place (as a foundation is placed down); but this was all manifested at the end of the Mosaic dispensation in your behalf and for your salvation,

---

**Who**

i.e., Christ.

**was foreknown**

*Proginosko.* See comments under 1:2, where the noun form of this verb occurs.

**before the foundation of the world**

The word "foundation," *katabole,* is a compound word made up of *kata,* down, and *ballo,* throw or cast. Hence, literally, a throwing, laying, or casting down. The picture is one of God "laying" or "casting" the world into place, as likened unto a man who has "thrown down" a foundation for a building. Here, of course, the word must be taken as a *figure of speech* and not pressed into something literal! See Jn. 17:24, and especially Eph. 1:4. The phrase is equivalent to "before the world was" (Jn. 17:5); i.e., before it existed. The phrase *"from* the foundation of the world" occurs in a similar setting in Matt. 13:35, 25:34.

Though the word "world" (*kosmos*) may also mean "age," it seems best here to leave it as it stands, for the phrase "before the foundation of the world" was a familiar expression, going back beyond *any* particular age or dispensation.

**but was manifested at the end of the times for your sake**

When was this time? When was the salvation of the world made available through the sacrifice of Christ? At the end of *what* times? The word "end," *eschatos,* means last, utmost, extreme. The making known of Christ's redemptive work was *at,* (*epi* upon, i.e., upon or at the conclusion of) the final stages of some period of history. It seems apparent that the reference can only be to the final times of the Mosaic period—the period of approximately fifteen hundred years in which the Law of Moses was in force. In Acts 2:17, Peter, quoting the prophecy of Joel, tells us, "And it shall come to pass in the *last days* (*eschatais hemerais*) . . ." which prophecy had very specific reference to the nation of Israel. Concerning the impending doom of the Jews, see under 2:12 and 4:7.

**1:21 who through him are believers in God, that raised him from the dead, and gave him glory; so that your faith and hope might be in God.**

### Expanded Translation

(you) who through him (Christ) are believers in God, the one who raised him up out of the dead ones and bestowed glory upon him, so that *your* faith and hope might be in God.

**who through him are believers in God**
The only way *any* man, Jew or Gentile, ever comes to know God is through the person of *Christ*. Jn. 14:6, Eph. 2:17-18.

**that raised him from the dead**
The resurrection and consequent glorification on God's right hand of Christ, gives us a *basis* or *reason* for confidence in *God*. It was obviously His working, and it caused us to believe on Him through Christ. Peter lays great stress on the importance of the resurrection, not only in his epistles, but also in his speeches recorded in the Book of Acts (Acts 2:32-36, 3:15, 4:10).

### 5.   Brotherly Love 1:22-25

**1:22-23 Seeing ye have purified your souls in your obedience to the truth unto unfeigned love of the brethren, love one another from the heart fervently: having been begotten again, not of corruptible seed, but of incurruptible, through the word of God, which liveth and abideth.**

### Expanded Translation

Having purified and cleansed your souls in your hearkening, submission, and obedience to the truth that issues into undisguised (i.e., real, sincere) love of the brethren, you must love one another out of your heart—intensely and fervently; having been begotten again (regenerated), not from corruptible or perishable seed, but from incorruptible or imperishable, through the Word of God which keeps on living and keeps on abiding.

**Seeing ye have purified**
All one word in the original. The perfect tense is used here, indicating action in the past with presently existing results. They *had been and were now* cleansed, and are to continue living in such a way as to *remain* pure.

**your souls**
i.e., their lives, beings, selves.

**in your obedience to the truth**
This is how the purification was accomplished—by responding

to and submitting to *the truth of God's Word*. Souls are not purified when one submits to false teaching or deceitful doctrines. "If
ye abide in my word, then are ye truly my disciples; and ye shall
know the truth, and the truth shall make you free" (Jn. 8:31-32).

### unto unfeigned love of the brethren

That is, one of the results or effects of a purified life is brotherly love. The word "unto" (*eis*), may signify here, "into the realm
of." Peter, it seems to me, is saying that one of the natural *out-
comes* of a life given over to Jesus IS brotherly love. The purified
life issues into the realm of brotherly affection.

### love one another

Imperative: "You must love one another . . ." But why do we
have here a further exhortation concerning brotherly love, when
the Apostle had just complimented them for possessing this virtue? Some say the reason for the second exhortation is found in
the two different words rendered "love." In the first (*philadel
phia*) we find *philos*, from the verb *phileo*, a word that is supposed to have personal pleasure or joy as a motive of the lover.
In the second "love" (*agapao*), we have a nobler word, where the
lover loses his affection on the *worthiness* and *preciousness* of the
thing or person loved. *If* this be a clear-cut distinction which holds
true here, Peter's exhortation is to further develop and grow from
a *phileo* type of love to an *agapao* type.*

### from the heart

Literally, out of the heart. Such love must be from *within* one.
How needful is this virtue among God's children!

### fervently

An adverb defined as earnestly, fervently, intensely. The adjective occurs in 4:8 ("being fervent"). The root verb from which
this word is derived signifies to stretch out or stretch forth, as
when one is *reaching out* to acquire something. *Effort* is involved
in true Christian brotherliness!

---

*See W. E. Vine, *Expository Dictionary of New Testament Words*, under
"love." He states that *phileo* (the first "love") more nearly represents tender
affection, and that the two verbs are never used indiscriminately in the same
passage. ". . . if each is used with reference to the same objects . . . each word
retains its distinctive and essential character."

**having been begotten again**

See 1:3, notes. The phrase looks to the whole process of regeneration.

**not of corruptible seed, but of incorruptible**

On "corruptible" see 1:18, on "incorruptible" see 1:4. God's Word has a permanent, imperishable, nondecaying quality. It shall never fade away (Matt. 24:35), and neither will those in whose hearts it is planted and in whose lives it is continually retained.

**through the Word of God, which liveth and abideth**

In our first birth the begetting was with perishable seed. Not so with the new birth!

The last two verbs, "liveth . . . abideth," are present participles in the original: ". . . the continually living word and the continually enduring word." Note the Expanded Translation. These verses, then, are inseparably connected with those that follow.

**1:24-25 For,**

>   **All flesh is as grass,**
>   **And all the glory thereof as the flower of grass.**
>   **The grass withereth, and the flower falleth;**
>   **But the Word of the Lord abideth for ever.**

**And this is the word of good tidings which was preached unto you.**

### Expanded Translation

Inasmuch as,
All flesh is like grass,
And all of its glory (splendor, brightness) is like the flower
    of grass.
The grass withers and dries up, and the flower falls off,
But the Word of the Lord remains and abides into the ages
    —forever.
And this word of good tidings is the very word which was
    preached unto you.

---

The passage here referred to is Isa. 40:6-8, but this is not an exact quotation. New Testament writers sometimes take their thought from an Old Testament passage without attempting to quote verbatim.

**For**

Or "inasmuch as" or "because." In these verses, then, we have added confirmation concerning the eternal nature of God's Word, "which liveth and abideth."

### All flesh is as grass
Both are temporal and transitory in nature.

### And all the glory thereof as the flower of grass
The word "thereof," *autes*, is feminine and must, therefore, refer back to the word "flesh," which is the same gender. The glory
of man is, like the glory of the flower, short-lived! The Psalmist
remarked concerning our days, "Yet is their pride but labor and
sorrow; for it is soon gone (A.V. "soon cut off"), and we fly
away" (Psa. 90:10).

### The grass withereth and the flower falleth
i.e., they both come to an end after a short life. The same is
true of man, and *also of man's word and wisdom.*

### But the Word of the Lord abideth forever
In view of what is stated in the latter part of the verse, it seems
this prophecy, though in all likelihood having *immediate* application to God's message to Israel through the prophet, had a *future*
reference to the Gospel Age and the teachings of Christ. Jesus
said, "Heaven and earth shall pass away, but my words shall not
pass away" (Matt. 24:35). Note that the prophecy just preceding
this one in Isaiah is also Messianic (Isa. 40:3).

Do not miss Peter's point! In v. 23 he speaks of our being begotten again, *not* with perishable seed as we were the first time
by our human parents, but with the *im*perishable seed from our
Heavenly Father by His Eternal Word. Verse 24 illustrates this
truth, by likening humanity to the grass of the field and its flower. *All* flesh (including human flesh with which we were first
begotten), is such as quickly perishes! *Not so with the Word of
God!**

### And this is the word of good tidings which was
### preached unto you
The term "good tidings," *evaggelidzo*, means, basically, to address with good tidings or news. But its most frequent *use* in the
New Testament is in reference to the Gospel Message, the message of salvation through the Son of God.**

This last phrase brings the whole subject of the Apostle's discussion to bear with great force upon the Christians. The *eternal*

---
*A similar thought is found in II Cor. 4:16-18.

---
**See further comments under 4:6.

word was not just the Old Testament message, but the Gospel that had been preached to *them, and by which they had been begotten!* We are begotten when we believe the Gospel, the good tidings of the New Testament.

Having been begotten again by such as the Word of God is, it should truly cause us to love one another, v. 22.

## QUESTIONS OVER CHAPTER ONE

1. What is the meaning of the name "Peter"?
2. Who are the elect?
3. How are Christians sojourners?
4. What was "the Dispersion" in the mind of a Jew? How is this term used in v. 1?
5. Define "foreknowledge."
6. How did God "beget us again"?
7. Why does a Christian have a living hope?
8. List four identifying marks of the Christian's inheritance.
9. How is our faith proved?
10. *Why* does a Christian "rejoice greatly with joy unspeakable and full of glory"?
11. What is the end of our faith in Christ?
12. What two classes or groups of persons are spoken of as being very interested in matters pertaining to our salvation?
13. What, specifically, did the prophets want to know?
14. By what Spirit did the prophets speak? (Explain your answer.)
15. How are a Christian's blessings superior to an angel's?
16. What is pictured in the phrase, "girding up the loins of your minds"?
17. How does Peter appeal to his readers to live holy lives? (13-16.)
18. How does God judge?
19. How does this compare with the judgment of man?
20. We were *not* redeemed with_____?
21. We *were* redeemed with_____?
22. When was Christ foreknown?
23. Where is our faith and hope to be?
25. What is the nature of the seed by which we were begotten?
26. All flesh is likened unto_____and its glory unto_____.
27. *To whom* was "this word of good tidings" preached?

# CHAPTER TWO

## 6. Things To Put Away 2:1

**2:1 Putting away therefore all wickedness, and all guile, and hypocrisies, and envies, and all evil speakings,**

### Expanded Translation

Laying down and renouncing therefore all ill-will, and all fraud, and hypocritical behavior, and envies and all slanderous remarks,

---

**Putting away**

The word indicates to lay off, lay down or aside, and is sometimes used of taking off or laying aside garments (Acts 7:58). Metaphorically, it signifies to lay aside, put off, or renounce. See Eph. 4:22-25.

**therefore**

Evidently referring to the teachings of Chapter 1:22-25. The idea is: "Because God's Word has regenerated you with new life, you should have therefore laid aside your former dispositions."

**wickedness**

Whereas it is true that *kakia* frequently carries the *general* idea of wickedness or evil, in this instance the King James ("malice") is probably more accurate. According to the lexicons, the word is sometimes used of a special kind of moral inferiority: malice, ill-will, malignity, desire to injure.

**guile**

Literally, a bait or contrivance for entrapping; hence, fraud, deceit, insidious artifice, guile.

**hypocrisies**

The Greek in English would be spelled *hupokrisis*. In the earlier days of Greek literature it referred to an actor on the stage, one who was portraying the life of another. Used here as a metaphor, it indicates pretence or simulation. An actor only *seems* to be the person he is portraying. But a *Christian* must *live* and *practice* the teachings of Christ from the heart. He must not only *appear* to be following the Saviour, but actually *be* following Him!

**envies**

Meaning envy, jealousy, spite. It is a feeling of discontent or mortification, usually coupled with ill-will, at seeing another's superiority, advantages, or success. Sometimes it also indicates a *desire for* some advantage possessed by another. The basic idea is that the one who harbors this evil is displeased and aggravated at another's good, success, or blessing. Christian, *guard against this sin!*

**evil-speakings**

*Katalalia,* refers to disparaging or belittling remarks about the reputation, worth, or character of another person. *Kata,* down, against, plus *lalia,* speech. Compare our term, "running a person down." It refers also to those who would make false and malicious statements about another. To use one word, "slander" would fit well. The same Greek word occurs in the verb form in 2:12, where it is translated "speak against." Employing this word, James exhorts us, "Speak not one against another, brethren . . ." (Jas. 4:11). Slander is not befitting of a Christian toward *anyone.* (Note the "all.") But how especially needful is this exhortation concerning our conduct *toward brethren,* who are to be special objects of our love (Gal. 6:10).

Peter had been speaking of the need of brotherly love (1:22). And it may be that he still has in mind the cultivation of that virtue when he demands that these things, so ruinous to true brotherliness, be put away.

### 7. Being Like Babies 2:2

**2:2 As newborn babes, long for the spiritual milk which is without guile, that ye may grow thereby unto salvation;**

### Expanded Translation

Just as newborn babies long for their physical milk, you must desire earnestly the spiritual milk which is without guile, that, by means of feeding on such food, you may grow unto salvation.

---

**As newborn babes**

The word "as" (*hos*) is an adverb, referring to *manner.* We are to act *like* babies, in the manner specified. We are not just to copy *babes,* but *newborn* babies, infants, small ones who have only recently been born. The reference here is not necessarily to one who has just embraced the faith, or been converted to Christ. The Apostle simply states that Christians—all Christians— should act *like* infants in their desire for nourishment. Just as *they* desire the physical nutriment, so *we* should long for the food that feeds the soul.

**long for**

*Epipotheo.* Literally, to desire besides . . . to desire earnestly, long for. By implication, to love, have affection for.

### the spiritual milk

Or "milk of the word" (King James Version). The word "spiritual" *logikos*, is an adjective and occurs in only one other instance in the New Testament—Rom. 12:1, where it is rendered "reasonable." Its meaning is: agreeable to reason, following reason. Both here and in Romans 12, the reference is to what Christians should be doing, as those whose primary interest is in that side of life which has to do with the cultivation of the mind and soul. We are to long for the milk which nourishes the soul of a person—his spiritual being, his inward person. "Spiritual milk," then, is in contrast here to mere physical milk, that only provides nourishment for the *body*.

Several times in the epistles of Paul the word "milk" is employed as a term for the less difficult truths of God's Word (Heb. 5:12-13, I Cor. 3:2). And, whereas this *may* also be true in the one passage before us, the *emphasis* here is on one's *desire for spiritual nourishment*.

### without guile

In verse 1 we saw that we were to put aside all guile (*dolos*). Here Peter merely adds the alpha negative to the same word, hence, *adolos*. The meaning is: without guile or deceit, without falsehood; pure, genuine. Such is God's Holy Word! Let us not "water down" his milk, and let us not take off the cream! (Prov. 30:5-6.)

### that ye may grow thereby unto salvation

i.e., by partaking regularly of the food for the soul.

Milk so constitutes an infant's food that they instinctively turn to their mother's breast as their only source of life. Their appetite is intense and frequent. They do not have to be urged and constantly admonished to seek that which causes them to grow. Contrarywise, they complain and cry if they do not get their food *regularly*, and plenty of it! Christians, how strong, how real, how intense is your desire for the word and will of God? Is it as strong as the small baby's desire for milk? It *should* be!

## 8. The Living Stone and Spiritual House 2:3-10

**2:3-4 if ye have tasted that the Lord is gracious: unto whom coming, a living stone rejected indeed of men, but with God elect, precious,**

## Expanded Translation

Presuming you have tasted and enjoyed the flavor of Christianity and that the Lord is helpful, kind, and meek; unto whom, as a living stone, you draw near; he who was indeed rejected by (the masses of) men, but with God he was picked out for special blessing and held in honor.

---

**tasted**

*Geuo,* means literally to taste or try the flavor of, hence to perceive the flavor of, or enjoy, experience. Evidently Peter was writing to those who had enjoyed the blessings of the Christian life. Compare Heb. 6:4-5.

**gracious**

*Chrestos.* Properly, picked for use, useful, virtuous. Secondly, the word signified manageable; that is, mild or pleasant (as opposed to being harsh, hard, sharp or bitter). When it is employed with reference to persons, it refers to one who is *kind* and *benevolent.* Such is the Lord we serve, for He Himself said, "My yoke is easy and my burden is light" (Matt. 11:30). "For this is the love of God, that we keep His commandments: and His commandments are not grievous" (I Jn. 5:3).

**unto whom coming**

With reference to approaching God, probably the act of coming to Him for salvation. While the masses of men had rejected Christ and turned *from* Him, Christians have come *to* Him. Compare Matt. 11:28 where salvation is pictured as coming to Christ. See also Rev. 22:17.

**a living stone**

Compare Isaiah 28:16 and also Psa. 118, 22. In contrast to the temple at Jerusalem and the Jewish synagogues, the church is made up of *living* materials—both the chief cornerstone and the bricks that make up the building (Christians). See Eph. 2:20-21.*

**rejected indeed of men**

The word rendered "reject" means basically to reject upon trial, or to reject after testing and examination. Christ, then, was rejected after the Jews had examined or tried Him and He did not fit their preconceived ideas about the Messiah. Also, He is rejected by all who refuse Him as Saviour (Matt. 12:30).

We have already seen that Christians regard Christ highly by coming to Him for salvation—though men (in general) reject Him. But we now see that *God also* esteems His Son highly . . .

**but with God elect**

See "elect" defined under 1:1.

**precious**

The word means held in honor, prized; hence, precious. It is well to compare this whole passage with Acts 4:11-12. Note there, that in sharp contrast to the foolish and unwise decisions of the Jews, God had placed Christ in the most important part of the building. The Jews, though they are termed "the builders," used poor judgment in leaving out this most important part of the building. God knew much more about good masonry and building than they did!

The statement in verse 4 probably was calculated to encourage the Christians as they made the same choice as God, though the world rejected Christ.

**2:5-6 ye also, as living stones, are built up a spiritual house, to be a holy priesthood, to offer up spiritual sacrifices, acceptable to God through Jesus Christ. Because it is contained in Scripture,**

> **Behold I lay in Zion a chief cornerstone, elect, precious:**
> **And he that believeth on him shall not be put to shame.**

### Expanded Translation

You yourselves also, as living stones, must be built up into a spiritual house, to be a holy priesthood, to offer up spiritual sacrifices, well-pleasing to God through Jesus Christ. Because it is contained within Scripture (Isa. 28:16),

> Look! I lay in Zion (Jerusalem) a chief cornerstone, carefully picked out (by God) for blessings and held in honor:
> And the one believing upon Him shall certainly not be disappointed or frustrated.

**ye also, as living stones**

In view of the fact that Christ is "a living stone" (v. 4), Christians are similarly described because they derive their life from His. (True, some *act* as if they are just *old dead bricks*, but we are *told* to be "lively stones"! (A.V.) We are not, as the old temple stones, plastered permanently into the wall! If we fail to be "doers of the Word," we will be "rejected indeed," not of men, perhaps, but of God, the master builder.

---

*Christ is also pictured as the *foundation* of a building (I Cor. 3:11), but do not confuse that metaphor with this one.

**a spiritual house**

God's house (church) *is* spiritual in nature (I Tim. 3:15). But if the former part of the verse be taken as imperative, Peter is here exhorting God's people to be certain they do their part to *keep* His house *spiritual*. (See the Expanded Translation.)

**to be a holy priesthood**

Compare the term *"royal* priesthood" (v. 9). Now the analogy seems to go from *a* building to a *particular* building, the temple of the Jews. Because saints have access to God and offer not external but spiritual sacrifices to God, they may be termed Jehovah's priesthood.

Our sacrifices are well-pleasing to God *only* when they are "through Jesus Christ." Compare Jn. 14:6. Thus our sacrifices differ in two basic ways from Old Testament offerings. They are to be: (1) spiritual, and (2) only offered through Christ. And what are our sacrifices to be? See Heb. 13:15, Rom. 12:1-2, Phil. 4:15-18.

**because it is contained in Scripture (Isa. 28:16) behold I lay in Zion a chief cornerstone**

Referring to the founding of the spiritual house. God made Christ the chief cornerstone of the church (Eph. 2:20) which began in Jerusalem (Zion), Acts 2.

Much has been said of the importance of the chief cornerstone in the construction of ancient buildings. It has been well established that it was first carefully cut and laid, the other parts of the building being measured and built from it. Thus great care was taken in selecting and shaping it properly.

**and he that believeth on him shall not be put to shame**

The phrase "put to shame," *kataischuno,* is variously rendered, but nearly all the modern scholars give it here the idea of "disappoint." Green's Lexicon and others state it is from the Hebrew, meaning to frustrate or disappoint. So we have, "No one who believes in it will ever be disappointed!"

**2:7-8 For you therefore that believe is the preciousness: but for such as disbelieve,**

**The stone which the builders rejected,**
**The same was made the head of the corner;**
**and,**
**A stone of stumbling, and a rock of offence;**
**for they stumble at the word, being disobedient: whereunto also they were appointed.**

### Expanded Translation

To you therefore who believe, He is precious and valuable, but for such as refuse to believe,
> The stone which the builders rejected (after examination)
> This has become the main corner stone;
> and,
> A rock which is an impediment and cause of stumbling.

They stub their toes at the word being disbelieving and incompliant: into which position they were appointed.

---

**For you therefore that believe is the preciousness**

Or, "He (Christ) is precious." The word "preciousness," rendered "honor" in 1:7, means a pricing, estimate of worth, etc. Then, a thing of price, something worthy of great price. Of course, in reality our Saviour is *priceless!*

**but for such as disbelieve**

i.e., on the Son of God. "Disbelieve" is in the present tense, indicating a persistent unwillingness to be convinced.

**the stone which the builders rejected, the same was made the head of the corner**

See comments, vss. 4, 6.

**and a stone of stumbling and a rock of offence**

These two phrases expressing basically the same thought, i.e., that Christ became a stone over which the Jews tripped and fell because He did not meet their preconceived ideas. It annoyed and offended the Jews that His words, deeds, career and particularly His ignominious death on the cross did not correspond to their expectations concerning the Messiah. They, therefore, despised and rejected Him, and by that crime brought upon themselves punishment. By their obstinancy and rebellion, they made shipwreck of salvation. See Rom. 9:32-33.

**for they stumble at the word, being disobedient**

Expressing a state of things which was still existing, as "being disobedient" is a present participle. The term *apeitheo* is composed of the alpha negative plus *peitho*, to *persuade*. Thus the lexicons: to be incompliant, to refuse to believe, disbelieve; to refuse belief and obedience, be stubbornly perverse or rebellious.

It is well to notice that the Saviour, as a stone, was *rejected* and cast out, *not* built into the wall. Note, also, that the builders themselves, according to Acts 4:11-12, rejected the precious stone of Christ, and were stumbling over Him. There seems to be here a picture of construction workers who were stumbling over the object they had cast out and left to the side of the building they were erecting.

**whereunto also they were appointed**

Literally, "into which they were placed." Into or unto what? The simplest interpretation from the context is the *disobedience*. "Being disobedient, into which state they were placed." Those who were not saved were, by the very nature of the case, destined to act in this manner. Actually, Peter has not as yet spoken of the *punishment* to which they were appointed, but only the *cause* of punishment—a life that is unyielding and unbending to the will of God.

It does no violence to the passage to attribute this appointing to God. He had even written of it beforehand (Jude 4, Isa. 8:14, 53:3). Therefore it was, in a sense, *appointed* that Christ should be an occasion of stumbling and falling to some, even as He was the Saviour to others. In either case, it was not a matter unforeseen by God. At the same time, no man who finds Christ to be such (i.e., disbelieves and rejects the Gospel) should take refuge in this as an excuse. Such are voluntary in *rejecting* the plan (though God knew some would reject it), the same as others voluntarily *accept* it (though this was also known and arranged for by God). Concerning those who rejected it, we may say they were not forced or compelled to do it; but it was seen that this consequence would follow, and the plan was laid to send the Saviour in spite of such knowledge.

The statement does not necessarily refer to their *eternal* doom. Notice Acts 3:17-19 and Acts 2:36-38. These very Jews who "were appointed" to the condition or circumstances mentioned here by Peter, were yet told to repent and turn to Christ, obey His Word and their sins would be forgiven. Yet, the verse before us is frequently cited by those who would teach that some are eternally destined beforehand by God to be everlastingly doomed, and that such individuals have no ability to turn to Christ—they being helpless victims of God's irrevocable edict that they should be forever lost.

Surely it is true in our present age, also, that some stumble at the Word because of their preconceived ideas when they study it.

An example of this is the modern Jew, who still is unwilling to accept Jesus Christ because of his false conceptions concerning the Messiah.

**2:9-10 But ye are an elect race, a royal priesthood, a holy nation, a people for God's own possession, that ye may show forth the excellencies of him who called you out of darkness into His marvelous light: who in times past were no people, are the people of God: who had not obtained mercy, but now have obtained mercy.**

### Expanded Translation

But you (in contrast to those of which I have just spoken) are a chosen and select race, a regal and royal priesthood, a holy and sanctified nation, a people belonging to God; in order that you may declare abroad the excellencies and perfections of him who called you out of the darkness of sin and into his admirable and wonderful light. You are the ones who formerly were no people, but now are the people belonging to God, the ones who had not received mercy (pity, compassion) but now have received mercy.

---

Notice the contrast between this verse and the three preceding verses. The phrase, "but ye," refers to the Christians. Whereas many of the Jews had found an occasion of stumbling in Christ because of their disobedience, those who accepted Him became "an elect race," etc. Surely this verse shows how God has elevated every person who has come into His fold!

#### race

The primary meaning of this word is "offspring. It refers to a family, stock, species, race or kindred. Notice that Peter tells us that we are not only a "race," but an "*elect* race." See 1:1 on "elect."

For over a thousand years the determining factor for becoming a member of God's "elect race" was *not* a new experience, or conversion. It was a physical birth. If one was born a Jew and obeyed the Law of Moses, he was a member of God's "elect race." Ex. 19:5-6 and Deut. 7:6 bear this out. But *now* the determining factor is a new birth, a birth of "water and the Spirit" (Jn. 3:5).

#### royal priesthood

See I Pet. 2:5 and compare Rev. 1:6.

Under the Law of Moses the priest constituted a special class empowered to officiate in worship and sacrifice to God. Inasmuch as all Christians are authorized to engage in the worship of God, all Christians are priests. We are a "priesthood of believers." This is contrary to the clergy-laity concept, prevalent in the Roman Catholic and some of the Protestant denominations. The church is a kingdom—a kingdom in which *all* the subjects are qualified to engage in offering sacrifice.

### holy nation

See 1:15 on "holy." The phrase now applies to all members of Christ's church, especially since the Israelites (in the past regarded as the nation consecrated to God) have been cast off and rejected as a whole because of their disobedience. All Christians now compose "the Israel of God" (Gal. 6:16).

### a people for God's own possession

A much better rendering than the King James Version, "a peculiar people." Christians belong to God and are His exclusive property (Eph. 1:14, Titus 2:14).

### that ye may show forth the excellencies of him who called you out of darkness into his marvelous light

The word "that," is a conjunction meaning "in order that." It is used here to show purpose or design. So in this verse we see *why* we were redeemed. God has called us to the high and holy position of being Christians for a specific reason. It is not that we might be egotistical, haughty or headstrong! See Luke 18:9-14. This is why physical Israel fell. They were proud of the fact that they were *God's chosen people.* Their attitude was, "God, you can't get along without us!" How easy it is for Christians to fall into this same attitude.

But notice that the real purpose of our lives is to "show forth the excellencies of Him . . ."

SHOW FORTH—that is, declare abroad, publish, make known. We may do this by both our lives and our words. What is it that we are to tell abroad?

EXCELLENCIES—a word signifying excellencies, perfections, beauties. It is used in II Pet. 1:3 of God's *power.*
The scope of reference in this phrase is to our whole manner of life as a Christian. Surely the text would include our work as personal evangelists to those who are unsaved. But in *every way* we are to be "reflectors" of God's glories.

God called or beckoned us *out* of something *into* something. Out of what were we called?

DARKNESS—used figuratively of ignorance respecting divine things and human duties. But, as Thayer says, it includes "the accompanying ungodliness and immorality, together with consequent misery." The ignorance and the *accompanying sinfulness* of the unsaved person is indicated. See Eph. 5:7-8. This is what we were called "out of." Now, what were we called "into"?

LIGHT—used to denote truth and its knowledge, together with the spiritual purity congruous with it. It especially denotes the *saving* truth embodied in Christ and by His love imparted to mankind. This "light" is called MARVELOUS. It is worthy of a Christian's admiration; excellent, wonderous, glorious.

What a picture of real conversion! Compare Col. 1:12-13.

God help us to never go back to the darkness!

### no people

The primary reference here is evidently to the Gentile nations. See Rom. 9:24-26. But it is also true, in a general way, of all who are without a saving knowledge of Jesus Christ. The Greeks were a people of great culture and learning. However, as far as usefulness to God was concerned, they were "nobodies," because they did not have Jesus Christ as their Saviour. The second chapter of Ephesians forms an excellent commentary on the phrase, "no people."

God is not primarily concerned with whether you are able to sing like Caruso, play the piano like Mendelsohn, scale the heights of political greatness, climb the pinnacle of oratorical excellence, or build a business that approaches Kaiser's. Although you may have done all of these things and more, as far as God is concerned you are "nobody" until you have turned your heart and soul over to Jesus Christ. Yes, God loves you, but your life is of no eternal profit until it is involved in His service!

### obtained mercy

*Eleeo*, "to feel sympathy with the misery of another, especially such sympathy as manifests itself in action, less frequently in word . . . a criminal begs *eleos* (the noun form of this word), of his judge"—Thayer.

It is well to note that the personal will of the individual is involved in accepting the mercy and love of God. We "had not obtained mercy" but now we "have obtained mercy." This *we* must do. We must accept the gracious offer of salvation that God lovingly extends. He will not force it upon us against our will. The prodigal's father ran out to embrace him, when the son left the pig-pen and returned to his family!

## 9.  Conduct As Sojourners 2:11,12

**2:11 Beloved, I beseech you as sojourners and pilgrims, to abstain from fleshly lusts, which war against the soul;**

### Expanded Translation

Loved ones, I implore you as foreigners and sojourners (whose fatherland is in heaven), to keep from yourselves and abstain from the passions and cravings of the flesh, which are at war against the soul;

---

**I beseech you as sojourners and pilgrims**

SOJOURNERS—*paroikos*, is from *para*, meaning "beside" and *oikos*, meaning "house." The word had reference to one who dwelt near another. In the Scriptures, it indicates a temporary resident, stranger, foreigner, one who lives in a place without the right of citizenship (Acts 7:6, 29). It is used in Eph. 2:19 with reference to those who are without citizenship in God's kingdom. Here the word is used of Christians, who live temporarily on earth as strangers or sojourners with their fatherland as heaven. Compare a similar thought in Phil. 3:20. Our citizenship papers are in heaven. We should be speaking the language of heaven and we should be observing the ways and customs that heaven has designed for its citizens. Compare "sojourning" (*paroikia*) of 1:17.

PILGRIMS—Compare I Pet. 1:1 where the same words are rendered "sojourners." It means to be a sojourner and stranger among another people, residing in another country not one's own, a sojourner, stranger. Compare Heb. 11:13. Souter says the word means "a stranger in a land not his own, a citizen with limited rights."

What is the difference between the word here rendered "sojourner" and "pilgrim"? The words are obviously very similar in meaning. However, in the latter word there is the idea of going through, or progressing through, a foreign country—an element not present in the former word.

Being foreigners and strangers, we are exhorted to be careful lest we succumb to the ways of lust, characteristic of the country in which we are temporarily dwelling.

**to abstain from fleshly lusts**

ABSTAIN—*apecho*, from *apo* (off, from) and *echo* (hold). It is used in the middle voice in our text and means to abstain from, hold one's self off from.

FLESHLY—*sarkikos*, means fleshly; pertaining to the body, corporeal, physical, carnal. According to Thayer it has reference to that which has "its seat in the animal nature, or aroused by the animal nature." Some of these evil desires are enumerated in Gal. 5:19-21.

**which war against the soul**

WAR—*strateuo* (comp. *strato*: an army): to perform military duty, serve as a soldier . . . to battle.

SOUL—*psuche*, is here best regarded as a moral being designed for everlasting life, as in v. 25. Ungodly lusts war against and tear down this soul and tend to make it unfit for its intended home with God.

**2:12 Having your behavior seemly among the Gentiles; that, wherein they speak against you as evil-doers, they may by your good works, which they behold, glorify God in the day of visitation.**

### Expanded Translation

Maintaining a behavior that is upright and honorable among the heathen (pagans, un-Christian people), that, wherein they are speaking against you as practicers of evil, or, perhaps *criminals*), they may, from observing your good works, glorify God in the day of visitation.

---

**Having your behavior seemly among the Gentiles, that wherever they speak against you as evil-doers**

SEEMLY—good, possessing moral excellence, worthy, upright, virtuous, beautiful. Our lives must be spiritually beautiful in a world of spiritual ugliness.

SPEAK AGAINST—*katalaleo*, also occurs in 3:16. The noun form is defined under 2:1.

EVIL-DOERS—*kakopoios*, an evil-doer, malefactor, or criminal. The same word is used in verse 14, 3:17, and 4:15. The word is frequently employed to refer to those who were committing some act which was legally wrong according to the laws of the land; a civil lawbreaker (Jn. 18:30).

**which they behold, glorify God**

BEHOLD—*epopteuo.* (*epi* — upon, plus a form of *horao* — to see): to look upon, be an eye-witness of, view attentively. The noun form, *epoptes*, "eyewitness," is rendered "eye witness" in II Pet. 1:16, where it appears in the plural.

With un-Christian people viewing our lives so attentively, we should be careful that they see the "good works" of which the text speaks. They are looking for anything off-color they can possibly find. Their original motive, no doubt, is often to find fault; but by our good (spiritually beautiful) lives, they are turned to "glorify God . . ."

GLORIFY—*doxadzo*, here means to extoll, magnify, adore or worship.

**day of visitation**

*Episkope*, means inspection, visitation. It is from *epi*—upon, and *skopeo*—to view attentively, see, observe. Thayer says of the word, "in Biblical Greek after the Hebrew, *pekudah*, that act by which God looks into and searches out the ways, deeds, and character of men in order to adjudge them their lot accordingly, whether joyous or sad; inspection, investigation, visitation."

There is considerable question as to just what day is "the day of visitation." Some refer it to the Judgment Day. That day shall be a time of Divine reward for some and a time of Divine judgment or condemnation for others. Each of us shall be "visited" on that final day through the judge God has appointed, Jesus Christ. He shall then search out our hearts and we shall receive that which he determines is proper for us: either eternal glory with Him, or eternal suffering with Satan and his cohorts. That day shall truly be a day of glorifying God to those who are saved.

A second possibility is the time that God "visits" the Gentiles (pagans), who were beholding the Christians' behavior, with *salvation*. Compare Psa. 106:4, "Remember me, oh Jehovah, with the favor that thou bearest unto thy people; *oh visit me with thy salvation.*"*

The third possibility is that the expression refers to the coming destruction of Jerusalem and the Jewish State. If the date we have assigned to the epistle is correct, that day, A.D. 70, was not far

---

*Pekudah* is used similarly in Ex. 3:16 of the *literal* deliverance of the Israelites from Egyptian slavery.

off. *Episkope* is used with this reference in Luke 19:44, where we have "the time of Thy visitation"—*ton kairon tes episkopes sou,* which is certainly similar to this passage, *en hemera episkopes.*

The Gentiles, having become Christians because of the influence of these disciples, would "glorify God" because they were *safe.* No Christian was harmed during that great catastrophe. Speaking of the Christians, Newman says:

"Shortly before the city had been invested by Titus (probably late in 69), they withdrew to Pella, in Perea, where under the leadership of Symeon, a cousin to the Lord, they remained until it was safe for them to return to Jerusalem."*

The possibility of this application to "the day of visitation" becomes very strong when we look at similar passages in the epistles (Heb. 10:25, Jas. 5:1-8) and the "day" of which they speak.

To the Jew, the "day of visitation" was proverbial, and is used of God's *divine punishment* in the Old Testament.**

There are admitted difficulties in this last interpretation, but on the whole, it seems to have the most in its favor. See further comments under 4:7.

## IV.  DUTIES TOWARD OTHERS
## 2:13 — 3:12
### 1.  Toward Civil Government 2:13-17

**2:13-14 Be subject to every ordinance of man for the Lord's sake: whether to the king as supreme; or unto governors, as sent by him for vengeance on evil-doers and for praise to them that do well.**

### Expanded Translation

Be submissive to every ordinance (literally, *creation*) of man for the Lord's sake (that is, as a part of your service to Him): whether to the (Roman) King or emperor as the one who is supreme (in the civil realm), or unto (Roman provincial) governors as sent by him to punish those who practice evil (criminals) and to commend and praise those who live righteously.

---

**Be subject to every ordinance of man for the Lord's sake:**

BE SUBJECT—*hupotasso.* Primarily a military term meaning

---

*A Manual of Church History, Vol. I, p. 118. His whole account of the destruction of the city (pp. 116-119) is excellent.
**Isa. 10:3, Jer. 10:15.

to place or rank under (as when lower officers were placed under higher officers). Hence, subject, put in subjection, submit.

ORDINANCE—*ktisis*. In Greek writing, the act of founding, establishing, building, etc. In the New Testament, the act of creating, creation (Rom. 1:20), then an institution, ordinance. The idea of the latter definition is apparently that laws, governments, etc., are "created" or *formed by human minds*, namely, the rulers of a nation or state.

Notice that we are to be in subjection to every ordinance of man, FOR THE LORD'S SAKE. That is, for the good of, or as a part of our obedience to, the Lord. We are to act in this manner as a part of our service to Christ. Compare Rom. 13:4-5 and Eph. 6:7.

**whether to the king as supreme; or unto governors,**

The specific reference here is to the Roman Emperor.

AS SUPREME—*hupercho*, literally indicates to hold above; hence, to stand out above . . . to be higher, superior. Compare Rom. 13:1: "Let every soul be in subjection to the higher powers . . ."

Of course, it is understood here that the things "ordained" by those in authority are not in themselves contrary to the laws of God as He has revealed them in His Word. Notice Acts 4:19, 5:27-29, where we find the principle that God's laws are to be obeyed first, should they come in conflict with laws or ordinances of men.

The commandment of Peter is particularly significant when we realize that these Christians were under a heathen government, and a wicked emperor (Nero?), yet were to heed this exhortation!

GOVERNORS—*hegemon*, a guide; a leader; a chieftain, prince (Matt. 2:6); a Roman provincial governor, under whatever title. Such was Pilate (Matt. 27-2).

Governors are sent for two reasons:

1. "Vengeance" on criminals. *Ekdikesis*, a revenging, vengeance, punishment, or the punishment by one. The word is from *ek*, meaning out of, and *dike*, meaning righteousness or justice. Hence, properly, the execution of right and justice,; and then the *meting or giving out of justice* to those who violate the laws of the land.

2. For "praise" to those who are well behaved. *Epainos, epi*—on or upon, plus *ainos*—praise; hence, praise, commendation, approbation, applause.

**2:15-16 For so is the will of God, that by well-doing ye should put to silence the ignorance of foolish men: as free, and not using your freedom for a cloak of wickedness, but as bond-servants of God.**

### Expanded Translation

Because this is the will and wish of God, that by doing good and living right you should reduce to silence the ignorant accusations and charges of foolish and inconsiderate men: as free and unbound by restraint, and yet not using your freedom as a veil over (i.e., means of hiding) evil, but living as God's slaves.

---

#### that by well-doing ye should put to silence the ignorance of foolish men

PUT TO SILENCE—*phimoo*, "to close the mouth with a muzzle." Note I Cor. 9:9: "for it is written in the Law of Moses, thou shalt not *muzzle* the ox when he treadeth out the corn." Metaphorically, to stop the mouth, make speechless, reduce to silence. Here, the word modifies "ignorance." Hence, "put a muzzle on the ignorant charges of foolish men."

FOOLISH—*aphron*. The word properly indicates without reason; hence, senseless, stupid, without reflection or intelligence, acting rashly. It is a stronger and more expressive word than would have been used if they had simply lacked information on a subject.

#### as free, and not using your freedom for a cloak of wickedness

FREE—*eleutheros* means free, exempt, unrestrained. The question here is, free from what? Some would say the Mosaic Law, as in Gal. 4:26. Others say it is from the bondage of sin, as in Jn. 8:36. It seems, from the context, that the last is the meaning in this passage.

CLOAK—*epikalumma*—a covering, veil. Metaphorically, a pretext, cloak. The "covering" here was used as a means of hiding or concealing one's sin. Their reasoning apparently was, "Are we not free? We are not bound by any restraint."

Freedom from sin, or the law, might be used to justify one's wicked ways; perhaps here even the breaking of civil law. But though we are free from the bondage of sin (II Pet. 2:18-19, Rom. 6:6) this does not mean we have no duties, responsibilities, or obligations toward God and man. Rather, we are to be bond-servants voluntarily. (See Rom. 6:15-18; I Cor. 9:21, II Cor. 4:5.)

**2:17 Honor all men. Love the brotherhood. Fear God. Honor the king.**

### Expanded Translation

Treat every person as a person of value, one to be honored. Love the band of brothers. Fear, reverence, and venerate God. Value and honor the king.

**Honor all men.**

HONOR—the word *timao*, means to estimate, fix the value, or price something; then, to have in honor, revere, venerate. The word is in the *aorist* imperative here, denoting a sharp, definite rule, to be adopted at once.

God tells us to venerate or hold in esteem all men. All men are God's creation or handiwork, made in His likeness, even though their lives may be sadly defaced and marred by sin. The "honor" would doubtless be shown in different ways to different people; but, in some sense, it is due *all* men. This is true even with regard to the worst harlot or backslider. Christians must learn to accept *people* (not their sin) where they are and strive to lead them from there to nobler things!

In the context here, Peter may have special reference to the Jews' attitude toward the idolatrous Gentiles around them.

**Love the brotherhood.**

LOVE—*agapao*. See notes on 1:22.

BROTHERHOOD—*adelphotes*, a band of brothers, i.e., of Christians. Peter is the only New Testament writer who employs this word and that only in this book. Compare 5:9.

**Fear God.**

Compare the use of "fear" (*phobeo*) in verse 18. The meaning here is: "to reverence, venerate, to treat with deference or reverential obedience." (Thayer). "It is the fear, not so much of punishment, as of his disapprobation; not so much the dread of suffering as the dread of doing wrong."—Barnes.

The fear of the *Judgment Day* and the agonies that follow in the punishment of the wicked, is cast out when a Christian is truly acting as he should toward God and his brother. See I Jn. 4:17-18 where we are told "perfect love casteth out fear." Fear of what? In that passage it is of the *Judgment Day*, and not of God. A Christian surely need not fear the Judgment Day, but we certainly should have a reverential fear and veneration for God. Hence, there is no contradiction between these two passages. We *are* to fear God, but as Christians, we have no fear of the Judgment. We are not terrorized or in dread of that day. Solomon is still right: "the fear of Jehovah is the beginning of knowledge" (Prov. 1:7a).

**Honor the King.**

(See II Pet. 2:10-11.) How would this be done? It could be accomplished in a number of ways, but probably here he is particularly speaking of their obedience. (See vss. 13-14.) Another way, we might add, for us to honor him is to pray for him (II Tim. 2:1-2). Compare Rom. 13:7 with this passage.

## 2.  Toward Masters 2:18-25

**2:18 Servants, be in subjection to your masters with all fear; not only to the good and gentle, but also to the froward."**

### Expanded Translation

You domestic servants (or household slaves), be subjecting yourselves to your master-owners, with all respect and deference; not only to the good (kind), and gentle (fair), but also to the perverse and ill-natured.

---

**Servants, be in subjection to your masters**

SERVANTS—*oiketes*, is equivalent to the Latin word *domesticus*, hence our word domestic, i.e., one who lives in the same house with another, spoken of all who are under the authority of one and the same householder, especially a servant. The word is more restricted in meaning than the normal word rendered "servant" (*doulos*), and designates one holding closer relations to the family than other slaves.

MASTER—*despotes*, meaning "a lord, master, especially of slaves." ". . . denotes absolute ownership and uncontrolled power" (Thayer). See discussion under "lord" in 3:6.

BE IN SUBJECTION—The phrase is here in the middle voice, indicating action with regard to one's self. Thus Young's literal translation: "be subjecting yourselves . . ."

**with all fear;**

*Phobos*, as we have seen in the verb of the previous verse, though *customarily* meaning fear, terror, or fright, is *here* used in

64

the sense of respect or deference. The latter word Webster defines: "a yielding of judgment or preference from respect to the wishes or opinions of another; courteous or complaisant regard for another's wishes."

Two types of masters are now described. We are to be in subjection to either type.

**not only to the good and gentle,**

GOOD—*agathos*. Benevolent, kind, generous, etc.

GENTLE—*epieikes*, equitable, fair mild. It expresses that considerateness that looks humanly and reasonably at the facts of a case. We all appreciate such men, and it is usually not difficult to submit to their oversight.

**but also to the froward.**

*Skolios* (whence the name of our disease, scoliosis), meaning crooked, curved; metaphorically, perverse, wicked, unfair, surly. It is when we must subject ourselves to *this type* of man that our real Christian character (or lack of it) is revealed. How blessed we are in the present age to have rulers who, as a rule, do not openly oppose and antagonize us as we pursue the Christ-like life.

**2:19-20 For this is acceptable, if for conscience toward God a man endureth griefs, suffering wrongfully. For what glory is it, if, when ye sin, and are buffeted for it, ye shall take it patiently? but if, when ye do well, and suffer for it, ye shall take it patiently, this is acceptable with God.**

## Expanded Translation

For this is what causes God to regard you with favor, if, because of consciousness of God, a man bears up under griefs and sorrows, suffering unjustly (undeservedly). For what credit is it to you to bear up patiently under it, if, being a sinner, you are punished (literally, beaten with the fist) for it?

**For this is acceptable,**

Acceptable—*charis*, so many times rendered "grace" in the Scriptures. Abbott-Smith says its basic meaning is "that which causes favorable regard," here, of course, in the eyes of God.

**if for conscience toward God**

Conscience—*suneidesis*. The normal definition is the soul as distinguishing between what is morally good and bad, prompting to do the former and shun the latter, commending the one and condemning the other. However, in this case our definition may be more simple. The phrase, "for conscience toward God," also may be read "because you are conscious of God," that is, His presence, His all-seeing eye, etc. Literally, the phrase reads "because of consciousness of God." Most modern translators have adopted the latter rendering.

**a man endureth griefs, suffering wrongfully.**

Wrongfully—*adikos*, is an adverb meaning unjustly, undeservedly, without fault.

**For what glory is it,**

Glory—*kleos*, properly rumour, report; then good report, praise, credit.

**if, when ye sin,**

Sin—is here a present participle, hence the meaning "when (as) you are sinning," or "being a sinful one," or "being a sinner." The word, *hamartano*, means literally "to miss the mark," hence to be guilty of wrong.

**and are buffeted for it,**

Buffeted—*kolaphidzo*, derived from *kolaphos* (a blow with the fiist), hence to beat with the fist, buffet. See especially Matt. 26:67 for a familiar example. It is likely here, however, that the specific term is used for the general meaning of *harsh treatment*.

**ye shall take it patiently,**

Patiently—literally, to stay or remain behind (when others have departed). Then to bear up under, endure, persevere.

On the whole passage, compare Matt. 5:10-12. See also Eph. 6:5, Col. 3:22-25.

**2:21-22 For hereunto were ye called: because Christ also suffered for you, leaving you an example, that ye should follow his steps: who did no sin, neither was guile found in his mouth.**

### Expanded Translation

For into this state (of suffering and bearing up under it properly) you have been called: Because Christ also suffered for you (and He Himself was *faultless*), leaving you an example to be copied, that you might tread in His footsteps; who did not commit an act of sin, neither was guile or deceit found in his mouth.

**For hereunto were ye called**

Or, "to such experience you have been called," or "that is the life to which you have been called"—that is, bearing up and enduring under trial and persecution. When accepting the call to follow Christ, we also accepted the call of a life of suffering and enduring, As Christ suffered and endured. (See Jn. 15:20.)

**because Christ also suffered for you**

This was prophesied and Christ knew it would be so, for it was necessary in God's plan of redeeming the world. But in another sense it was "wrongfully"—see v. 22. Christ was given an unfair trial, wrongfully accused, etc. Thus He was a perfect illustration of the type of suffering that is *virtuous*, that type of suffering of which Peter just spoke (v. 20).

**leaving you an example,**

EXAMPLE—*hupogrammos*, means basically a writing-copy, including all the letters of the alphabet, given to beginners as an aid while learning to draw them. Hence, an example that is set before one.

Who has not, in his younger days, experienced the difficulty of following the perfect examples of written letters in his copy-book? However, if we would have continually striven to copy the letters after the perfect example in our book, we would surely have improved with time. The fault in most of our writing is that we do not continually pattern it after a perfect model. This is also the frequent fault of Christian people. Instead of copying Christ, their perfect "copy-book," they are following the poor example of their fellow man or their own lives.

**that ye should follow his steps**

FOLLOW—*epakoloutheo*, means to follow close upon, to follow after. Metaphorically it is used here of treading in another's footsteps, that is, imitating another's example, for we have here the phrase, "that ye should follow his steps." There is a picture here of one walking, whose steps as he proceeds are visible (as when one walks in the dust or snow). Following such a person, we are not to follow his trail carelessly, but rather, place our footsteps in His.

The particular way that we are to follow in the very steps of Christ is in suffering wrongfully and yet being obedient—in spite of the harshest persecution.

Notice who says this! Perhaps, as he wrote, it was with reflection upon his own life, when he (Peter) did *not* follow this very exhortation.

**neither was guile found in his mouth.**

GUILE—see definition under 2:1, and its opposite "without guile"—under 2:2.

FOUND—*heurisko* generally indicates to find or discover after searching, to find a thing sought after.

Notice especially that Jesus suffered though He was sinless, and thus suffered "wrongfully." The inference is that you as a Christian may be called upon to suffer *even though you are living as Christ lived*. We should not be alarmed, therefore, if we suffer, even though we *know* of no particular reason for it. Christ was *perfect*, but He still suffered. Verse 22 shows His perfection in both deed and word.

Concerning Christ's sufferings we may say:

1. He *did* suffer, and we will also if we are living as He did.
2. He suffered *unjustly*, no real crime being proven against Him. So should it be with us.
3. He suffered for the good and benefit of others.
4. His manner of conduct in suffering provides a Divine copy for us to follow.

**2:23 who, when he was reviled, reviled not again; when he suffered, threatened not; but committed himself to him that judgeth righteously:**

### Expanded Translation

Who being reviled did not revile back (did not return the same type of abusive speech); Suffering, was not threatening, but was committing himself to him who judges righteously and justly:

**who, when he was reviled,**

REVILED—*loidoreo* means to reproach, rail at, heap abuse upon. See its usage in Jn. 9:28, Acts 23:4, I Cor. 4:12.

**reviled not again**

Literally, did not revile back; that is, Jesus did not retaliate with the same type of abuse that was given Him. He lived what He taught: Matt. 5:38-48.

**when he suffered, threatened not;**

THREATENED—*apeileo*, to threaten, menace, rebuke. Compare Acts 4:17.

Our Saviour knew He was in the safe hands of His Father. He also knew His Father would render justice to those who had *unjustly* treated Him. But that was the Father's duty, not His

(Rom. 12:17-21).

**2:24-25 who his own self bare our sins in his body upon the tree, that we, having died unto sins, might live unto righteousness; by whose stripes ye were healed. For ye were going astray like sheep; but are now returned unto the Shepherd and Bishop of your souls.**

### Expanded Translation

who himself carried the burden of our sins in his own body upon the cross, in order that we, after having died (ceased from) sin, might live for righteousness; by whose bloody wounds ye were healed, (restored from a state of sin and condemnation). For you were misled and wandering about like lost sheep, but are now returned (brought back) unto the Shepherd and Overseer of your souls.

_____ ___

**who his own self bare our sins in his body**

The first part of v. 24 emphasizes the part of Christ in our redemption. It was *Christ Himself* who underwent such affliction *for* us. Why? That: (1) We might die to sin and (2) *Having died that death,* live for righteousness.

**having died unto sins**

The words "having died" carries the basic idea of being removed from. When we die physically, the spirit is removed from the body. When we die to sin, we should be alienated from its influence and practice in our lives.

**by whose stripes**

Stripes, *molops.* Literally, the mark of a blow, then, a wound, a wound that bleeds. By enduring such suffering, involving both mental and physical agony, we were made spiritually whole. By His *wounds* on the *cross,* our *spiritual* wounds were healed.

**ye were healed**

The Bible in several places refers to our spiritual restoration as "healing" from our previous state of sickness: Isa. 1:5, 6, Matt. 13:15, Heb. 12:12-13.

**shepherd and bishop of your souls**

"Bishop" would be better rendered overseer or watcher. Christ is our guide, protector, guardian, and provider. Such care is ours, if we will only commit ourselves into His hands. (See comments, 5:2-3.)

### QUESTIONS OVER CHAPTER TWO

1. Of what significance is the "therefore" of 2:1?
2. To what *particular* evil does the word "wickedness" most likely refer? (2:1)

3. What is *guile*?
4. What did *hypocrite* mean before the word took on a religious significance?
5. How many times does *all* occur in v. 1?
6. Are we to be like newborn babies in every way possible? Explain.
7. In what sense *does* Peter specify we are to imitate the newborn babe?
8. The term "long for" (v. 2) is usually translated _____ in the Bible?
9. What is necessary if we are to grow into salvation, according to Peter?
10. How does one "taste" the graciousness of the Lord?
11. What kind of stones are Christians to be?
12. They are "built up a _____ house."
13. Explain how Christians are "a holy priesthood."
14. What *kind* of sacrifices do these priests offer? Illustrate.
15. Give two basic ways in which our sacrifices differ from those of the Old Testament Priests.
16. What is the significance of Christ being called the chief cornerstone?
17. Who are "the builders" of v. 7?
18. How do God's actions contrast with theirs?
19. Why was Jesus a "stone of stumbling" to the Jews?
20. Why, specifically, did they "stumble at the word"?
21. Do you remember another rendering of the term "were appointed"? (v. 8)
22. Explain, simply and briefly, the expression "Whereunto also they were appointed." (v.8.)
23. To what does v. 9 stand in contrast?
24. Name at least three ways in which Christians (the church) are pictured here as "the Israel of God."
25. For what *purpose* do we occupy this exalted position?
26. Of what is "darkness" and "light" a picture? (v. 9.)
27. In what way are un-Christian people "no people"?
28. How is a sojourner and a pilgrim different from a tramp?
29. Against what do the lusts of the flesh make war?
30. In the phrase, "having your behavior seemly among the Gentiles," what does "seemly" mean? Who are the "Gentiles" here?

31. Give three possible periods of time which may be referred to in the expression "day of visitation." Which seems most correct to you?
32. *Why* are we to be subject to "every ordinance of man"?
33. Are there any limitations on this? Explain.
34. Peter gives two reasons God ordained civil authority. Can you name them?
35. How should Christians *not* use their freedom?
36. Please complete v. 17 without the use of your Bible: "Honor _____ _____. Love _____ _____. Fear _____. Honor _____ _____."
37. In what sense are Christians to "fear" God?
38. Who are the "froward" masters? Should they be feared and obeyed?
39. What should always be the reason behind the suffering and persecution one receives from the world?
40. In what *particular* way did Christ leave an example for *these* Christians?
41. In this example, how closely should He be followed?
42. In what two areas of life was Christ found sinless? (v. 22.)
43. Into whose hands did He commit Himself?
44. Christ gave His life on the cross "that we, having _____ unto sin, might _____ unto righteousness."
45. ". . . by whose stripes ye are healed" is spoken of Christ. What Old Testament prophet spoke this? Where?
46. Christ is the _____ and _____ of the Christian's soul.

## CHAPTER THREE
### 3. Toward Husbands 3:1-6

**3:1-2 In like manner, ye wives, be in subjection to your own husbands; that, even if any obey not the word, they may without the word be gained by the behavior of their wives; beholding your chaste behavior coupled with fear.**

### Expanded Translation

In the same way you wives be subjecting yourselves to and obeying your own husbands, in order that (for this purpose:) even if any (of the husbands) refuse to yield and comply to the word (teachings of Scripture) they may be won over (to Christ) without a word (talking, speech), but rather by means of the behavior and conduct of their wives, when they behold your pure and chaste behavior joined with reverence and respect (of your husband).

**In like manner,**
Relating this passage to the previous context, especially Chap. 2:13-25. Peter had previously written to citizens and servants to relate all of life to God, behaving as Christians at all times and in all circumstances. Actually, the subject of the previous verses has been *obedient subjection*—even if one is mistreated. The case had just been cited of Christ, who suffered wrongfully and yet did not sin or rise up in rebellion against those who mistreated Him.

**ye wives, be in subjection**
See the same word defined in 2:18.

**to your own husbands; that,**

OWN HUSBANDS—Compare Eph. 5:22.

THAT—The Greek word expresses purpose; herefore, we have here the purpose of her subjection to her husband.

**obey not**
See our notes in 2:8 where the same word is translated "disobedient." Previously Peter had exhorted servants to be in subjection to their masters even if their masters were "froward." Here he exhorts wives how to act even if they have un-Christian mates.

**the word**
i.e., the Gospel Message. They have not been obedient to the teachings of Christ.

**they may without the word be gained by the behavior**
BE GAINED—*kerdaino*, means "to gain" in various senses in the New Testament. Here, to win over, to embrace the Gospel. See I Cor. 9:19-22.

BEHAVIOR—*anastrophe*, mode of life, conduct, deportment. The King James "conversation" now conveys a thought too limited for this word, though *anastrophe* would certainly *include her* speech.

What does this latter statement mean? There are at least two possibilities: (1) That the phrase "the word" is used here as it is previously in the verse to refer to the Gospel Message. The idea would then be that the husband is influenced much more by the *conduct* of the wife than he is by the Gospel Message. However, this interpretation would seem to minimize the value of the Gospel teaching. We know of nothing in the entire New Testament which indicates that *any* person could ever come to know Christ without previously having been taught something about Him. In the Book of Acts, for example, one is consistently taught the Word before he is baptized. (2) That the phrase "the word" in its second appearance in the verse, has reference to the speech or verbal statements (teachings?) of the wife to her un-Christian husband.  In the original language, the first "word" has the definite article. But the second "word" has no article. As a result, almost every modern speech translation renders this last phrase "that they may, without a word, be won . . ." or, "that they may be won over without argument through the behavior . . ."

Peter is emphasizing the influence of a Christian wife's conduct upon her un-Christian husband. Rather than trying to argue, contend, or out-talk one's husband on religious issues, the Apostle  would instruct the wives to let their consecrated lives, their humble subjection, their meek and quiet spirit, to be of such a nature that it would stand out in bold relief against his ungodliness and rebellion. Comp. 2:12. There is also a similarity to the thought expressed here and the one in Rom. 12:20.

ᐧ Her behavior, her Christian conduct, her humble demeanor, Peter knew, would do ten times as much good as a trainload of sermons from her lips. How true to life is this statement! Observe that un-Christian husband—the one who for years has turned down the Gospel Message. Finally, he yields his heart to Christ. Now observe the conduct of the same man's wife. It invariably meets the requirements of this very verse!

**beholding your chaste behavior**

BEHOLDING—Defined under 2:12.

CHASTE—*hagnos*, pure, chaste, modest, innocent, blameless. The word first of all had reference to purity of morals. But sometimes it was used in the more *general* sense of one's over-all conduct; innocent, blameless. The more primary meaning is assumed by most translators here, and is nearly always necessary in the behavior of a Christian wife if her un-Christian husband is to be turned to Christ.

**coupled with fear**

See our discussion of the word "fear" under 2:18. The meaning is similar here.

Certainly, if this exhortation is heeded, the husband will be turned to Christ many times when other means fail and particu-

larly when her attempts at teaching, rebuking and verbally condemning him accomplish little. He realizes she means business.
She *practices* her religion. Her *example* proves the sincerity of her
claims. All of her sweet-spirited Christian conduct, it is hoped,
will serve to shame him in his disobedience and lead to his repentance and conversion.

**3:3-4 Whose adorning let it not be the outward adorning of braid-
ing the hair, and of wearing jewels of gold, or of putting on apparel; but let it be the hidden man of the heart, in the incorruptible
apparel of a meek and quiet spirit, which is in the sight of God
of great price.**

## Expanded Translation

Whose adornment must not be outward or external: braiding
(plaiting) of the hair, and putting on things made of gold or
wearing garments; but rather let it be the hidden person of the
heart that receives your primary attention, in the incorruptible
(imperishable) clothing of a meek and tranquil spirit which is in
the sight of God, of surpassing value.

---

**outward adorning of braiding the hair,**

BRAIDING THE HAIR—*emplokes*, braiding or plaiting (of
hair). It frequently had reference to "an elaborate gathering of
the hair into knots."—Thayer.

**and of wearing jewels of gold,**

This is all one word in the original—*chrusios*. The literal translation here, because the word is in the plural, is "of gold things"
or "things of gold." The word means golden, made or adorned
with gold, golden in color or appearance. Moulton & Milligan say
the word was used first of a gold coin, and secondly of gold ornaments (here). They cite a statement written in a letter about A.D.
260: "When you come bring your *gold ornaments*, but do not
wear them in the boat."

**or of putting on apparel**

APPAREL—*himation*—garments, clothes, raiment. The word
consistently refers to exterior or outer clothing in the New Testament, the "coat" rather than the "cloak" (Matt. 5:40).

**outward adorning**

ADORNING—This is the final word in the Greek text, though
it appears at the front of the sentence in the English text. *Kosmos*
is a word of wide significance in the original. Here it is used in the
more primary sense of "order." Thayer says of it, "1. in Greek

writing, from Homer down, an apt and harmonious arrangement or constitution, order. 2. As in Greek writing from Homer down, ornament, decoration, adornment." Compare here I Tim. 2:9, where the context is very similar.

**let it be the hidden man of the heart,**

HIDDEN—*kruptos*—hidden, concealed, secret, clandestine. A similar word, *kruptle*, means a vault or closet, a cell for storage. Compare our English words cryptic, cryptogram, etc.

**in the incorruptible apparel**

INCORRUPTIBLE—*aphthartos*. See our comments under 1:4, where the same word is defined. Here, as there, the meaning is perpetuity in contrast to decay. The clothes and garments of the *outward* person will soon pass away. But the benefits of a meek and quiet spirit will last into eternity.

**of a meek and quiet spirit**

MEEK—*praos*: gentle, mild, meek.

QUIET—*hesuchios*: quiet, tranquil, peaceful. Note its only other appearance in the New Testament, I Tim. 2:12. The prophet said "in quietness and in confidence shall be your strength" (Isa. 30:15).

**of great price**

*Poluteles* (from *polu*, much, and *telos*, revenue): precious, excellent, expensive, of surpassing value, requiring a great outlay.

Here we have what God esteems as very valuable and important in the life of a woman—the proper adornment of her *inward* person. But what is it that the twentieth century woman is so bent on adorning? It is just the opposite! To her, the *outward* person is "of surpassing value," and she is often willing to give "a great outlay" if she thinks by that means she will add to her external beauty. "My ways are not your ways, saith Jehovah."

On the above verses there is an excellent statement in Bush's *Illustrations of the Holy Scriptures*, p. 642, where he quotes Paxton:

> "The eastern females wear their hair, which the prophet emphatically calls the 'instrument of their pride,' very long, and divided into a great number of tresses. In Barbary, the ladies all affect to have their hair hang down to the ground, which, after they have collected into one lock, they bind and plait with ribands; a piece of finery which the apostle marks with disapprobation:" [and this

very passage is quoted in its entirety.] "Not that he condemns in absolute terms all regard to neatness and elegance in dress and appearance, but only an undue attention to these things. His meaning plainly is: 'Whose adorning, let it not chiefly consist in that outward adorning of plaiting the hair,' but rather let it be the hidden man of the heart, in that which is not corruptible, even the ornament of a meek and quiet spirit, which is, in the sight of God, of great price.' The way in which the apostle uses the negative particle in this text, is a decisive proof that this is his true meaning; it extends to every member of the sentence; and by consequence, if it prohibits the plaiting of hair, it equally prohibits the putting on of apparel. But it never could be his design to forbid women to wear clothes, or to be decently and neatly dressed; therefore, the negative must have only a comparative sense, instructing us in the propriety and necessity of attending more to the dispositions of the mind, than to the adorning of the body. . . . The men in the East, Chardin observes, are shaved; the women nourish their hair with great fondness, which they lengthen by tresses, and tufts of silk, down to the heels."

**3:5-6 For after this manner aforetime the holy women also, who hoped in God, adorned themselves, being in subjection to their own husbands: as Sarah obeyed Abraham, calling him Lord: whose children ye now are, if ye do well, and are not put in fear by any terror.**

### Expanded Translation

For after this manner (that I have just mentioned) the holy women of past time also, who placed their hope in God, adorned themselves: being submissive to their own husbands. As an example of this, I cite the case of Sarah, who obeyed Abraham, calling him Lord (sir, master); whose children (daughters) you have now become, if you will do well (live right) and not be put in a state of fear by any thing or person which causes terror.

---

**after this manner**

Referring to the manner described in verses 1-4, i.e., an *inward* subjecting of themselves to their husbands—innocent and blameless behavior, with reverential fear. They were to have a meek and quiet spirit, as they subjected themselves.

**who hoped in God**

Compare 1:3. It is true that the position of Sarah and the holy women of the Old Testament was one of *expectancy*, or looking forward to the fulfillment of some promise—of a son. Some have thought, then, that the description of them as hopeful women is intended to make the readers feel the superiority of their own position. God's promises to them (such as that of the coming Messiah) were fulfilled, not just hoped for.

The meaning, however, may be more general, and have reference simply to their unqualified trust in Jehovah as they went about their daily lives. Notice the similarity of Paul's description of the "widow indeed" in I Tim. 5:5: "Now she that is a widow indeed, and desolate, hath her hope set on God, and continueth in supplications and prayers night and day."

**adorn themselves, being**

Their adornment was *this type of subjection.*

**after this manner**

Referring to the manner described in verses 1:4.

**calling him Lord**

LORD—*kurios*, a title of reverence and respect. Thayer's definition is "He to whom a person or thing belongs, about which he has the power of deciding; master, lord. The word is properly translated "sir" a number of times in the New Testament: Luke 13:25, Jn. 4:11, 15, 19, 5:7. It is to be carefully distinguished from *masters* (*despotes*) in I Peter 2:18. Trench says, "a man, according to the latter Greek grammarians, was *despotes* (master) in respect of his slaves . . . therefore *oikodespotes* (housemaster), but *kurios* (lord) in regard of his wife and children; who in speaking either to him or of him, would give him this title of honor . . . Undoubtedly there lives in *kurios* (lord) the sense of an authority owning limitations—moral limitations it may be; it is implied, too, that the wielder of his authority will not exclude, in wielding it, a consideration of their good over whom it is exercised; while the *despotes* (master) exercises a more unrestricted power and absolute domination, confessing no such limitations or restraints."*

---

*Synonyms of the New Testament*, p. 96.

The actual occurrence of Sarah referring to Abraham as "Lord" is in Genesis 18:12.

**whose children ye are**

Still addressing the wives of (un-Christian) husbands. See 1:14 on "children." They were her daughters when they behaved as she did.

**if ye do well and are not put in fear by any terror**

Note the Expanded Translation. Thayer would render the latter part of this phrase, "to be afraid with terror." Notice the similarity to Prov. 3:25: "Be not afraid of sudden fear, neither of the desolation of the wicked, when it cometh."

To be afraid of sudden alarms and panics argues a lack of trust in God's providence, power, and protection. Such a disposition would, therefore, be unbecoming to the daughters of Sarah, who "hoped in God." The "alarms" which they naturally might fear are, of course, quite general; but especially here, we may suppose, dread of what their unbelieving husbands might do to them. They must quietly, serenely, trustingly live the life to which God has called them.

### 4. Toward Wives 3:7

**3:7 Ye husbands, in like manner, dwell with your wives according to knowledge, giving honor unto the woman, as unto the weaker vessel, as being also joint-heirs of the grace of life; to the end that your prayers be not hindered.**

### Expanded Translation

In the same conscientious manner, you husbands must dwell with your wives in accordance with knowledge (governed by intelligence and wisdom), treating her as one of honor and value, as the weaker vessel, as being those who are joint-heirs of (physical) life; in order that your prayers be not rendered ineffectual.

---

**Ye husbands, in like manner,**

Just as wives are exhorted to be in subjection to their own husbands, so husbands also must do what is right and proper toward their wives. Peter certainly does not mean here that a husband is to be in subjection to his wife, just as she is to be in subjection to him. This would be a gross contradiction. The idea is, that he must be just as considerate and careful to maintain his God-given relationship to his wife, as she is in maintaining her rightful relationship to him.

His conduct in this relationship is to be considered a *part of his Christianity*. This, I believe, is the "common denominator" of the term "in like manner" as it occurs here and in verse 1. There was something about the slave's relationship to his master that the Christian wife was to do "in like manner" toward her husband. And there was something about the wife's conduct (and perhaps the slave's) that a husband was to do "in like manner." In each instance, the Christian being exhorted is told to act in a manner befitting a true child of God in the particular relationship discussed.

### according to knowledge
*Gnosis*, here meaning intelligence, understanding, etc. He must strive to know and understand those matters, principles, and facts which will encourage, help, and edify his wife. He must be a *considerate* and *thoughtful* husband. He ought to know her physical, spiritual and emotional needs and how to fulfill them. How many marriages go on the rocks because of *ignorance!*

### giving honor unto the woman
See under 1:7 where the word "honor" (*time*) is defined.

### as unto the weaker vessel
The word "vessel," *skeuos*, means literally a vessel, bowl, pottery, etc. The weaker the vessels, the greater must be the care lest they be broken. If one has a vase that is thin and fragile, he takes more care and caution with it than with the heavier, more sturdy container. Using Bible language, he "honors" it. The wife here is pictured as a vase or vessel that will not stand harsh or careless treatment.

### as being joint-heirs of the grace of life
It is difficult to know precisely what is meant by this phrase. Evidently the Apostle wants to emphasize that *both* the husband and wife are heirs of this grace. But to what "life" is he referring? Some would refer it to God's precious gift of everlasting life. Others, to "the life which now is"—the Christian life. But it is not *stated* in this passage that both husband and wife are Christians. (The "your prayers," may refer only to the prayers of *husbands*, rather than to the prayers of both mates.) It seems more probable that the reference here is to the gift of *human* life. God has seen fit to bring both into the world and sustain them up to the present hour. For this, they should both be thankful. The husband, particularly, should recognize the fact that God saw fit to bless his wife with this life just as much as himself.

**that your prayers be not hindered**

*Ekkopto* (*ek*, from, off, and *kopto*, to cut) to cut out; to cut off, metaphorically, to cut off occasion, remove, prevent, render ineffectual.

Sin in the heart and life is devastating to effectual prayer! Particularly is this so when squabbles, fights, hatreds, and animosities are present in the home. In the first place, the very desire to pray will probably be lost. How many husbands and wives who are continually at odds with one another, encourage one another to pray? How many times do you see such couples praying together at all? Even if such mates should pray, their sinful home life would clog up God's channel of blessing. "Behold, Jehovah's hand is not shortened, that it cannot save; neither His ear heavy, that it cannot hear: but your *iniquities* have separated between you and your God, and your *sins* have hid His face from you, so that He will not hear" (Isa. 59:1-2).

No, friend, you cannot be acting wrongly toward your mate, and be right with God!

## 5. Toward Christian Brethren 3:8

**3:8-9 Finally, be ye all likeminded, compassionate, loving as brethren, tenderhearted, humbleminded; not rendering evil for evil, or reviling for reviling; but contrariwise blessing; for hereunto were ye called, that ye should inherit a blessing.**

### Expanded Translation

Finally (besides these particular groups to whom I have been writing), *all* of you be concordant and agreeable, sympathetic and compassionate, loving your Christian brothers and sisters, tender and kind from the heart, humbleminded; not refunding evil for evil, or reviling (railing, abusive speech) for reviling, but, on the contrary, blessing (them); for unto this type of life were you called, in order that you might inherit a blessing.

---

From the various groups he has treated within the church (servants, wives, husbands), he now turns to the entire Christian society.

**be ye all likeminded, compassionate,**

LIKEMINDED—*homophron*—of like mind, of the same mind, concordant "of one mind (intent, purpose)"—Thayer. It expresses an *attitude* of the mind which strives for harmony. We must, as Christians, be "giving diligence to keep the unity of the Spirit in the bond of peace" (Eph. 4:3). Compare I Cor. 1:10. Few of us always agree on how to carry out the thousand details of everyday life. But we should ever strive to have the same basic goals, purposes and motives, that provide the very foundations of Christianity.

COMPASSIONATE—*sumpathes* (*sun*, meaning with, and *pascho*, to suffer, be afflicted): suffering or feeling the like with another, sympathetic. The verb form of this word is used of Christ in Heb. 4:15 ("with the feeling").

The exhortation of Rom. 12:15 demonstrates what would happen when this virtue was actually practiced: "Rejoice with them that rejoice; weep with them that weep." When two tuning forks are set on a table, one across from the other, and one is plucked, the other vibrates also. Iikewise, when the heartstrings of our brethren are plucked, ours will not fail to vibrate with them.

### loving as brethren,

This is all one word in the Greek, *philadelphos*: loving brother or sister, loving one like a brother. Notice the similar word *philadelphia* in 1:22.

### tenderhearted, humbleminded

TENDERHEARTED—*eusplagchnos* (from *eu*, good, well, kind, tender, and *splagnon*, meaning the inward parts): thus compassionate, tenderhearted; i.e., being tender and kind from the very heart or inside. Such a person would be easily moved by the sorrows or joys of others. See this word also in Eph. 4:32.

HUMBLEMINDED—*tapeinophron* (from *tapeinos*, "not rising far from the ground," hence, lowly, plus *phran*, meaning *mind*): humbleminded, i.e., having a modest opinion of one's self. In secular writing, this word had the bad sense of being *pusillanimous* or cowardly. In the Christian life, however, it is a virtue which rises when one has a *true* estimate of his own worth, ability, and limitations.

### not rendering

RENDERING—*apodidomi*, a common word that sometimes means: to give back, restore, refund, retaliate.

### evil for evil

Literally, "evil against evil." That is, one should not retaliate with evil when evil is done to him.

### reviling for reviling

Again, literally, "reviling against reviling." Peter does not endorse the "eye for eye" or "tooth for tooth" teaching. In this regard we have the perfect example of Christ, as we saw in 2:23. On this whole subject see Matt. 5:38-42, Rom. 12:17-21, I Thess. 5:15.

## 6. Toward Revilers 3:9-12

**but contrariwise blessing**

*Eulogeo* (*eu*, meaning good, well, plus *logos*, word, discourse): to speak well of. Hence in the New Testament, to bless, ascribe praise or glorification. We should *not* try to pay them back in their own coin.

**for hereunto were ye called that ye should inherit a blessing**

This phrase may be taken in two ways: One, you were called to bless others in order that you may, in the future, inherit a blessing (heaven). Two, Christians bless others, not *in order that* they should inherit a blessing, but because it is God's will and their duty as Christians to so act; that duty *follow from the fact* that God has made them inheritors of His blessings . . . God has blessed them, therefore, they must bless others. See comments, 3:10-11.

**3:10-12 For,**

> He that would love life,
> And see good days,
> Let him refrain his tongue from evil,
> And his lips that they speak no guile:
> And let him turn away from evil, and do good;
> Let him seek peace, and pursue it.
>
> For the eyes of the Lord are upon the righteous,
> And His ears unto their supplication:
> But the face of the Lord is upon them that do evil.

### Expanded Translation

Because,
> He who wants (literally, is willing) to love life and
>     enjoy it,
> And see good, happy, delightful days,
> Let him not use his lips to speak words of guile.
> And he must turn aside from (the path of) evil, and
>     must practice good (virtue, right);
> He must seek and search for peace—even chase after it.
> For the eyes of the Lord are (favorably) upon the
>     righteous ones
> And His ears unto their entreaty (supplication, prayer),
> But the face of the Lord is (unfavorably) upon the
>     ones practicing evil.

It seems best to regard vss. 10-12 as an illustration of the truth expressed in v. 9; i.e., that those who live righteously are blessed of God.

**He that would love life**

The word "love" here, *agapao*, is assumed by most critics to be used in the sense of "enjoy." If then, we would *get the most out of life*, living it to its fullest and richest extent, we must follow the exhortations of these verses!

**And see good days**

The word rendered "good" (*agathos*), is here evidently used in the sense of happy, delightful, or satisfying.

**Let him refrain his tongue from evil**

The word, "evil," *kakos*, may mean, among other things, malediction, that is, a curse, a slander.

**And his lips that they speak no guile**

See the word "guile," *dolos*, defined under 2:1. Would we be truly happy? Would we arise each morning looking forward to the day ahead? Would we make the most out of our lives? God has the formula! *His* prescription must be taken to find *real* happiness! He calls for *obedience*. Then we may

Let our life and lips confess
The Holy Gospel we profess.

**let him turn away**

The word *ekklino* (*ek*, meaning out, out of, etc., plus *klino*, properly, to slope or bend; to bow down): to deflect, deviate (Rom. 3:12), to decline or turn away from, avoid (Rom. 16:17). The word is sometimes used of one turning away from the *right* path (Rom. 3:12), and sometimes from the *evil* path. The exhortation here reminds one of Prov. 4:14-15:

Enter not into the path of the wicked,
And walk not in the way of evil men.
Avoid it, pass not by it;
Turn from it, and pass on.

**Let him seek peace, and pursue it**

SEEK—*zeteo*: usually indicates simply to seek, to look for. It is not as strong as the next word.

PURSUE—*dioko*: to put in rapid motion; to pursue; to follow, pursue the direction of. This same word is sometimes rendered "persecute" in the Scriptures.

This last sentence is evidently climactic. "Let him seek peace, *even* (for so may the word 'and,' *kai*, be rendered) pursue it." How many of us are looking for peace with the diligence this verse requires? "Blessed are the peacemakers" (Matt. 5:9).

## V.  SUFFERING AND THE GLORIES TO FOLLOW
### 3:13 — 4:19

### 1.  Proper Conduct When Suffering For Righteousness
### 3:13-17

**3:13-14  And who is he that will harm you, if ye be zealous of that which is good? But even if ye should suffer for righteousness' sake, blessed are ye: and fear not their fear, neither be troubled;**

### Expanded Translation

And who is he that will be harming you, if you are eager and zealous to do what is good and right? But even if you might suffer in behalf of (or, on account of) righteousness, you are blessed. And do not fear their fear (i.e., the things they do which would cause fear), neither let your mind be troubled, disquieted, or terrified.

---

### he that will harm you

HARM—*kakoo* (from the same root as *kakos*, "evil," which occurred once each in verses 10, 11 and 12): to maltreat, cause evil to, oppress, afflict, harm.

### if ye be zealous

ZEALOUS—*zelotes*. The primary meaning is one burning with zeal; a zealot. Hence, one most eagerly desirous of something, zealous for a thing, a diligent aspirant, a devoted adherent. It is from the root word *zeo* which meant, according to Thayer, "to boil with heat, be hot"—a word sometimes used by ancient classic writers of *boiling water*.

The idea of the passage is, "if you live such a life as just recommended in my previous exhortation, you need not fear."

There are two basic interpretations of these verses:

1. Christians are *generally* safe. Thus Macknight: "Besides, in ordinary cases, we will have the favor of men; for few will do you evil, if ye be . . ." Similarly, Matthew Henry states: "this, I suppose, is spoken of Christians in an ordinary condition, not in the heat of persecution. 'Ordinarily, there will be but few so diabolical and impious as to harm those who live so innocently and usefully as you do.' " Worthy of thought under this consideration is the statement of Gal. 5:23, where, after listing the fruits of the Spirit that should be evident in a Christian's life, Paul said, "against such there is no law."

2. That we will not *really* be harmed (actually or permanently). Those who hold this view would cite such passages as Matt. 10:28, Mark 10:29, 30, Rom. 8:28. So Lange states: "the sense is not: nobody will have any mind to harm you. Peter, at least, knew the world differently, and his Master had foretold differently" (Ch. 2:12, 18, 3:9; Matt. 10:22, 23, 38-39. Likewise, Pulpit Commentary: "St. Peter does not mean, Who will have the heart to harm you? He knew the temper of the Jews and heathen; he knew, also, the Saviour's prophecies of coming persecution too well to say that." Similarly, Zerr, Ellicott, and others.

In view of what is stated in v. 14 however, it seems this passage expresses *ordinary* circumstances, but that persecution would sometimes be their lot.

**fear not their fear**

i.e., the things they (the persecutors) do which would cause fear. "Be not afraid of the terror which they cause." ". . . do not dread or be afraid of their threats"—Amplified N. T. They are not to be upset and fretful over the terror which their enemies would seek to instill.

**neither be troubled**

TROUBLED—*terrasso*: to cause one inward commotion, take away his calmness of mind, disquiet, make restless . . . strike one's spirit with fear or dread.

**3:15 but sanctify in your hearts Christ as Lord: being ready always to give answer to every man that asketh you a reason concerning the hope that is in you, yet with meekness and fear:**

### Expanded Translation

But in your hearts, sanctify and reverence Christ as Lord; being ready and prepared at any and every time to give answer (make a defense) to every person who asks you a reason (asks you to give an account) concerning the hope that lies within you, yet with meekness, mildness, forbearance, along with reverence and respect.

---

**but sanctify in your hearts Christ as Lord**

Other translations of this passage could be "but sanctify in your hearts the Lord Christ" or ". . . sanctify the Christ as Lord."

SANCTIFY—*hagiadzo*. See our complete definition of the adjective form of the same word (*hagios*) in 1:15. Thayer says this word has its more primary meaning here, listing it along with Matt. 6:9 and Luke 11:2, as meaning: "to render or acknowledge to be venerable, to hallow."

The reference here may especially be with a view to Christ as our *protector*.

**Being ready always to give answer to every man**

READY—*hetoimos*: "of persons; ready, prepared . . . for (the doing of) a thing."—Thayer. See also Tit. 3:1 where the same word is used and in a similar sense.

ALWAYS—*aei* (a word closely related to *aion*, a word which occurs many times in the Scriptures and usually translated "age" or "eternal"). The word is an adverb and means *always;* i.e., (1) perpetually, incessantly (Acts 7:51, Tit. 1:12); (2) invariably, at any and every time (here). Notice the relationship of the Greek word to our word *aye*. It is from this Greek word that the old English word was derived.

GIVE ANSWER—*apologia* (whence our word apologetic), verbal defense, speech in defense. Originally a speech made by a prisoner in his defense, it was later applied to the treatises written in defense of the Christian faith. Compare I Cor. 9:3, "defense."

**yet with meekness and fear**

"Meekness" is defined and discussed under 2:17, 18, 3:2, and "fear" under 2:18. Note the Expanded Translation.

Concerning the testimony about our hope in Christ, this verse demands:

1. We must be prepared or ready to give it.
2. We must be such always—at any and every time.
3. We must be able to do "to every man."
4. We must do so "with meekness and respect."

Do you meet these qualifications?

**3:16-17 Having a good conscience; that, wherein ye are spoken against, they may be put to shame who revile your good manner of life in Christ. For it is better, if the will of God should so will, that ye suffer for well-doing than for evil-doing.**

### Expanded Translation

Having a good (pure, clear, approving) conscience; so that, wherein you are spoken against (slandered, abused with words), they may be made ashamed who revile (falsely accuse) your good conduct in Christ. For it is more excellent to suffer for doing good, if the will of God should so will, than for doing evil.

---

**Having a good conscience**

See also 2:19, 3:21. The word *suneidesis*, is defined fully by

Thayer as "the soul as distinguishing between what is morally good and bad, prompting to do the former and shun the latter, commending the one, condemning the other." When one has a "conscience" about a subject or matter, he has a sense or consciousness of right or wrong concerning that subject. But here the Apostle exhorts us to have a "*good* conscience." What would this include? Probably here a *good* conscience refers to an *approving* one. Notice the context. In spite of the ridicules and jeers of the worldling that spoke against them, they were to have a conscience that approved of their actions so that they inwardly felt that God was with them.

Taking a broader view of the term "good conscience," according to the Scriptures, it is commendable to have:

1. An informed conscience (I Cor. 8:1-8).
2. A pure conscience (Heb. 9:13-14, I Tim. 3:9).
3. A sensitive, responsive, or tender conscience. (Notice I Tim. 4:1-2, which describes the opposite.)
4. A good conscience (here).

Some may have an approving conscience when they are really in sin. This can easily happen if we do not constantly inform and educate our conscience that it might properly approve what the Scriptures approve. It would sting us and prick us when the Bible's teachings condemn our actions. A thermostat is an excellent help in keeping your house warmed by the heat of the furnace, if it is in good working order. So with the conscience. If it is properly informed, sensitive and pure, then it will approve what is endorsed by God's Word.

**they may be put to shame**

This is all one word in the original. See it defined under 2:6 (*kataischuno*).

**who revile your good manner**

REVILE—*epereadzo*. Compare *epereia*, spiteful abuse, to insult, treat abusively, use despitefully, revile. Thayer says it is here used in a forensic sense, meaning to accuse falsely.

**For it is better**

BETTER—*kreitton*, means more excellent, superior, more valuable; hence, more conducive to good.

**if the will of God should so will**

Literally, if wills the will of God.

Suffering for *well*-doing is to our *credit*—a compliment to us. See Matt. 5:10-12, and in this book, Ch. 4:14-16 and 2:19-20. Suffering for evil-doing is to our *dis*credit, and is something to be ashamed of.

## 2.   *The Example Of Christ 3:18 — 4:6*

**3:18-19 Because Christ also suffered for sins once, the righteous for the unrighteous, that he might bring us to God; being put to death in the flesh, but made alive in the spirit, in which also he went and preached unto the spirits in prison,**

### *Expanded Translation*

Because Christ also suffered (some MSS have *died*) for sins (or possibly, sinners) once for all, the righteous one in behalf of the unrighteous ones, in order that he might bring us into the good graces of God (by reconciling us to Him); having been put to death indeed in the realm of the flesh, but made alive in the realm of the spirit; in which form he (Christ) also went and preached (by means of such men as Noah) unto the spirits (presently) in prison,

---

**suffered for sins once**

ONCE—*hapax*, is an adverb usually meaning simply once (II Cor. 11:25), but sometimes *once for all*: Heb. 6:4, 9:26. Thayer says the word here is used of what is so done as to be of perpetual validity and never need repetition.

**the righteous for the unrighteous**

"Righteous" is singular, referring to Christ, while "unrighteous" is plural, referring to the lost. The word "for," *huper*, may be rendered "in behalf of" or "for the sake of." On this whole phrase see also Rom. 5.6, II Cor. 5:21, Heb. 9:28. Christ so suffered when He died for *you* and *me!*

The reason for this statement is evidently to show us that we have a divine example and pattern for those who suffer for well-doing. He was just, innocent and guiltless, yet He *suffered*.

**that he might bring us to God**

*Prosago*, meaning to lead or conduct to, bring. This word was sometimes used in a nautical sense of a ship or craft that was approaching land, particularly a harbor (Acts 27:27). How good it is when Christ, our Captain, pilots us out of the stormy seas of life and into God's serene harbor, the Church.

The death of Christ on the cross was the means of reconciling sinners to God (Eph. 2:14-18). Peter opens up one of the deeper aspects of the death of Christ. The veil that hid the Holy of Holies was then rent in twain, and believers were invited and encouraged to draw near into the immediate presence of God.

The reference to His sufferings leads Peter (vss. 18-20) into a statement of the various ways in which Christ suffered, and of His ultimate triumph. By His example in His sufferings, and by His final victory, the Apostle would encourage those whom he addressed to bear with patience the sorrows to which their religion exposed them.

**being put to death in the flesh, but made alive in the spirit**

The article "the" is not in the Greek, either before "flesh" or before "spirit." We observe the absence of any article or preposition in the original, and the exact balance and correspondence of these two clauses. The two datives, beginning with "in" must be taken in the same sense; it is impossible to regard one as the dative of the sphere, and the other as the dative of the instrument; both are evidently datives of the sphere to which a general predicate is to be limited. They limit the extent of the participles "being put to death" and "made alive." Thus the literal translation is, "being put to death in flesh, but quickened in spirit."

(Another point that shows the balance of these two phrases is the existence of *men* in the first phrase and *de* in the second— a common way of showing contrast in the original.)

To what does the term "spirit" refer in this verse? There are at least three possibilities: (1) The Holy Spirit, part of the Godhead; (2) That eternal part of man that God gave him upon birth, and which returns to Him upon death (Eccl. 12:7); and (3) That inner principle which stands in contrast with flesh. Hence, that which Jesus possessed in common with all men, and which was not affected by His death.

It is our opinion that the last is referred to in this passage in view of Peter's purpose in writing these words. The Apostle is evidently trying to show that though Christ suffered death, this, far from terminating His existence or destroying His influence, only enabled Him to be brought to life in the realm or sphere of the spirit. When the Lord said, "Father, into Thy hands I commend my spirit"; when he bowed His head and gave up the spirit —that spirit passed into a new life.

This explanation seems to fit into the context more smoothly, as it is universally true. All of us will some day have this same experience. To those of us who are Christians and faithful, when we are "made alive in the spirit" we shall be living with our heavenly Father forever. Hence, regardless of the sufferings we may have to endure here, the end will be glorious.

**in which also he went and preached**

IN WHICH—The word here rendered "in" may also be translated "by" or "through"—that is, the spirit previously referred to — Christ's. It would seem untenable that we should make "spirit" here refer to anything different than we did in verse 18. The preaching that Christ is spoken of as doing here, He had to do outside of the realm or sphere of His corporeal body. This preaching was done by Christ in His spirit before His incarnation —but (as we will see in verse 20) it was done *through* Noah. It was done to the antediluvians.

Notice the similarity of language in 1:11. The Old Testament prophets spoke "by the Spirit of Christ."

In Gen. 6:3, God said, *"My Spirit* shall not strive with man forever, for that he also is flesh." *How* was God's Spirit striving with those ancient peoples? What *means* did He use? II Pet. 2:5 tells us *Noah* was a preacher (*kerux*) of righteousness during that period.

PREACHED—*kerusso*, means first to publish, proclaim as a herald (I Cor. 9:27). Then, to announce openly and publicly, noise abroad, preach.

**unto the spirits in prison**

The term *prison*, as it is used in the New Testament, might refer to: (1) the act of guarding, or watching; (2) those who kept watch; hence, a guard or sentinel; (3) the place where persons are kept under guard, a prison. This is its most common usage in the New Testament. Compare Acts 5:19, II Cor. 6:5.

But how or in what way are the spirits of man in prison? There is a sense in which each person's spirit is "imprisoned" at death. It is then confined to Hades—the abode of the dead.

The spirits were not in prison when Noah preached to them, but when Peter was penning these words. The Syriac version has "sheol" here instead of "prison," with reference to the place of departed spirits. They are (Peter is saying) *presently* confined, and will be until the resurrection, on the last day, when they shall receive their condemnation. See also II Pet. 2:4, Jude 6.

How do we *know* when the preaching was done to these spirits? The next verse tells us plainly. It is the only place in the passage where the Apostle refers to the time element. It was done "while the ark was a preparing."

How does this whole verse relate to the context? In the patience and forbearance of Christ and also of His mouthpiece, Noah, during this previous age of great sinfulness, *we* are encouraged to be patient in *our* attempt to do good to others though *we also* are offended, persecuted and abused.

On these two verses, and particularly the question "Did Christ go to hell?" be sure to read the *Special Study* of Brother Fields on the subject. You will find it in the final pages of "The Glorious Church," his book on Ephesians. His work forms an excellent commentary on this passage as well as Eph. 4:9.

**3:20 that aforetime were disobedient, when the longsuffering of God waited in the days of Noah, while the ark was a preparing, wherein few, that is, eight souls, were saved through water:**

### Expanded Translation

(spirits) that aforetime refused to believe and obey, when the longsuffering (patience, self-restraint) of God waited it out in the days of Noah, while the ark was being prepared, inside of which few, that is eight souls (persons) were saved by means of water.

---

#### that aforetime were disobedient

(See the latter word defined in 2:8.)

This phrase certainly shows *when* these imprisoned spirits were disobedient. And, unless all other plain teachings of the Scriptures be cast aside, we can only believe that the preaching was done to them *at the time of their disobedience*, and while they still had opportunity to repent, that is, while they were still living beings and in the flesh. (Note questions, end of chapter.)

#### when the longsuffering of God waited in the days of Noah

LONGSUFFERING—*makrothumia*, is generally used in reference to a man who perseveres patiently and bravely, particularly in the enduring of misfortunes and troubles. Trench says that it is "the self-restraint which does not hastily retaliate a wrong." The word stands in contrast to one who would become quickly full of wrath or revenge. How grateful we may be that we serve such a God!

### while the ark was a preparing

It is our opinion that the preaching mentioned in verse 19 was also to the imprisoned spirits during this same period of time. II Pet. 2:5 speaks of Noah as "a preacher of righteousness." Gen. 6:3 states that God allowed 120 years between the time he decided to destroy the earth and the time of its actual destruction by the flood. Precisely how much of this 120 years Noah spent preaching is not known.

"Was a preparing"—one word in the original, *kataskevadzo*—a word meaning to prepare, put in readiness, hence to construct, build.

In view of the fact that the antediluvians as a whole did not believe Noah's preaching, he and his immediate family must have done most of the "preparing" themselves.

### wherein few, that is, eight souls, were saved

The "eight souls" are mentioned in Gen. 7:7.

SAVED—*diasodzo* (from *dia*), through, and *sodzo*, to save, to bring safe through, to convey in safety; but passively, as here: to reach a place or state of safety; hence, be saved, out of danger, rescued.

### through water

That is, the ark was held up by water. Water was employed in their preservation in an important way and they, in a definite sense, owed their safety to that element. Though water spelled the damnation of the rebellious, it meant the salvation of the obedient. In like manner, we ourselves owe our salvation in an important way, to the same component. The stress in the illustration is not on the *mode* used, but rather that the same *element* was present in *both* cases—their salvation and ours.

It is striking to see the importance of water in connection with salvation down through the ages. It played an important role in the salvation of Noah and his family. It certainly was important in the deliverance of the Israelites when they were "baptized in the cloud and in the sea" as they escaped from the pursuing Egyptians. It was an important element as they crossed the Jordan and entered into the Promised Land. And even in the rites and ceremonies of the Old Testament Jew, water played an integral part. Should we, then, be so amazed that water should have an important place in the salvation of mankind in the Christian age?

**3:21** which also after a true likeness doth now save you, even baptism, not the putting away of the filth of the flesh, but the interrogation of a good conscience toward God, through the resurrection of Jesus Christ;

### Expanded Translation

Which (that is, water) also now saves you in the antitype-baptism, which does not have to do with the removal of dirt from the flesh (i.e., the body, the *outside* of one), but to provide ground or reason for having a good conscience toward God (which comes when one is right on the *inside*). All this is possible because of the resurrection of Jesus Christ;

---

#### which also after a true likeness doth now save you

LIKENESS—*antitupos*, meant first of all a thing formed after some pattern (Heb. 9:24), then a thing resembling another, its counterpart; hence, something in the Messianic times which answers to the type prefiguring it in the Old Testament. It is this very word from which we have the English word, "antitype."

We understand that *God* was responsible for their salvation, and it was through His mercy and love that He provided a means whereby they could escape the doom of the world. But the means He chose was *water*. Had Noah refused to accept the means God had provided, we could only call him rebellious, and he would have been lost.

Today, God has also provided a means whereby *we* may avail ourselves of His salvation, and where we may meet the blood of Christ. He has provided it in His mercy, kindness and love, *but we must accept what He has provided.* The Holy Spirit says baptism "doth now save you." God saves us through the *blood of Christ*, BUT THE MEANS HE HAS CHOSEN IS WATER!

#### not the putting away of the filth of the flesh

FILTH—*hrupos*, filth, squalor, dirt. The purpose of baptism is not to obtain an outward cleansing. We can take care of that matter in the bathtub.

#### but the interrogation of a good conscience toward God

INTERROGATION—*eperotema*. W. E. Vine states that the word is not here to be rendered "answer." It was used by the Greeks in a legal sense, as a demand or appeal. The word is often rendered "seeking." The meaning is easily seen when this phrase is compared with the previous. The purpose of baptism is not to cleanse the outside. Rather, it is to gain a clean inside, that is, to *gain* or *obtain* a clear conscience toward God. Any true Christian can testify to the truthfulness of this verse in his own experience. When he met the blood of Christ in the baptismal waters by faith, and arose to walk in newness of life, his conscience no longer condemned him and the purpose for which he was immersed— to meet the blood of Christ—was fulfilled. He was "seeking" and he found! "Blessed is the man whose transgression is forgiven, whose sin is covered" (Psa. 32:1). If you have not obtained a clear conscience in baptism, then it has *not fulfilled its purpose in your life!*

**through the resurrection of Jesus Christ**
That is, all this is possible through the resurrection of Christ. If He had not arisen, our baptism would have been in vain and Christ would have no power to save us. See I Cor. 15:12-14. His resurrection showed His power over death. For the exact relationship between His resurrection and our baptism, see Rom. 6:1-6.

**3:22 who is on the right hand of God, having gone into heaven; angels and authorities and powers being made subject unto him.**

### Expanded Translation
who is on the right hand of God (i.e., in a place of honor), having departed (from earth) and gone into heaven; angels, and (heavenly) authorities or princes, and (heavenly) beings excelling in power being arranged under and in subjection to him.

---

**who is at the right hand**
That is, at a place of power, prestige and esteem.

**angels, authorities and powers**
The latter part of the verse could very well read: "Angels— even those in places of authority and power, were made subject unto Him." The "authorities" are evidently a certain class of angels or spiritual potentates. The same is also likely of "powers." Note how these words, "authorities" and "powers" occur in the same order with reference to heavenly beings in Eph. 3:10, Col. 2:10, I Cor. 15:24.

Do not miss the *purpose* of this verse, for it forms a vital conclusion to the discussion which began in v. 17. Our Saviour, though He suffered, was victorious! He *triumphed* over sin and the grave! As a result of His sufferings, we have salvation and He has been glorified in Heaven, and all authority has been given unto Him in heaven and on earth (Matt. 28:18).

## QUESTIONS OVER CHAPTER THREE
### CONCERNING WIVES, Vss. 1-6

1. The first verse tells us wives are to be in subjection to their husbands "in like manner." Like what or whom?
2. What other Scriptures can you cite in the New Testament concerning a wife's subjection to her husband?
3. What expression does Peter use to describe the unchristian husband?
4. How might an unchristian husband be won "without the word"? Give two possible explanations of this expression.
5. An unchristian husband then, primarily observes the _____ of his wife?
6. Her chaste behavior is to be "coupled with fear." Define "fear" as it is used here.
7. What three outward adornments of a woman are here mentioned?
8. Concerning this outward adornment, the Apostle said, "let it not be . . ." Is this latter statement to be understood as a total ban on these things? (Explain why or why not before proceeding to the next question.)
9. How do we *know* he is not abolishing their use entirely?
10. What is to receive a woman's primary attention?
11. What kind of spirit is she to have?
12. What Old Testament woman is used here as an illustration of subjection?
13. What title did she give her husband?
14. May a woman today be a daughter of Sarah? How?
15. The Christian woman is not to be "put in fear by any terror." Explain this statement in its context.

### CONCERNING HUSBANDS V. 7

16. How does a husband act toward his wife "in like manner"?
17. Describe how a husband would act who dwelt with his wife "according to knowledge."
18. In what way is a wife "the weaker vessel"?
19. Husband and wife are joint-heirs of "the grace of life." What is this?
20. Describe how poor domestic relations can hinder prayer life. (Note: Wives are to memorize 3:1-6, and husbands, 3:7, plus another New Testament passage, such as Eph. 5:25-30.)

LETTERS FROM PETER

21. Define "likeminded" and "compassionate." (V. 8.)
22. Rather than render evil for evil, or reviling for reviling, we should _____.
23. What is God's prescription for happiness?
24. How is this prescription seen in vss. 10 and 11?
25. Give two explanations of v. 13.
26. Which one is favored in view of v. 14?
27. Explain the phrase "fear not their fear," v. 14.
28. Memorize (including where found), vss. 15-16.
29. What elements are found in a good conscience?
30. For what should a Christian *not* suffer?
31. What should *always* be the reason a Christian suffers mistreatment?
32. Why does Peter bring the death of Christ into the picture here?
33. Explain: "being put to death in the flesh, but made alive in the spirit," v. 28.
34. Who or what are the spirits in prison?
35. *How* did Christ preach to them?
36. *When* did this preaching take place?
37. When were these spirits "disobedient"?
38. If you believe Christ preached to these spirits between His death on the cross and His resurrection, please explain the following:
    a. What did He preach to them?
    b. Why were these particular people (the dead antidiluvians) preached to and not others?
    c. Could Christ have preached the message of Salvation to them? If so, how is II Pet. 2:4-5, 9, to be understood?
    d. Could He have preached the *Gospel*, including His resurrection? (See I Cor. 15.)
    e. How do you reconcile Luke 16:24-28 with this teaching? (It is understood that a doctrine may be true even though all its details may not be understood, yet a doctrine must *harmonize* with other Biblical teachings.)
39. How was Noah's family saved "through water"?
40. Of what is this a "true likeness"?
41. How can *water* save us? Is not the principle of the Jews true, "who can forgive sins, but God alone"? (Luke 5:21.)
42. What is baptism *not* for, according to Peter?

43. What *does* it obtain for one?
44. Explain the phrase "interrogation of a good conscience toward God," v. 21.
45. Baptism is effectual because of what great event in the life of Jesus?
46. Who *are* the angels, authorities, and powers of v. 22?
47. What does v. 22 show about the final outcome of Christ's sufferings?

## CHAPTER FOUR

**4:1-2 Forasmuch then as Christ suffered in the flesh, arm ye yourselves also with the same mind; for he that hath suffered in the flesh hath ceased from sin; that ye no longer should live the rest of your time in the flesh to the lusts of men, but to the will of God.**

### Expanded Translation

Inasmuch then as Christ suffered in the flesh, you also must equip yourself with the same frame of mind (as He possessed) for the one (Christian) who has had suffering in the flesh has ceased from (the practices of) sin; in order that you might not from now on live the rest of your time in the flesh to the lusts of men, but to the will of God.

---

**as Christ suffered in the flesh**
SUFFERED—*pascho*, see 2:19.

**arm ye yourselves**
ARM—*hoplidzo*: to arm, equip; in the middle voice (here) to arm one's self, equip one's self.

**with the same mind**
MIND—*ennoia*, knowledge, insight, understanding, manner of thinking or feeling. In Heb. 4:12 it is rendered "intents." The same word is used in a similar setting by Paul: "Have this *mind* in you, which was also in Christ Jesus" (Philip. 2:5). We should, therefore, take on the same mind or attitude that Christ did—a readiness and willingness to suffer for God and His kingdom.

**for he that hath suffered in the flesh hath ceased from sin**
Some would refer this phrase to Christ. However, the more likely reference is to Christians in general. Christ never "ceased" practicing sin—He was without it (2:22). The true disciple who wishes to profit from the example of Christ, will cease his life of sin even though he must suffer persecution for it. Suffering endured with a Christian attitude *will have a purifying influence upon one's life!*

97

**that ye no longer should live the rest of your time in the flesh**

Suffering, persecution, and trial provide no excuse for falling into sin. Rather, such times grant to us opportunity for spiritual growth and development. Watch that person who has learned how to keep a strong grip on the Saviour in time of great stress and difficulty—observe him over the years—and you will also be observing one who is *conquering sin.*

**to the lusts of men . . .will of God**

The two stand in direct contrast, and they always have: Isa. 55:6-9. The true follower of Christ casts off the former lusts and submits himself without reserve to the will of God.

**4:3 For the time past may suffice to have wrought the desire of the Gentiles, and to have walked in lasciviousness, lusts, wine-bibbings, revellings, carousings, and abominable idolatries:**

### Expanded Translation

For the time which has passed by (in our former unregenerated state) is sufficient (enough, adequate) to have worked out the desires and wishes of the Gentiles (heathens, pagans) and to have walked in intemperance (outrageous behavior), lusts (cravings of the flesh), drunkenness, revellings (wild group behavior), liquor-drinking contests, and idolatries which are (in God's sight) lawless and profane;

---

**to have wrought the desire**

DESIRE—*boulema*, desire, purpose, will.*

**walked in lasciviousness**

LACIVIOUSNESS—*aselgeia*, intemperance; licentiousness, lasciviousness (Rom. 13:13, etc.), insolence, outrageous behavior (Mark 7:22).

Thayer says, "The conduct and character of one who is *aselges* (a word which some suppose to be compounded of the alpha negative and *selge*, the name of a city in Pisidia whose citizens excelled in strictness of morals) . . ."

(Others give a different origin of the word, saying it is the combination of the alpha negative, plus *selgo*, a word meaning "not affecting pleasantly, exciting disgust." But the later Lexicons favor the first idea on its etymology.)

---

*For you who would like a more complete definition of this word, consult Thayer's Greek Lexicon under *thelo*.

Trench says it "is best described as wanton lawless insolence
. . . The *aselges*, as Passow observes . . . being one who acknowl-
edges no restraints, who dares whatsoever his caprice and wanton
petulance may suggest . . . the fundamental notion . . . of *aselgeia*,
lawless and insolence and wanton caprice."
See II Pet. 2:7 where the same word occurs in the plural.

### lust, wine-bibbings

LUSTS—*epithumia*. See "desire" under 1:2. The Apostle here
means those unbridled and uninhibited cravings of the flesh—
stirred up and perpetuated by Satan.

WINEBIBBINGS—*oinophlugia* (from *oinos*—wine, and *phulo*
—to bubble over, overflow): to debauch with wine, drunkenness,
sottishness.

"commonly . . . it is used for a debauch; no single word rendering it better than this; being as it is an extravagant indulgence
in potations long drawn out . . . such as may induce permanent
mischiefs on the body . . . as did, for instance, that fatal debauch
to which, adopting one of the reports current in antiquity, Arrian
inclines to ascribe the death of Alexander the Great . . ." Trench.

REVELLINGS—*komoss* properly, a festive procession, a merry-
making; in the New Testament, a revel, lascivious feasting. See
Rom. 13:13 ("rioting"), Gal. 5:21. Trench states that the word
contains both an element of riot and of revelry. *Komoss* was often
used of the company of revelers themselves; always of a festal
and disorderly company, but not of *necessity* riotous and drunken.
Still, he says, the word generally implies as much, being applied
in a special sense to the troop of drunken revelers who at the late
close of a revel, with garlands on their heads, and torches in their
hands, with shout and song, pass to the harlots' houses or otherwise wander through the streets, with insult and wanton outrage
for everyone whom they met.

Do we not see very similar acts in our society today? Midnight
parties, high school and college dances, and other late-hour
gatherings of the world are frequently concluded in a similar
fashion. In fact, attend any such get-together in this, our "cul-
tured" twentieth century, and nearly all of the sins mentioned in
this passage will be committed!

CAROUSINGS—*potos*: a drinking; a drinking together, drink-
ing-bout, compotation. This word would be descriptive of a couple
or group who sat down at a drinking place and competed against
one another to see who could drink the most.

## and abominable idolatries

*Athemitos* (alpha negative, plus *themitos*—lawful), hence, unlawful, wicked. In this passage, the meaning is that it is *divinely* unlawful, hence lawless, profane, ungodly.

**4:4 wherein they think it strange that ye run not with them into the same excess of riot, speaking evil of you:**

### Expanded Translation

in which (sinful ways just described) they are amazed that you do not keep company with them, indulging in the same excess, (overflowing) of riot (profligacy, debauchery), speaking against you.

---

### wherein they think it strange

STRANGE—*xenidzo*, means first of all to receive as a guest, entertain (Acts 10:23), or, in the passive, to be entertained as a guest, to lodge or reside with (Acts 10:6). However, the word is derived from *xenos*, the primary meaning of which is foreign, alien, strange. Hence, in this verb form the meaning is sometimes (as here) to be struck with surprise, be amazed, be astonished at the novelty or strangeness of a thing.

### that ye run not with them

RUN WITH—*suntrecho*, means literally, to run or flock together (Mark 6:33, Acts 3:11). Here it is used as a metaphor of one who runs in company with others.

### into the same excess of riot,

EXCESS—*anachusis*: a pouring out; metaphorically, excess, an overflowing, an overabundance.

OF RIOT—*asotia* (*a*-alpha negative, plus *sodzo*, to save), hence, properly either of one who is abandoned (a hopeless, incorrigible individual), or, one who *does not save* (himself, his means, his time, etc.). The adverb form occurs in the story of the Prodigal Son (Luke 15:13, "riotous"), and is evidently why we have entitled that narrative as we have.

I cannot resist here to quote again from Richard Trench:

". . . more commonly the *asotos* is one who himself cannot save or spare—'prodigus': or, again, to use a good old English word more than once employed by Spenser, but which we have let go, a 'scatterling.' "

"But it is easy to see that one who is *asotos* in this sense of spending too much, of laying out his expenditure on

100

a more magnificent scheme than his means will warrant, slides easily, under the fatal influence of flatterers, and of all those temptations with which he has surrounded himself, into a spending *of his own lusts and appetities* of that with which he parts so freely, laying it out for the gratification of his own sensual desires. Thus the word takes on a new colour, and indicates how not only one of a too expensive, but also and chiefly, of a dissolute, debauched, profligate manner of living . . ."
"In this sense *asotia* is used in the N.T. . . . The waster of his goods will be very often a waster of everything besides, will lay waste himself—his time, his faculties, his powers; and, we may add, uniting the active and passive meanings of the word, will be himself laid waste; he at once loses himself, and is lost."
Thus the Lexicons define *asotia*: An abandoned, dissolute life, profligacy, prodigality, debauchery.

**speaking evil of you:**
*Blasphemeo* (hence our word blaspheme): to speak reproachfully, rail at, revile, accuse falsely and maliciously. (As in I Tim. 1:20.)

**4:5-6 who shall give account to him that is ready to judge the living and the dead. For unto this end was the gospel preached, even to the dead, that they might be judged indeed according to men in the flesh, but live according to God in the Spirit.**

### Expanded Translation
These wicked persons shall render an account (report) to him (Christ) who is ready and prepared to judge those living and those dead. For unto this purpose was the good news (of salvation) preached also to those (now) dead, in order that they might be judged (condemned?) in accordance with (the judgment proper for) men who live in the realm of the flesh, but that (others) might live in harmony with God, and his will in the realm of the Spirit.

---

**who shall give account**
ACCOUNT—*logos*, usually rendered "word" in the Scriptures, is translated "reason" in 3:15. Here it means account, report; an answer or explanation.
**to him that is ready to judge**
That is, Christ: Jn. 5:22-23, Acts 17:31.

### the living and the dead

A phrase which has been variously interpreted.

Some believe the terms *living* and *dead* are to be understood of one's *spiritual* state. "And you did he make alive, when ye were dead through your trespasses and sins" ((Eph. 2:1). ". . . thou hast a name that thou livest, and thou are dead" (Rev. 3:1). "But she that giveth herself to pleasure is dead while she liveth" (I Tim. 5:6).

Most scholars, however, have simply understood the phrase as referring to the universality or comprehensiveness of the judgment, as in II Tim. 4:18. Many are familiar with the committal which concludes concerning the body in the grave:

". . . there to await the day of resurrection
When the earth and sea will give up their dead,
To appear before our Lord Jesus Christ,
The Righteous Judge of the living and the dead."

See II Cor. 5:10, Rev. 20:12-13.

### for to this end was the gospel preached, even to the dead

If we have placed the right construction on the phrase "living and dead," then the *gospel* must have been preached to many who were, at the time of Peter's epistle, in their tombs. The thought here is so similar to that expressed in 3:19 that we dare not separate them. The "spirits in prison" there, is equivalent to "the dead" here.

We have commonly limited the term "preach the gospel" to the death, burial, resurrection and ascension of Christ, and the fact that salvation is offered by this One who is the Son of God. True, I Cor. 15 *does* so define the Gospel, and this *message of salvation through the resurrected Christ* is by far the most frequent usage of the word *evangelidzo* in the New Testament. Peter himself so uses it in 1:12, 25, and the noun form (*euangelion*, "gospel") in 4:17.

But this specific definition of the term is only an *application* of its basic meaning: to proclaim or announce good tidings. Several times in the Septuagint, and in a number of New Testament passages it is used in this *basic* sense (Rev. 10:7, 14:6; Matt. 11:5). Sometimes the writer obviously did *not* have salvation through the resurrected Christ, as such, in mind, but simply the *message of salvation*, which is surely "good news," whether preached in the Patriarchal, Mosaic, or Christian dispensation.

"But they (the Jews) did not all hearken to the *glad tidings*. For Isaiah saith, Lord, who hath believed our report" (Rom. 10:16).

Again the Apostle Paul speaks of the disobedient Jews, this time during the days of Moses:

"Seeing therefore it remaineth that some should enter thereinto, and they to whom the *good tidings* were before preached failed to enter in because of disobedience . . ." (Heb. 4:6).

The message to those of a previous era which provided salvation, then, may Scripturally be called good tidings, joyful message, good news, glad tidings, or gospel. This, I believe, was the "gospel preached even to the dead," including the antediluvians (3:19-20), who were, at the time Peter wrote, dead, and whose spirits were in prison. They did not, for the most part, accept this gospel, but it was preached to them nevertheless. Caton pointedly remarks that if *all* are to be judged by the Gospel of Christ as promulgated by the Apostles, then there must be a post-mortem preaching of the same, or else there would be a failure of justice on the part of God.

### that they (the dead) might be judged indeed according to men in the flesh

Referring to those who had refused to believe, accept, and obey the *Gospel*, the message of salvation.

The fact that they had the good news proclaimed to them but *refused* it, made their condemnation even more justifiable. Knatchbull translates, "that they who live according to men in the flesh may be condemned . . ."—a quite frequent sense of "judged" in the New Testament; and a definite possibility here.

### but live according to God in the Spirit

Or "but (they who live) according to God in the Spirit may live." The words "Indeed . . . but . . ." (*men . . . de*) represent a definite contrast in the original: "on the one hand . . . on the other . . ." The contrast is between people who live in two realms or spheres, the flesh and Spirit. Though men living in the realm of the flesh condemned them and abused them by their evilspeaking, *they* were living in the spirit-realm with the approbation of God upon their lives.

103

## 3. Service to God and Christians Enjoined in View of Impending Calamity 4:7-19

**4:7 But the end of all things is at hand: be ye therefore of sound mind, and be sober unto prayer:**

### Expanded Translation

But the end (conclusion, termination) of all things is near. You must therefore be soberminded and self-controlled; and be calm, that you might be able to pray.

---

### But the end of all things is at hand

The "all things" mentioned here does not necessarily refer to all the world. There are a number of places in the New Testament where the term "all" is not to be taken in a literal sense. See for example, Matt. 10:22. But whatever he has reference to, he tells us it is "at hand." The word here so translated (*engidzo*) occurs 43 times in the Greek New Testament. It is usually rendered "at hand," "draw near," etc. Sometimes it is used in regard to place or position, and sometimes with reference to time, as in this instance. When referring to time, it invariably refers to what is imminent or impending. However, some commentators believe the word frequently does not carry this idea in a literal sense, because, they say, there are certain contexts where placing this significance on the word is impossible. Something could be "near," they say, *as far as God is concerned*, and yet cover thousands of years. ". . . one day is with the Lord as a thousand years, and a thousand years as one day" (II Pet. 3:8). The following passages have been cited as proof of this usage of *engidzo*: Matt. 3:2, Rom. 13:12, Heb. 10:25, James 5:8. Also Phil. 4:5, where the adverb form (*engus*) appears. All of these passages, they point out, are as yet unfulfilled. Thus they believe that the word covers a period of more than 1900 years, and reaching unto the second coming of the Lord, and the end of the world.*

That the above construction on the word "near" as it occurs here, *could* be true, it is conceded. But I am not convinced, after examining the above 43 passages, that *engidzo* is never used in this loose sense by any New Testament writer.

By carefully checking each of the above cited Scriptures in their own contexts, one will find that it is at least very possible,

---

*See, for example, *Jesus Is Coming* by Blackstone, pp. 83-88. Alson Johnstone's Commentary on Jas. 5:8.

if not likely, that they have *all* been fulfilled. (In the last passage cited (Phil. 4:5) where the word is rendered "near," there may simply be a reference to Christ's *presence*. That is, the Lord was close to them, hence a comforting influence.)

If we take the term "at hand" literally here, how shall we understand this verse? It appears to me that we once again have a reference to the destruction of Jerusalem and the Jewish state. (See comments, 2:12.) So great was this event, so far-reaching was its influence in the Roman world, that it could be spoken of by the people of that age as "the end of all things." (Compare the use of "the last days" with reference to the same event, Jas. 5:1-9.)**

### be ye therefore of sound mind

Note that the exhortation here is *based on* the fact just stated: things were soon coming to an end. All those who were true to Christ would have nothing to fear—if they were mentally and spiritually prepared! (See 1:13.) To be of sound mind (*sophroneo*) is to be so ruled by one's mind that he is self-controlled and temperate. Some persons are impulsive and ruled by emotions. But the quality spoken of here consists of the government of such passions, so that on all occasions we behave with prudence.

### and be sober unto prayer

The word "sober" (*nepho*) literally meaning not intoxicated, is used in the New Testament of one who is calm and collected in spirit, temperate. (See comments, 5:8.)

In view of the coming catastrophes, persecutions, and confusion all about them, it would have been easy for the Christians to become alarmed, bewildered, and fearful. The Apostle exhorts them not to be rash or impetuous, but rather to be calm, that they might be able to pray. Their sobriety was to be "unto" (*eis*) prayer—*in order that* they might be in a state of mind which was conducive to prayer life. (See Expanded Translation.)

### 4:8-9 above all things being fervent in your love among yourselves; for love covereth a multitude of sins: using hospitality one to another without murmuring:

**It would help the student see the far-reaching consequences of that great holocaust, by reading in *Wars of the Jews*, by Flavius Josephus, Book VI, Chapters VIII, IX and X.

## Expanded Translation

in preference to everything else, having an intense, earnest and fervent love among yourselves; for love covers (conceals, hides) a multitude of sins. Be hospitable toward one another without sulking and grumbling.

### above all things being fervent in your love among yourselves

The last word is emphatic in the original. Why is this virtue so important? Peter had just spoken of the great calamity that was to fall round about them. Times were already difficult, and the persecution, trials, and hardships were soon to increase. Under such trying and extenuating circumstances, the *church* must be a loving and harmonious unit.

BEING FERVENT—See under 1:22, where we have a very similar exhortation.

### love covereth a multitude of sins

That is, when love dominates a person's life and being, he is not a fault-finder or crank. The constant practice of sin should certainly arrest our attention—whether in our life or in another's. But when love is the controlling force in our lives, we will not be *looking* for sins in our brothers' lives. "Hatred stirreth up strifes," the Wise Man said, "but love covereth all transgressions" (Prov. 10:12). This same thought is expressed by Paul in his great eulogy on Love, when he said that love "taketh not account of evil (I Cor. 13:5).

God also covers our sins when He forgives us (Psa. 32:1, Jas. 5:20). For that reason, some have thought *God's* love and forgiveness is here cited as an example to be imitated. The phrase may, however, simply be taken as a general truth.

### using hospitality one to another

The word *philoxenos* comes from *phileo*, to love and *xenos*, stranger. Thus literally; kind to strangers, loving strangers. But "strangers" here is obviously to be taken in the sense of *others* (*guests*), that is, those outside your immediate household. We are to practice this virtue among *ourselves* as Christians. More is involved in this than *just* having Christian guests in our home. We should *want* them there, and treat them kindly and helpfully.

All too often this virtue is practiced by a few in the church who (bless their generous hearts) are thoughtful of those in need. Others, it seems, practice hospitality to a few of their select friends, while those who need assistance most go unhelped.

Hospitality among ourselves is to be practiced . . .

**without murmuring**

The way all of God's work is to be done (Philip. 2:14). The word "murmuring" (*goggusmos*) sometimes referred merely to low and suppressed discourse, a *muttering* (Jn. 7:12). But more often, as here, it is an expression of secret and sullen discontent —*complaining* or grumbling. Hospitality so rendered represents represents no virtue at all—it only shows you have grudgingly complied to duty. Won't those guests feel so comfortable and relaxed in your home as you show your "love for guests" in this manner? God help us to serve Him and others out of a cheerful and ready mind!

**4:10-11 according as each hath received a gift, ministering it among yourselves, as good stewards of the manifold grace of God; if any man speaketh, speaking as it were oracles of God; if any man ministereth, ministering as of the strength which God supplieth: that in all things God may be glorified through Jesus Christ, whose is the glory and the dominion for ever and ever. Amen.**

### Expanded Translation

According as every man was gifted by God, employing this same gift, be serving and ministering among yourselves as good stewards (caretakers, managers) of the grace of God which is abundant and many-sided. If any man speaks, let his words be uttered as words of God. If any man is performing a service, let him do so as one who serves out of the strength which God supplies, that in everything God may receive glory through Jesus Christ, whose is the glory and the might (power, dominion) for ever and ever. (Literally, into the ages of the ages). Amen.

**according as each has received a gift**

Or "gifted" as above. It is difficult here to know for certain whether the Holy Spirit has reference to extraordinary powers and manifestations of the Holy Spirit (as in Rom. 12:6, I Cor. 12:4, 31, etc.), or if the reference is simply to natural talents with which God has equipped every person, though not in the same measure or with the same gifts. The literal meaning of "gift," according to Thayer is: "a gift of grace; a favor which one receives without any merit of his own." Many would refer its usage here to the class of extraordinary powers. However, in such passages as II Cor. 1:11, I Cor. 7:7, and possibly Rom. 11:29, the word has a more *general* significance. Thus Moulton and Milligan tells us it is used of gifts *generally.* . . . They list several such usages in the Papyri. This general usage of the word—referring to *whatever* abilities or talents one might be able to use for Christ —seems to be intended here. That it included *more* than the direct miraculous work of the Holy Spirit, seems to me to be shown in v. 11, for such a "gift" was certainly not necessary to qualify as a *server* or even as a deacon.

The idea, I believe, is that *whatever* we have, we must use *in God's service.*

### ministering it among yourselves

*Diakoneo.* One immediately notices the relationship of this word to the word "deacon," as it is the verb form of the word so translated. Hence, several lexicographers give it the meaning "perform the duties of a deacon" or some similar rendering. This is a possibility here, but again it is probably better to take the word in a general rather than a specific sense, as in 1:12.*

### as good stewards of the manifold grace of God

A "steward" was commonly a superior slave of proven character, who looked after the accounts and functions of the household. We are managers, caretakers, and overseers of God's gifts of grace to us! How, Christian, are you using what God has given to you? Are you a competent and careful steward of that which he has loaned you for a while—or are you foolishly squandering it for *your* good and pleasure? We should be stewards that have the best interests of our Master at heart—employing our time and energy for His benefit!

### if any man speaketh, speaking as it were oracles of God

An "oracle" is a word or message. If the *gift* of verse 10 had reference to natural endowments, verse 11 provides a further exhortation to cultivate such capacities and use them profitably in the Lord's service.

If *gift* in verse 10 has reference to the spiritual gifts (miraculous), then the exhortation here would be to rightly use such a gift (prophesy?) so that others would know that that person was speaking from God.

### if any man ministereth, ministering as of the strength
### which God supplieth

Referring to the same one who is ministering his gift among the congregation (v. 10). He must recognize, acknowledge, and

---

*Also so used in Jn. 12:26, Acts 19:22, Philem. 13.

call upon the power of God, "for in Him we live, and move, and have our being" (Acts 17:28).

**that in all things God may be glorified**

The ultimate purpose of all our service: "whether therefore ye eat, or drink, or whatsoever ye do, do all to the glory of God" (I Cor. 10:31).

**4:12-13 Beloved, think it not strange concerning the fiery trials among you, which cometh upon you to prove you, as though a strange thing happened unto you: but insomuch as ye are partakers of Christ's sufferings, rejoice; that at the revelation of His glory also ye may rejoice with exceeding joy.**

### Expanded Translation

Loved ones, you must not be surprised (amazed, astonished, shocked) concerning the fiery trial among you, which comes upon you to prove (test, try) you: as though something strange, unexpected, or surprising is happening to you: But insomuch as you are sharers (partners, partakers) in the sufferings of Christ, rejoice! that you may also rejoice greatly and exceedingly at the revelation (disclosure, appearance) of His glory when He comes again.

---

Note the close similarity of 1:6-9, 3:17, 18, 4:1-2.

**Beloved, think it not strange**

The trial was already upon them, and evidently to become more severe (v. 7). They were not to be surprised or amazed at this, but should rather have *expected* it as a natural consequence of living the Christ-like life. ("Think it strange" (*xenidzo*) is defined in v. 4.)

**concerning the fiery trial among you**

i.e., trying, severe, and difficult trials. Fire is painful, but fire is also necessary in the refining process.

**which cometh upon you to prove you**

See comments, 1:7.

**as though a strange thing happened unto you**

We should be mentally and spiritually prepared for such tests (see under 1:13). "Yea, and all that would live godly in Christ Jesus shall suffer persecution" (II Tim. 3:12).

**but insomuch as ye are partakers of Christ's sufferings, rejoice**

Christ was without fault of any kind, yet He suffered (2:21-23). He suffered as a result of *living righteously*. We should suffer for

109

the *same reason* as our Master. "A servant is not greater than his Lord," Jesus told His disciples. "If they persecuted me, they will also persecute you . . ." (Jn. 15:20).

We cannot return to the hill of Calvary and agonize with our Lord there. Yet our fellowship with Him is not as it should be until we are so living from day to day so that times of suffering *similar to His* are our lot. "For as the sufferings of Christ abound unto us, even so our comfort also aboundeth through Christ" (II Cor. 1:5). Paul not only wanted to know the power of Christ's resurrection, but "the fellowship of His sufferings" (Phil. 3:10).

When our suffering is a result of patterning our behavior after His Divine example, then we may truly have reason for rejoicing. Our consoling thought may then be, "Because I am acting like Christ, I am being treated like Christ."

### that at the revelation of His glory

When He comes the second time. No one will welcome that day more than those who have suffered (and are suffering) for Him! The *hope* of His coming and the joys to follow have sustained and encouraged these Christians through life. But their faith and hope will then become sight! Those in trial and affliction, above all people, are qualified to be "looking for and earnestly desiring the coming of the day of God" (II Pet. 3:12).

**4:14-16 If ye are reproached for the name of Christ, blessed are ye; because the Spirit of glory and the Spirit of God resteth upon you. For let none of you suffer as a murderer, or a thief, or an evil-doer, or as a meddler in other men's matters; but if a man suffer as a Christian, let him not be ashamed; but let him glorify God in this name.**

### Expanded Translation

If you are censured (railed at, reproached) for professing and living by the name of Christ, blessed are you, because the glorious Spirit of God is resting upon you. For none of you must suffer as a murderer, or a thief, or an evil-doer (criminal?) or as a busybody in the affairs of others: but if a person suffers as a Christian, let him not be ashamed; rather, let him be glorifying God in (or *by*, or *through*) this name ("Christian").

---

### If ye are reproached

The latter word (*oneididzo*) meaning to censure, attack vehemently in words, insult. It is rendered "upbraid" in Jas. 1:5.

**for the name of Christ**

Several other translations are possible (see above), but the meaning is altered little. We must suffer because we profess and live by the name of our Saviour.

**blessed are ye**

i.e., God's favor and blessings are upon us. Our lot is a happy one, though this is sometimes difficult to perceive in our weakness of faith!

Peter specifies *why* we should consider it a privilege and favor to be so treated:

**because the spirit of glory and the Spirit of God resteth upon you**

Not two *different* spirits, but two ways of describing the same one. (Note the Expanded Translation.) Another translation might be: because the Spirit of glory even the Spirit of God resteth upon you. This *blessing* upon us when being reviled or otherwise mistreated far outweighs the suffering endured by the assaults of the world. We will not be left or forsaken. God's glorious Spirit will be with us.

There is a very close parallel with this passage in Matt. 5:10-12. Please look it up. How many likenesses can you name?

**for let none of you suffer as a murderer, thief, evil-doer, meddler in other men's matters**

Suffering for these things is only receiving one's just deserts (Cp. 2:12, 20). We ought to be ashamed of ourselves and humbly ask God for forgiveness if we suffer for doing any of these (including the last!).

The word *evil-doer* may be rendered "criminal" as in 2:12. The word frequently had reference to one who broke *civil* laws, the laws of the land. Souter thinks the reference here is to a sorcerer, magician, or poisoner.

**meddler in other men's matters**

All one word in the original, *allotrioepiskopos.* It is, in turn, from two words: *allotrios,* belonging to another, and *episkopos,* an overseer, inspector, watcher, guardian (sometimes rendered "bishop"). The reference, then, is to a person who takes upon himself the supervision or oversight of affairs pertaining to others

111

and in no wise to himself. Don't be a "bishop" of another man's business! See II Thes. 3:11, I Tim. 5:13.*

### but if any man suffer as a Christian

As a follower of Christ. This name appears only three times in the New Testament: Acts 11:26, 26:28, and here.

Isaiah prophesied that God's people would be called by "another name" and a "new name, *which the mouth of Jehovah shall name.*" (Isa. 65:15, 62:1-2.) The name *Christian* is the only one that is *new*, for in the Old Testament we have Godly people called saints (Psa. 16:3), brethren (Psa. 133:1), and disciples (Isa. 8:16). I therefore believe this name was given to us by *God*, and not by the heathens or Gentiles.**

The phrase "suffer as a Christian" is here equivalent to "when ye do well" (2:20), "zealous for that which is good" (3:13), and "for righteousness' sake" (3:14).

### let him not be ashamed

Note Barnes' Comment here:

> "He is to regard his religion in every way honorable, and all that fairly results from it in time and eternity as in every respect desirable. He is not to be ashamed to be called a Christian; he is not to be ashamed of the doctrines taught by his religion; he is not to be ashamed of the Saviour whom he professes to love; he is not to be ashamed of the society and fellowship of those who are true Christians, poor and despised though they may be; he is not to be ashamed to perform any of the duties de-

---

*Thayer (and others) believe "other men" here has reference to the *Gentiles.* Citing this very passage, he states: ". . . the writer seems to refer to those who, with holy but intemperate zeal, meddle with the affairs of the Gentiles

—whether public or private, civil or sacred—in order to make them conform to the Christian standard." This interpretation sems likely to me for two reasons: (1) ALL the previous sins mentioned (murder, thievery, evil-doer) were crimes against society or the public at large; (2) The Gentile (or outsider) could easily be referred to by *allotrios* ("other men's"). In Matt. 17:25-26 it, is very properly translated "strangers." And in Heb. 11:34 our translators have rendered it *aliens.*

---

**See the various commentators (particularly McGarvey) on Acts 11:26 and the term "were called" (*chrematidzo*).

manded by his religion; he is not to be ashamed to have his name cast out, and himself subjected to reproach and scorn. A man should be ashamed only of that which is wrong. He should glory in that which is right, whatever may be the consequence to himself . . . His views may be regarded as bigoted, narrow, severe. Opprobrious epithets, on account of his opinions, may be applied to him. His former friends and companions may leave him because he has become a Christian. A wicked father, or a gay and worldly mother, may oppose a child, or a husband may revile a wife, on account of their religion. In all these cases, the same spirit essentially is required which was enjoined on the early Christian martyrs. We are never to be ashamed of our religion, whatever results may follow from our attachment to it."

**4:17-18 For the time is come for judgment to begin at the house of God: and if it begin first at us, what shall be the end of them that obey not the Gospel of God? And if the righteous is scarcely saved where shall the ungodly and sinner appear?**

### Expanded Translation

For the specific time has come for the judgment (of trial, persecution, or affliction) to begin at the house of God. And if this judgment begins first at us, what shall be the end (ultimate destiny) of the ones who do not believe and obey (yield to) the good tidings of God? And if the righteous is saved accompanied with difficult times (under the disciplining hand of God), where shall the ungodly (irreverent, irreligious) and sinner appear?

---

**For the time is come for judgment to begin at the house of God**

What judgment? The word *krima* is employed in many different senses in the New Testament. It especially refers to the sentence of God as a judge. Sometimes this meant a *condemnatory* sentence: II Pet. 2:3 ("sentence"), Jude 4 ("condemnation"). But surely *this* is not the judgment God has in mind for the *house of God!* It is true that some will be condemned who *seem* to be in His true house.* But the Apostle speaks of *their* fate in the same verses.

---

*As the Parable of the Dragnet shows, Matt. 13:47-50, and which Paul also confirms, I Tim. 5:24-25.

We know Peter did not mean *final* judgment here, for he stated "the time *is come.*" Literally, the forepart of the verse reads, "because it is the time of the beginning of the judgment." It was something impending upon the church *at that time.*

It is the opinion of most commentators that the Holy Spirit is here speaking of a severe trial and time of persecution.*

God, the all-wise judge, allows such to come upon Christians to purify and refine them.**

**and if it begin first at us, what shall be the end of them that obey not the Gospel of God?**

"Obey not" (*apeitheo*) is a present participle: ". . . those not yielding to the Gospel . . ." It is defined under 2:8 where we also have a present participle: "being disobedient."

The Church is the special object of God's care, concern, and love, yet it is soon to be tried, persecuted, and afflicted! If our merciful and loving Father allows such for His *children,* how much *greater* will be the hardship and misery of those who refuse to believe and obey Him? What shall be *their* outcome?

**and if the righteous is scarcely saved**

Or, saved *with difficulty,* or, saved *with hardship.**** (See the Expanded Translation.) *God's* strength is not so limited and impotent that He "scarcely" or *barely* saves us: II Pet. 1:10, 11; II Tim. 1:12, Heb. 7:25, Isa. 59:1. Some, it is true, are *almost* lost before they are saved (Jude 23). But this is not because of God's inability.

**where shall the ungodly and sinner appear?**

What shall be their ultimate destiny? They shall certainly not appear in heaven.

If a Christian is *saved* under the disciplining and chastening hand of God, what will be true concerning the *future life* of the *unsaved?* If there are *difficulties* involved in saving a Godly and holy man, how much *more* difficult is it for one to be saved who does *not have* the reassuring promises of the Gospel? The salvation of such a man is not only difficult—it is impossible!

*Zerr, Lange, Brown, The Pulpit Commentary, Barnes, Wood, etc.

---

**Perhaps these were also *chastening* judgments. Compare the use of *krino* (the verb) in I Cor. 11:32.
***Compare the use of *molis* in the Book of Acts: 14:18 ("scarce"), 27:7, 8, 16 ("with difficulty"). The idea of "barely" is present, but the thought of *difficulty* seems uppermost.

**4:19 Wherefore let them also that suffer according to the will of God commit their souls in well-doing unto a faithful creator.**

### Expanded Translation

And consequently (because these things are true) those that are suffering according to the will of God must give over their souls in well-doing to a creator worthy of trust and confidence.

In Verses 17-18 we learned:

1. That God, as the good judge, was about to allow hardship and stress to come upon Christians. He has promised to save us if we will cling to Him—but He has *not* promised that life would be without its hardships.

This brings to mind the well-known words of Annie Johnson Flint:

God hath not promised skies always blue
　Flower-strewn pathways all our lives through;
God hath not promised sun without rain,
　Joy without sorrow, peace without pain.

God hath not promised we shall not know
　Toil and temptation, trouble and woe;
He hath not told us we shall not bear
　Many a burden, many a care.

God hath not promised smooth roads and wide,
　Swift, easy travel, needing no guide;
Never a mountain rocky and steep,
　Never a river, turbid and deep.

But God hath promised strength for the day,
　Rest for the labor, light for the way,
Grace for the trials, help from above,
　Unfailing sympathy, undying love.

2. That God is just in condemning the wicked to *eternal* punishment. Someone says, "Would God be so cruel, harsh, and *brutal* as to let people suffer in the fires of hell?" What shallow insight into the mind of God! He allows His *very own children* to suffer here on earth—sometimes for years on end! And during the same years, the unconverted may be "enjoying the pleasures of sin for a season" (Heb. 11:25). Why, then, would not Jehovah allow the *sons of Satan* to suffer in the *world to come?* The Christian chooses to embrace Christ and suffer temporarily on earth

115

(II Tim. 3:12). The unregenerated man chooses the ways of the devil, and suffers eternally in the future life. In fact, even in *this* life it is often true that "the way of the transgressor is hard" (Prov. 13:15).

In view of the *superiority* of the Christian's position, then, let him place all his trust in his God. Let him suffer only for doing right, but when times of affliction are his lot, he must learn to lean heavily on the strong and sustaining arm of his loving Father.

## QUESTIONS OVER CHAPTER FOUR
### I. Vss. 1-6

1. In what way are we to have the same mind as Christ (v. 1)?
2. Does the expression (v. 1) "he that hath suffered in the flesh hath ceased from sin," refer to Christ or Christians? Explain your answer.
3. Multiple choice: "Gentiles" in this book is used of:
   a. all who were not of Hebrew extraction,
   b. the Greeks,
   c. the Romans,
   d. non-Jews who were not Christians.
   (The term appears in 2:12 and 4:3.)
4. Define, in everyday words, the meaning of the sins mentioned in v. 3.
5. Do Christians seek out the company of sinners?
6. Who thinks it is strange that we do not go along with them?
7. What expression we have studied shows that though a man dies, his life will still be judged?
8. When was the Gospel preached to "the dead"?
9. Why was the preaching done?
10. What does it mean to be "judged according to men in the flesh"?
11. Look at v. 6. With what verses we have previously studied would you connect this one?

### II. Vss. 7-11

12. When Peter said, "But the end of all things is at hand," do you think he was prophesying of the end of the world? Explain answer.
13. If this statement refers to the destruction of Jerusalem, how do you explain the "all things"?
14. How is one "sober unto prayer"?

116

15. Without using your Bible, finish this statement: "Above all things being ——— ——— ——— ——— among yourselves . . ."
16. Explain: "love covereth a multitude of sins."
17. Finish: "using hospitality one to another ——————— ———————."
18. Notice v. 10. What two types of "gifts" could be in the mind of Peter?
19. How would you apply v. 10 and 11 to Christians *today*?
20. What is the highest motive for all of our service?

### III. Vss. 12-19

21. Name two things fire does that trial in a Christian's life should also accomplish?
22. Note v. 12. Of what previous verses does this remind you?
23. How are we partakers (sharers) in Christ's sufferings?
24. For what reason should a Christian be reproached?
25. For what reasons should he *not* suffer (according to this chapter)?
26. In what name should a Saint glorify God?
27. In what other Scriptures does the name "Christian" appear? Who gave us this name?
28. Make a list of five circumstances in life where one is tempted by Satan to be ashamed, but where being ashamed would be sinful.
29. What is the "judgment" about to come on the church at this time?
30. How are the righteous "scarcely saved"?
31. Answer the question the Holy Spirit asks in v. 17. In v. 18.
32. According to the final verse of this chapter, we must commit our souls "unto a faithful ———————" in times of suffering.

## CHAPTER FIVE
### VI. EXHORTATIONS TO ELDERS
### 5:1-4

**5:1 The elders therefore among you I exhort, who am a fellow-elder, and a witness of the sufferings of Christ, who am also a partaker of the glory that shall be revealed:**

### Expanded Translation

Therefore (because the judgment of trial is engulfing the church), I exhort and appeal to the elders (presbyters) among you, being a fellow-elder and a witness or testifier of the sufferings of Christ, and being a sharer (partner, partaker) in the glory which shall be revealed (uncovered).

**The elders therefore among you I exhort,**

THE ELDERS—*presbuteros*, whence our words presbyter, presbyterian, etc. The word primarily means "the older" if two ages were being compared (Luke 15:25). More generally, it refers to an *older person* (see V. 5, I Tim. 5:1). Seventeen times in the New Testament this word is used, as here, of those who are shepherds, overseers and caretakers of the house of God. The term was evidently taken from the Jewish "elders" in the Sanhedrin, but their function is certainly different in many respects.

There are two other terms used in the New Testament for this office:

1: Bishop or overseer (*episkopos*). Compare Acts 20:17 with 20:28, or Tit. 1:5 with 1:7.

2. Shepherd or Pastor (*poimen*). In sixteen occurrences of this Greek word in the New Testament, it is rendered *shepherd*. In one instance (Eph. 4:11), it is translated *pastor*. And who is to be performing the duties of a spiritual shepherd over God's flock? In Acts 20:28 the *Overseers* (bishops) are so exhorted, and in the passage before us the *elders* are told to perform such duties.

Using Bible terminology, then, the names *elder, bishop* and *pastor* all refer to the same person.

**therefore I exhort**

In view of these matters of which I have just spoken. Note especially 4:17-19. When the church is under great stress, its spiritual overseers much attend to their responsibilities with diligence. Paul exhorted the Ephesian elders when the flock was in danger (Acts 20:28-35).

**who am a fellow-elder**

Peter was still an apostle (1:1), but he here mentions an area of commonness with these elders. It was more than a likeness in age—he actually held the same office, probably in the church at Babylon (5:13).

It is well to note that the apostle does *not* say he was *the* or even *a* head-bishop or chief-elder! Yet, if he was writing from and was soon to be elevated to the Pontificate (as the Romanists claim), one would think that a title of greater esteem would be more appropriate! We know that an elder must be an older man. And by the time II Peter is penned, Peter's sojourn on earth was soon to conclude (II Pet. 1:13-14). But strange indeed is the utter silence concerning the promotion of this man who our Roman Catholic acquaintances tell us was "Lord God The Pope!"*

*Strange, too, that the "future Pope" is not so much as greeted by the Apostle Paul in his lengthy list of persons to salute in his epistle to the Romans, Chap. 16.

**and a witness of the sufferings of Christ**

A witness (*martus*) is one who testifies, or *can* testify, concerning what he himself has seen, heard, or knows by some means; but particularly one who can verify what he has *seen*. To his apostles Jesus could say concerning the great events of his life. "Ye are witnesses of these things" (Luke 24:28).* Like John (I Jn. 1:1-2), Peter could speak or write of that which he had seen, heard, and handled. He had seen the Lord bound, mistreated, and delivered into the hands of wicked men. True, he was sometimes "afar off" from this suffering, but he could still speak from personal observation.**

**who am also a partaker of the glory that shall be revealed**

This glory is evidently the same as the "salvation ready to be revealed in the last time" (1:5).

Peter, then, was a brother-elder and a sharer in the coming reward of eternal life. These things he had in common with those he exhorted. But he shows his preëminent qualification for exhorting them in a time of suffering, by reminding them that he was a personal witness of Christ's sufferings.***

**5:2-3 Tend the flock of God which is among you, exercising the oversight, not of constraint, but willingly, according to the will of God; not yet for filthy lucre, but of a ready mind; neither as lording it over the charge allotted to you, but making yourselves ensamples to the flock.**

## Expanded Translation

Tend, feed, and shepherd the flock (church, Acts 20:28) of God which is among you, performing the duties of an overseer and superintendent, not because you are forced to do it, but voluntarily and willingly in accordance with the will and mind of God; nor yet in a spirit of eagerness for base gain, but with a cheerful readiness; neither as lording it over or being domineering over your portion (i.e., that part of God's universal church over which you rule), but making your lives exemplary patterns (examples suitable for imitation) to the flock.

---

*Especially could such be said of Peter, one of the "inner circle" apostles. See the *Introduction*.
**Matt. 26:58, Luke 22:54, Mk. 14:54, and perhaps he is included among "all His acquaintance," Luke 23:49.
***Comp. II Pet. 1:16-18, where his personal witness of the transfiguration is mentioned.

## Tend the flock of God which is among you

The King James Version's "feed" in place of "tend," expresses only part of the meaning of *poimaino*, which means to tend a flock, keep sheep. It is employed in Acts 20:28 thus: ". . . to *feed* the church of the Lord which He purchased with his own blood." A Scriptural elder is a shepherd (Eph. 4:11) and here he is told to do the *work* of one.

What is the work of a shepherd? He is

a. To protect the flock from those who would destroy or scatter it. (Jn. 10:12-13, I Sam. 17:34-36.) (For this reason the ancient shepherd carried a staff or rod, and sometimes a sling (Psa. 23:4, I Sam. 17:40).

b. To go before them, lead them, and guide them safely. See Psa. 23.

c. To find feed for them. "The chief care of the shepherd is to see that the sheep find plenty to eat and drink. The flocks are not fed in pens or folds, but, summer and winter, must depend upon foraging for their sustenance" (Psa. 23.2).*

d. To watch the flock carefully. He tries to keep them from straying, but if one goes astray, he goes after it and brings it back to the fold (Luke 15:3-7).

## exercising the oversight

One word in the original—*episkopeo*. Just as the previous duty was the verb form of the word "pastor" or "shepherd," this word is the verb form of *episkopos*, "bishop" or "overseer." It might be loosely rendered "to do the work of an overseer." It means to look upon, inspect, oversee, look after, care for. The Greek word *skopeo* would have been enough to express the thought of "to look at," or "to inspect," for that is its meaning. But to this verb is added the emphatic particle *epi* (on, upon, over). Thus our word means more than just gawking, looking, or gazing, but looking *with a sense of care and concern* toward the object or person upon whom the attention is centered. This essential element of the meaning is accurately brought out by the translators in the only other occurrence of the word in the New Testament, Heb. 12:15. Paul exhorts the Hebrew Christians to be *"looking carefully"* (*episkopeo*) lest there be any man that falleth short of the grace of God . . ."

---

*The *International Standard Bible Encyclopedia*, Vol. IV, p. 2763.

### not of constraint, but willingly

The word "constraint" (*anagkastos*) means by force, or compulsion; unwillingly. It is opposed to (and the opposite of) *hekousios*: voluntarily, spontaneously, of one's own accord. The latter word occurs only one other time in the New Testament—in the familiar Heb. 10:26, "For if we sin willfully . . ."

### according to the will of God

Literally, "according to God," i.e., God would have it *this* way —"willingly."

### nor yet for filthy lucre, but of a ready mind

These two stand in sharp contrast. When one is laboring "in a spirit of eagerness for base gain,"* he is *not* working spontaneously and zealously for *Christ.*

One of the qualifications of an elder is that he be "no lover of money" (I Tim. 3:3)** and "not greedy of filthy lucre" (Tit. 1:7, I Tim. 3:8).*** Thus he is to be free from this trait in his everyday life before he is qualified, and after he is in the office he is to be free from it as a motivating force in his work as an elder. This duty is especially fitting when we remember that some elders are to receive financial support (I Tim. 5:17-18).

When one's work is done "of a ready mind" (*prothumos*) it is done eagerly, promptly, heartily and cheerfully. Broken down, this word is from *pro*, which here means *with*, and *thumos*, glow, ardor. Stronger in meaning than *hekousios* ("willingly") it implies zeal and enthusiasm. How desirous are these traits in the lives of every Christian!

### neither as lording it over the charge allotted to you but making yourselves ensamples to the flock

Again we have a negative and positive exhortation in direct contrast to each other. He is *not* to "lord it over" his subjects. *Katakurieuo* means to gain or exercise dominion over (see Acts

---

*Souter.
**Where we have *aphilarguros.*
***Where we have *aischrokerdes*, the noun form of the very word under consideration, *aischrokerdos.* Contained within this word is *aischros*, which means indecorous, dishonorable, vile. The reference, then, is not simply to one who is greedy of money, but to a man who so loves money that he will, without hesitation, stoop to low practices to make a "quick buck." In biblical language, "*filthy* lucre' is not *all* money, but money gained dishonorably.

19:16, "mastered"). The significance here is doubtless the same as that given to it by Jesus, when He called the Apostles unto Him and said:

"Ye know that the rulers of the Gentiles *lord it over* (*kata-kurieuo*) them, and their great ones exercise authority over them. *Not so shall it be among you:* but whosoever shall become great among you shall be your minister; and whosoever would be first among you shall be your servant" (Matt. 20:25-27). (By "Gentiles" Jesus evidently had particularly the *Romans* in mind, for they were the ruling power in Judaea and the whole Mediterranean world at that time.) So Barnes says of this word, "it refers properly to that kind of jurisdiction which civil rulers or magistrates exercise. This is an exercise of AUTHORITY, as contradistinguished from the influence of reason, persuasion, and example."

Rather than ruling with an iron hand and making much of his authority, he must lead primarily by his example (*tupos*). Tracing the history of this word, it was first the mark or strike of a blow (from *tupto*, to strike, smite, beat). See Jn. 20:25, "print." Then it meant a *figure formed* by such a blow or impression, or a die (Acts 7:43). After examining the 13 other passages where the word is employed in the New Testament, *apart* from this literal sense, it is my opinion that the word could have been consistently rendered "outline" or "pattern." It is this very word which we would use, if we were Greeks writing 2,000 years ago about a dress *pattern* or *blueprint* for a house. But it is variously translated "form," "ensample," "example," "figure," and "pattern." in the Scriptures. Thus the elder should be one who so lives in his everyday life that he provides a pattern for imitation to the members of the congregation.

**5:4 And when the chief Shepherd shall be manifested, ye shall receive the crown of glory that fadeth not away.**

### Expanded Translation

And when the chief (head) Shepherd appears, you will obtain for yourselves the crown (or wreath, or garland) of glory, that never fades—never loses its original brightness, lustre, or beauty.

---

### And when the chief Shepherd shall be manifested

i.e., Christ, when He returns, cp. 2:25.* He is the head of the church, his flock, and the elders are his under-shepherds. Note

---

*Peter says much of the second coming of Christ and the glories of our future home: 1:3-9, II Pet. 3:10-14.

the similarity of expression in Acts 20:28.

**ye shall receive the crown of glory that fadeth not away**
The word "crown" (*stephanos*) had usual reference to some
type of wreath or garland, such as those given for winners of the
athletic contests (I Cor. 9:25). Such prizes were given as a *reward*. Earthly accomplishments quickly wilt, fade, and crumble.
Even *golden* crowns soon tarnish. Not so with our eternal reward!
(See the term "fadeth not away" discussed under 1:4.)

## VII. FINAL EXHORTATIONS TO BE SUBMISSIVE, HUMBLE, TRUSTFUL AND WATCHFUL 5:5-11

**5:5 Likewise, ye younger, be subject unto the elder. Yea, all of you
gird yourselves with humility, to serve one another; for God resisteth the proud, but giveth grace to the humble.**

### Expanded Translation
Also, the younger ones must arrange themselves under the older
ones. Indeed, all of you must be clothed with a lowly opinion of
yourselves [subjecting yourselves to one another];* because God
opposes and resists the high-minded and arrogant, but gives grace
and favor to those who are humble, lowly, and condescending.

---

**Likewise, ye younger, be subject unto the elder**
The "elder" here mentioned is plural in the Greek, and is the
same Greek word so rendered in verse 1. But the exhortation here
is apparently a *general* one concerning conduct among Christian
brethren. That the "elder ones" here refers to the elderly in the
congregation and not to the bishop as such, I submit the following reasons:

1. It is in plain contrast here to the "younger" (*neoteroi*)
which invariably has reference to *age* in the New Testament.

2. The term "elder" (*presbuteros*) is elsewhere used in its literal significance. Why not here? Compare Luke 15:12 with 15:
25. See also Acts 2: 17.

3. A very parallel passage is I Tim. 5:1-2, where the same contrast is found, even in the original. And note there, as here, the
previous context concerns the office of the eldership (I Tim. 3:
1-7, 4:14).

But in what way are younger Christians to be *submissive* to
older ones? They are to "arrange themselves under" them (see
3:1, where *hupotasso* is defined). They must be respectful, kind,
courteous, and thoughtful of them.**

---
*Omitted in some MSS.
**Compare II Kings 2:23-25, Lev. 19:32, Prov. 16:31, 20:29, Lam. 5:12.

**yea, all of you gird yourselves with humility**

That is, surround and clothe yourself with it. Humility (*tapeininophrosune*) is "the having a deep sense of one's (moral) littleness; modesty, lowliness of mind."***

**to serve one another**

What a different way is the Christian life from that of the world's "dog eat dog" philosophy! Compare 3:8-9; Phil. 2:3-4.

**for God resisteth the proud, but giveth grace to the humble**

See the same phrase in Jas. 4:6. The proud, arrogant, and haughty are opposed and resisted by God, though this opposition is not always immediately discernable. But just as certain is his *favorable* regard for the humble (*tapeinos*—literally, low, not rising far from the ground; hence lowly in his own estimation of himself, lowly in spirit). Only the humble are *in a position* to receive the spiritual blessings and kindnesses God has to offer him.

**5:6-7 Humble yourselves therefore under the mighty hand of God, that he may exalt you in due time; casting all your anxiety upon him, because he careth for you.**

## Expanded Translation

You must be humble, submit, and lower yourselves therefore under the strong and powerful hand of God, in order that you might be elevated and exalted at the proper time. Throw all your worry and anxious care upon him, because he is concerned about your welfare and cares for you.

---

**Humble yourselves therefore**

In view of the truth just stated—that the Almighty resists those who lift themselves up in arrogance and has blessings in store for the lowly.

**casting all your anxiety upon him**

The word "anxiety" (*merimna*) means literally to draw (the mind) in different directions. Those things which cause worry or anxious care must be cast upon our God! Many of such cares are concerning an impending or anticipated ill and the painful uneasiness of mind that comes from dwelling upon them. How easy it is to take these burdens upon *ourselves*, believing *we* can solve them! Even when the greatest calamity has befallen us let us say with Job, "Jehovah gave, and Jehovah hath taken away; blessed be the name of Jehovah" (Job 1:21).

***Thayer's Greek Lexicon. See also Trench, *Synonyms of the N.T.*, XLii. Also, note our discussion of *tapeinophron* under 3:8.

As we have seen, the recipients of this epistle were already in the midst of tribulation and about to undergo trials of even greater intensity. If any group of Christians had the "right" to be anxious, they did. The apostle's exhortation was timely.

It appears that the Psalmist learned the lesson that Peter would here have us all heed, particularly concerning anxiety over our bodily safety.

"I laid me down and slept.
I awaked; for Jehovah sustaineth me.
I will not be afraid of ten thousands of the people
That have set themselves against me round about."
—Psa. 3:5-6.

"In peace will I both lay me down and sleep;
For thou, Jehovah, alone maketh me dwell in safety."
—Psa. 4:8.

**because he careth for you**

More than anyone else! See Heb. 13:5-6.

**5:8-9 Be sober, be watchful: your adversary the devil, as a roaring lion, walketh about, seeking whom he may devour; whom withstand stedfast in your faith, knowing that the same sufferings are accomplished in your brethren who are in the world.**

### Expanded Translation

Be calm (sober, self-controlled), be wide awake (watchful and vigilant): Your adversary (enemy, opponent) the devil, as a roaring lion is stalking about, seeking those whom he may gulp down (swallow, devour, gobble). Whom you must oppose with firm faith, knowing (considering, realizing) that the same experiences of suffering are endured by your (Christian) brethren who are in (other parts of) the world.

**Be sober**

*nepho* (see discussions under 1:13 and 4:7). Literally meaning not intoxicated, in the New Testament it is used only figuratively: "Be free from every form of mental and spiritual drunkenness —from excess, passion, rashness, etc." In Apostolic usage, it refers to one who is well-balanced or self-controled. Here (as in II Tim. 4:5 and I Thes. 5:6), Arndt and Gingrich would translate: "be self-possessed under all circumstances."

**be watchful**

*gregoreo* literally signifies "to be awake" or "watch" (Matt.
26:38-40). Metaphorically, as here, to be watchful, vigilant, cir-
cumspect; give strict attention to, be cautious. Through careless-
ness, neglect, and lack of careful attention, our souls can drift
away from Christ and become easy prey to Satan. "Watch and
pray, that ye enter not into temptation" (Matt. 26:41).

Both "be sober" and "be watchful" are aorist imperatives, indicating sharp commands to be heeded at once.

**your adversary, the devil**

The term "adversary" (*antidikos*) sometimes refers to an opponent in a lawsuit (Matt. 5:25, Luke 12:58, 18:3). This has
caused some to believe the devil is called our "adversary" because
he accuses men before God (tries to get a "case" against us) so
God, as judge, may sentence us. However, the word is commonly
used in ancient Greek literature (including the Septuagint) to
simply indicate an enemy, adversary, or opponent; and, I believe,
should so be understood here.

Christ is our *friend!* All that he does to or for us, he does out
of a heart of love and for our good. Not so with Satan! He may,
and o.ften does, *appear* as a friend, BUT HE HAS NOTHING
BUT OUR HARM, DAMAGE, AND RUIN in mind. May we
never forget this truth!

**as a roaring lion walketh about**

Many beasts roar or howl when they are *hungry*. Perhaps we
may so understand this phrase. Satan is hungry and eager for
souls! Watch out!

**seeking whom he may devour**

The words "walking" and "seeking" are in the present tense,
showing constancy of action. You may let down your guard and
go to sleep on the job, BUT SATAN DOES NOT! He is at his
task of consuming unwary saints *at all hours!*

His allurements may, and often do, look attractive. But what
is his real purpose? To destroy our souls! He seeks those he may
"gulp down." If Satan's subtlety and slyness are portrayed when
he appeared as a serpent (Gen. 3:1), his ferocity and meanness
are pictured in this simile of a lion. He is a brutal, ravaging, wild
beast! What must we have to ward off such a beast? Peter tells
us . . .

**whom withstand stedfast in your faith**

The term "in" (*en*) may be taken as instrumental: with or by means of faith; or locative: in faith.

Our faith is to be rigid, strong, firm, solid, and immovable, for this is the meaning of "stedfast." Homer used this word to describe *rocks*. God needs people with a "rock-like" faith!

Equipped with such a trust, we are to resist and oppose Satan. "But resist the devil and he will flee from you" (James 4:7).

**knowing that the same sufferings are accomplished in your brethren who are in the world**

Note the Expanded Translation. There are some who believe the "brethren" here are the Jewish people who were undergoing trials over the world. This is particularly held by those who believe the book was exclusively addressed to Hebrew Christians, the "brethren who are in the world" referring to non-Christian Jews who were undergoing persecutions at the hands of the Romans.

Whereas the above is a possibility, the whole scope of the verse concerns *Christians*. The term "brethren" occurs throughout the book with this significance (1:22, 2:17, 3:8). Realizing that *other* brethren in other parts of the globe are bearing up under trials similar to our own provides us with spiritual encouragement. (Compare Rom. 1:12.)

**5:10-11 And the God of all grace, who called you unto his eternal glory in Christ, after that ye have suffered a little while shall himself perfect, establish, strengthen\* you. To him be the dominion for ever and ever. Amen.**

### Expanded Translation

And after you have suffered a little (while), the God of all grace, favor, and kindness, who called you into his eternal glory in Christ (or, by Christ), shall himself put you in proper order, confirm, strengthen you. To him be the might and dominion for ever and ever (literally, *unto the ages of the ages*). Amen.

---

\*Many manuscripts add the word *settle (themelioo)*. Its meaning is: firmly establish, ground, render firm and unwavering, make stable. It is omitted in the Vatican and Alexanderian manuscripts, but included in the Sinaitic and other manuscripts and versions. Nestle's text includes it, but most modern translations omit it.

**And the God of all grace**

All the blessings of our lives we can trace to God's goodness (Jas. 1:17). Salvation, that grace by which we are saved, comes from him as its Author and Source.

**after that ye have suffered a little while**

Literally, a little. The word may refer to the degree, as well as to the duration, of the sufferings. They are transient and passing; the glory is eternal. "For our light affliction, which is for the moment, worketh for us more and more exceedingly an eternal weight of glory" (II Cor. 4:17).

**shall himself perfect, establish, strengthen you**

Here is what *God* can do!

PERFECT—*katartizo*. This word basically means to finish, complete, or repair. It is used in the account of the calling of Peter, Andrew, James and John, by the Sea of Galilee, when the latter two were in the boat with Zebedee, their father, *mending* (*katartizontas*) their nets. That is, they were putting them in good shape. God will repair, adjust, and place in proper order what is lacking or maladjusted in the character of his people, if we will conscientiously strive to adhere to his word. He can make us fit vessels for the tasks he has given us to accomplish!

ESTABLISH—*sterizo*. Literally, to set up, fix firmly, support. ("And besides all this, between us and you there is a great gulf *fixed* . . ." Luke 16:26.) Figuratively, it means to confirm, establish, or strengthen. Jesus had said to this very apostle, "When thou art converted, *strengthen* thy brethren" (Luke 22:32), employing this same word.

STRENGTHEN—*sthenoo*, a word similar in meaning to the previous: to make strong, put strength into.

**to him be the dominion for ever and ever**

See also 4:11. This seems to be a spontaneous outburst of praise, honor, and glory to God, straight from the heart of the apostle.

## VIII. PERSONAL MATTERS AND SALUTATIONS
## 5:12-14

**5:12 By Silvanus, our faithful brother, as I account him, I have written unto you briefly, exhorting, and testifying that this is the true grace of God: stand ye fast therein.**

### Expanded Translation

By (or through, or by means of) Silvanus (Silas) your faithful and trustworthy brother, as I estimate him, I have written you this short letter, exhorting (or, perhaps, *encouraging*) you, and bearing my testimony that this is the true (real) grace of God: stand fast (stay put) in it!*

## By Silvanus

Silas is a contracted form of this man's name. I see no reason to doubt, as some do, that this is the same man who traveled extensively with Paul. He is always referred to as Silas in Acts, and as Silvanus in the epistles. He may have been Peter's secretary, or scribe, but more than likely he only served as the messenger. See the *Introduction*.

## exhorting

*Parakaleo*, which sometimes combines the ideas of exhorting, encouraging, and comforting.

## and testifying that this is the true grace of God

*Epimartureo*, signifies to bear testimony, testify solemnly, establish by testimony, usually with the thought of *giving evidence*. So Peter had done regarding those matters that make up the life of the real Christian—the life that is in the sphere of God's true grace. They had experienced this grace in conversion and in the blessedness and progress of their life with Christ. This was no delusion, as they were tempted to suppose by their troubles and afflictions, *but the genuine grace of God!*

## stand ye fast therein

That is, in the realm of the grace of God, Christ's church, the place where God's grace is diffused. "Wherefore, my beloved brethren, be ye stedfast, unmoveable, always abounding in the work of the Lord, forasmuch as ye know that your labor is not vain in the Lord" (I Cor. 15:58).

**5:13-14 She that is in Babylon, elect together with you, saluteth you; and so doth Mark my son. Salute one another with a kiss of love.**

**Peace be unto you all that are in Christ.**

### Expanded Translation

She (the church) that is in Babylon, who have been elected to Gospel privileges along with you, greet (salute, express good wishes to) you; also Mark my son. Greet one another with a kiss,

---

*Thayer and others would give *eis* the meaning of "enter" here, rather than "in," translating "enter and stand fast." But the simple meaning "in" seems more appropriate to me.

which is an expression of (your Christian) love.
Peace and tranquility be to all of you that are in fellowship with Christ.

---

### She that is in Babylon

The word "church" (*ekklesia*) is feminine in gender, and the salute here given is to be taken as from the congregation of believers in the city of Babylon.* Babylon was not as yet *entirely* destroyed, and there seems to be no real reason for believing *Rome* is meant here, or some Babylon of another country. See the *Introduction*.

### Mark my son

Peter may have been instrumental in turning this man to Christ and therefore refers to him in this endearing manner. Paul spoke of Timothy and Titus as his children: I Tim. 1:2, II Tim. 1:2, 2:1, Tit. 1:4.

### salute one another with a kiss of love

Evidently the same as the "holy kiss" mentioned in Paul's writings (Rom. 16:16, etc.). Greeting by means of a kiss seems to have been a common practice in the early church and for several centuries following the apostolic era.**
There is reason to believe that, as a rule, men only thus greeted men, and women, women.'" The eastern kiss was on the cheek, forehead, beard, hands, and even feet, but not the lips. In modern times, Christendom has substituted the kissing of the altar, the "sacred elements," or the stole of the clergy.***

### peace be unto you all that are in Christ

Others do not have such an assurance. The peace Christ gives is "not as the world gives" (Jn. 14:27), but far more lasting and satisfying. If our trust is in him, the peace of God, which passes all understanding, shall guard our hearts and thoughts in Christ Jesus (Phil. 4:7).

---

*"Church" actually appears in Syriac and Vulgate versions.
**See *The Anti-Nicene Fathers*, Vol. 2, p. 291 and Vol. 7, p. 422.
***This point is made by the *Shaff-Herzog Ency.*, *The International Standard Bible Ency.*, Woods.

I PETER

## QUESTIONS OVER CHAPTER V

1. Do you believe Peter occupied the office of an elder in the church, or was he just an older man at this time? Why?
2. At what time was Peter a witness of Christ's sufferings?
3. In what way was he a partaker of "the glory that shall be revealed"?
4. Name at least three things a good shepherd must do when he tends a flock.
6. Rather than exercising the oversight out of constraint, the elder is to do so _____?
5. Explain the *feeding* of the flock.
7. What is "filthy lucre" as far as the Bible is concerned?
8. What is the opposite force that *should* motivate the elder?
9. Who did *Jesus* say lorded it over others?
10. What is the better method of helping people according to the Holy Spirit?
11. Who is the chief Shepherd? Where is he mentioned elsewhere in I Peter?
12. What quality does the crown of glory have?
13. What are the younger ones to do?
14. With what are we to gird ourselves?
15. Name some ways we can "serve one another."
16. "God _____ the proud, but giveth _____ to the humble."
17. When will the humble be exalted?
18. What is anxiety?
19. What is to be done with it?
20. What reason does Peter give for doing this?
21. Define "Be sober.'
22. To what animal is the devil likened?
23. What is he *doing?* What does this indicate?
24. How is he to be overpowered?
25. Who were their "brethren who are in the world" (v. 20)?
26. Jehovah is here called "the God of all _____"?
27. How were they to suffer?
28. Just what does God do when he "perfects" us (v. 10)?
29. Who was Silvanus?
30. What compliment does Peter give him?
31. Did Peter consider this a long letter? (Do you?)
32. What is the true grace of God?
33. How is it to be regarded or treated?

131

34. Is "She that is in Babylon" Peter's wife?
35. Does "Babylon" here mean "Rome" as in Revelation? Give a reason(s) for your answer.
36. What affectionate title does Peter give Mark?
37. Identify Mark in the Book of Acts. (Was he "washed up" when he returned to Jerusalem?)
38. With what were the recipients to greet one another?
39. Upon what group does Peter wish peace?

## INTRODUCTION TO II PETER

I.   THE RECIPIENTS.

This letter is addressed "to them that have obtained a like precious faith with us" (1:1). More specifically, it was intended for the same people as was I Peter; i.e., "the elect who are sojourners of the Dispersion in Pontus, Galatia, Cappadocia, Asia, and Bithynia" (I Pet. 1:1), for Peter himself states in 3:1, "This is now, beloved, the *second* epistle that I write unto you . . ."

II.  PLACE OF WRITING.

It is not known. Among places conjectured have been Rome, Egypt, Palestine, and Asia. Perhaps he is still in Babylon (I Pet. 5:13).

III. TIME OF WRITING.

It is generally accepted that second Peter was written toward the end of the first century, and is one of the latest New Testament books. How do we arrive at such a conclusion?

a. Peter speaks of his death as near, 1:14,15.
b. Apparently, most or *all* of Paul's epistles had already been written, 3:15,16.
c. Paul's Epistles had existed long enough to be perverted, 3:16. His letters cover the years between 62 A.D. (I Thes.) to 66 A.D. (II Tim.).
d. Heresies dealt with in the epistle did not become a real problem until the latter part of the first Century. (Compare the book of Jude, where there are many parallels to this book in thought and language.)

Thus the date has been set at about 66 or 67 A.D., perhaps even later.

IV.  THE HUMAN AUTHOR AND THE
GENUINENESS OF THE BOOK.

No book in the entire New Testament has had its genuineness questioned more than the second epistle of Peter. It is placed among the seven books called *The Antilegomena*, or disputed books, about which certain questions arose which prevented them from being received into the canon until a later date. At the core of these disputes concerning the epistle's authenticity lies this question: Is the Apostle Peter its true author?

Some have rejected this book as the work of Peter because of statements made by early "Church Fathers." So Eusebius says, "One epistle of Peter, called the first, is acknowledged. This the presbyters of ancient times have quoted in their writings, as undoubtedly genuine. But that called his second, we have been informed by tradition, has not been received as a part of the New Testament. Nevertheless, appearing to many to be useful, it hath been carefully studied with the other Scriptures."[*]

Again, Eusebius states: "Among the contradicted [books] but yet well known to many [or approved by many], are that called the Epistle of James, and that of Jude, and the second of Peter, and the second and third of John . . ."[**]

Origen is the first writer to mention II Peter *by name*, about 240 A.D.[***] Later, he quotes II Peter 1:4, "partakers of the divine nature," and labels it "Scripture." But he adds: "Peter has left one acknowledged Epistle, and perhaps a second, for this is contested."

Jerome, though including it in his Vulgate Version, knew of the scruples which many entertained concerning it. His own uncertainty, he said, stemmed from "a difference in style from I Peter."

The book is not mentioned in the writings of Tertullian, Cyprian, Clement of Alexandria, Muratori's Canon, or the older (Peshitta) Syriac Version (the *later* Syriac has it). This is *not* to say these sources did not *know* of the book—only that they did not mention it by the name as a part of Scripture.

Over against these statements, which may seem weighty *against* our acceptance of this book as the inspired work of Peter, we would submit both external and internal evidences *in favor of its acceptance* as the genuine work of the inspired apostle whose name it bears.

---

[*]Eusebius, *Ecclesiastical History*, lib. ii.c.3. (about 325 A.D.)
[**]*Ibid*, lib. iii.c.25.
[***]In his *Homily* on Joshua; also in his 4th *Homily* on Leviticus and 13th on Numbers.

LETTERS FROM PETER

1. EXTERNAL EVIDENCE.

a. Traces of acquaintance with it appears at a very early date. Hermas, who flourished about 140, is best known for the book we call *The Shepherd of Hermas*. In *Vision* 3:7 we have "They have left their true way" (Cp. Pet. 2:15 where it is closely parallel in the Greek) and in *Vision* 4:3, "Thou hast escaped this world" (Cp. II Pet. 2:20). In *Similes* 6:4 we have "luxury in the day . . . luxuriating with their own deceivings"; (Cp. II Pet. 2:13 in the Greek). Clement of Rome, whose *Epistle to the Corinthians* (96 A.D.) is one of the most valuable works of the early church, may allude to it in 7:9 and 10. Concerning Noah's preaching and Lot's deliverance, he said, "the Lord making it known that he does not abandon those that trust in Him, but appoints those otherwise inclined to Judgment" (Cp. II Pet. 2:5-9). Irenaeus (died about 192) uses the phrase "the day of the Lord is as a thousand years" as does Justin Martyr (100-165) —a statement we immediately connect with II Pet. 3:8. Hippolytus (3rd Century), in *The Antichrist*, seems to refer to II Pet. 1:21 in these words: "The prophets spoke not of their own private [individual] ability and will, but what was [revealed] to them alone by God."

b. Though there were scholars of the early church who rejected it, other learned men, of equal ability, *accepted* it. Among these were Firmilian of Caesarea in Cappadocia (died, 264),* Athanasius (293-373), Epiphanius (315-403), Cyril of Jerusalem (315-386),** Rufinus (345-410), and Augustine (354-430).

c. It is included in the Sinaitic MS. (350), The Alexandrian (450)—and the Vatican (325-350), or in all the "big 3" manuscripts. Let us remember that the scholars and teachers of the fourth century, when the canon of the New Testament was fixed, had, in many ways, more evidence to go upon than we now possess. It was only as a result of careful examination that *any* writing was admitted as part of the canonical Scriptures.

---

*This evidence is found in his *Epistle ad Cyprian*, where he speaks of Peter's *Epistles* as warning us to avoid heretics—an admonition which occurs in the *second* letter. Note that Cappadocia is one of the countries addressed in both epistles (I Pet. 1:1, II Pet. 3:1), and it is certainly striking that from this country we have the earliest decisive testimony. "Internally, it claims to be written by Peter, and this claim is confirmed by the Christians of that very region in whose custody it *ought* to have been found."—Tregelles.
**who enumerates seven Catholic General Epistles, including II Peter.

II PETER

d. The *Antelegomena* (disputed) books are to be carefully distinguished from those regarded as *Spurious* and false. The former designation merely separated them from the *Homologoumena*—those books universally accepted as canonical. By the middle of the fourth century, *all* of the *Antelegomena* books were accepted as canonical.* Included among the *Spurious* were *The Gospel of Peter, The Apocolypse of Peter,* and *The Acts of Peter,* but not the second epistle of Peter! Now to say a book is pseudopigraphal or spurious is one thing, and to say it is *contested* is another. To know that a book was carefully examined by the most critical scholars shortly after it was written, and then *accepted as genuine,* is reassuring evidence in favor of its authenticity.

2. INTERNAL EVIDENCE.

a. The direct claim of Peter's authorship, 1:1.

b. He states he had already written to the same people he was now addressing—3:1.

c. The author mentions that he, along with the other apostles, was one of the eyewitnesses of Christ and with Him on the mount of transfiguration, 1:16-18.

d. The writer was apparently an older man, and expecting death soon—appropriate for *Peter,* 1:13-14.

e. Although there is considerable difference in style, yet there is also considerable *similarity* between this epistle and I Peter. There are a good number of words and phrases *common* to both epistles, but rarely or *never* found in other New Testament books.** Also, words and phrases employed in *both* epistles are also found to be similar to those used by Peter in the Book of Acts.

*These include: II Peter, James, II and III John, Jude, Hebrews and Revelation.
**See the *New Bible Commentary,* p. 1143, for a comprehensive list of these similarities. Also, the *International Standard Bible Encyclopedia,* Vol. IV, pp. 2355-2356.

## I. INTRODUCTION AND GREETING 1:1,2
## CHAPTER I

**1:1-2 Simon Peter, a servant and apostle of Jesus Christ, to them that have obtained a like precious faith with us in the righteousness of our God and the Saviour Jesus Christ: Grace to you and peace be multiplied in the knowledge of God and of Jesus our Lord;**

### Expanded Translation

Simon Peter, a servant (bondman, slave) and apostle (commissioned messenger sent forth with orders) of Jesus Christ, to those having obtained an equally precious faith with us, in the righteousness of our God and Saviour Jesus Christ. Grace, favour, and blessing be upon you and peace be increased and multiplied as you acquire a full and accurate knowledge of God and of Jesus our Lord.

---

### Simon Peter, a servant and apostle of Jesus Christ

(See I Pet. 1:1.) This inscription varies from that of the first letter in two particulars:

1. He adds his original name, Simon (Jn. 1:40-42).

2. Besides verifying his apostleship, he adds that he is a *sérvant* (*doulos*) of Jesus Christ.

What is a *doulos?* This word normally means a bondman, a slave, one who sustains a permanent servile relation to another. (But it sometimes indicates subjection without the idea of bondage.) Jesus employs this very word when he said to his apostles, ". . . whosoever would become great among you shall be your minister (*diakonos*); and whosoever would be first among you shall be your servant (*doulos*) . . ." (See Matt. 20:20-28, also Luke 22:24-27). We become great in God's eyes when we forget our own glory and become servants!

It is significant that most of the epistles were written by men who chose to wear the title of *servant*: Rom. 1:1, Jas. 1:1, Jude 1:1, etc. They were bondmen and slaves of Christ, happy and joyous that they could maintain such a relationship!

### to them that have obtained a like-precious faith with us

The word "obtained" (*lagchano*) means to obtain by lot. They had been allotted a faith that was just as precious and valuable as the apostle's (if that is who is meant by "us").*

What is the faith here spoken of? I would refer it to the *life* of faith, or the Gospel with all its privileges (as in Gal. 1:12). It cannot be subjective (belief), for it is given to us by God.**

### in the righteousness of our God and the Saviour Jesus Christ

Or, "our God and Saviour Jesus Christ." Christ is God: Acts 20:28 (some MSS), Jn. 1:1, 10:30, I Jn. 5:20. In the realm or sphere of *his* righteousness (not our own merit) we have obtained our salvation.

### grace to you and peace be multiplied

A repetition of I Pet. 1:2.

### in the knowledge of God and of Jesus our Lord

The word "knowledge" (*epignosis*) is a very important word in this second epistle, occurring again in 1:3, 8, 2:20, and the verb (*epiginosko*) in 2:21. It will be worth our time to notice a quote from Trench concerning it:

> Of *epignosis*, as compared to *ginosis* (knowledge), it will be sufficient to say that *epi* must be regarded as intensive, giving to the compound word a greater strength than the simple possessed . . . a deeper and more intimate knowledge and acquaintance . . . St. Paul, it will be remembered, exchanges the *ginosko*, which expresses his present and fragmentary knowledge, for *epignosomai*, which would express his future intuitive and perfect knowledge (I Cor. XIII. 12) . . . It is bringing me better acquainted with a thing I saw before afar off.***

It is thus more than knowledge; it is a precise and correct knowledge. It is more than acquiring a bundle of facts and placing them in the memory; it is *understanding* those facts and their relation to one another. It denotes exact or full knowledge, and expresses a greater care and concern on the part of the knower.

---

*I have a hard time believing that the "us" here refers to the *Jews* generally, as some assert. Peter's first epistle was *largely* to Jewish *Christians* and this epistle was to the same group (II Pet. 3:1).

**A careful examination of Eph. 2:8 will also reveal that "the gift of God" in that passage is not faith, but salvation. Belief is something *we* must exercise after the evidence is presented.

***Trench, *Synonyms of The N.T.*, p. 285. See also Lightfoot's commentary on Col. 1:9.

## II. THE CHRISTIAN'S GROWTH, 1:3-21
### 1. Exhortations to Grow in the Full Knowledge of Christ
### 1:3-15

**1:3 seeing that his divine power hath granted unto us all things that pertain unto life and godliness, through the knowledge of him that called us by his own glory and virtue;**

### Expanded Translation

We realize* that his (God's) divine power and ability has given (granted, bestowed) to us all the things which pertain to the (spiritual) life and godliness (piety, true religion), through (by means of) the exact and full knowledge of the one (Christ) who called us by that glory and moral goodness which was uniquely his own.

---

**seeing that his divine power hath granted unto us all things that pertain unto life and godliness**

Cp. Jas. 1:17-18, II Tim. 3:16-17. The word "divine" (*theios*), from *theos*, (God) is used here of God's *power*, and in v. 4 of his *nature*; in both instances it refers to that which proceeds or emanates from God. The "life" here is the *spiritual* life— the life of Christian conduct. "Godliness" (*eusebeia*) is a compound word made up of *eu*, well, good, and *sebomai*, to be devout or religious.

It denotes that piety which, characterized by a Godward attitude, does that which is pleasing unto him.

To live the Christ-like life, our Father has provided every need —"all things." It is well to remember that God has given us *all* —mankind cannot improve upon it, nor can he rightfully add any more necessary things. What he supplies for the spiritual life cannot be improved upon.

**through the knowledge**

(*epignosis*, see comments, v. 2.)

**of him that called us by his own glory and virtue**

When the real knowledge of Christ is ours, and when it is carefully preserved and cultivated, the blessings which enable us to live a full, rich and prosperous Christian life shall be ours!

Christ called us by his *own* (*idios*) glory and virtue—not ours! But by living in close union with him, we shall be sharers in the divine nature (v. 4).

---

*hos with the genitive absolute presents the matter spoken of (Thayer) and in this case a truth is stated, hence an "editorial 'we'" seems appropriate.

Notice that the grace and peace Peter wishes upon his readers is granted *through this type of knowledge concerning God and Christ.* Friend, do you *know* your Saviour, or are you only casually acquainted? This verse should not only cause the Christian to see his need of studying the Scriptures, but of cultivating his friendship with this "Friend of friends" in *every* way.

**1:4 whereby he hath granted unto us his precious and exceeding great promises; that through these ye may become partakers of the divine nature, having escaped from the corruption that is in the world by lust.**

## Expanded Translation

Through which (glories and virtues) he has freely given us the precious (properly, held as of great price) and very great promises, in order that through them you might become sharers (partakers, fellowshippers) in the divine nature, having fled and escaped from the (moral, spiritual) corruption and destruction that is in the world through lust (strong passions of the flesh).

---

### whereby he hath granted unto us his precious and exceeding great promises

Promises it is well for us to stop and enumerate frequently. The word *doreomai* ("hath granted") which also occurred in verse 3, means to give freely, present, bestow; conveying the idea of generosity. In its only other New Testament appearance it is used, strangely enough, of the Roman procurator Pilate, when he *granted* the corpse of Jesus to Joseph of Arimathaea (Mk. 15:45).

God always fulfills his promises, for he cannot lie (see Titus 1:2). Solomon could say in his prayer as he dedicated the temple, "Blessed be Jehovah, that hath given rest unto his people Israel, according to all that he promised; *there hath not failed one word of all his good promise,* which he promised by Moses his servant" (I Kings 8:56).

### that through these ye may become partakers of the divine nature

Peter had previously stated that he was "a *partaker* of the glory that shall be revealed" (I Pet. 5:1). The word *koinonos* means basically to be a partner or fellow (so *koinonia,* fellowship); then, to be a sharer, partaker, participant. We, as God's children, should partake in the nature of our Father, becoming like him in holiness (I Pet. 1:14-19).

139

**having escaped from the corruption that is in the world by lust**

The word *apopheugo* is an emphatic form of the common word *pheugo* (to flee, seek safety by flight). It is used only by Peter in the New Testament (here, 2:18, 20), always with reference to those who have fled from the world, its people, or its defilements. Many, alas, are still behind Satan's Iron Curtain and have never escaped to the freedom that is in Christ.

CORRUPTION—*phthora*, signifies a bringing or being brought into a worse condition, a destruction or corruption. Mankind has deteriorated in its morals and spiritual character. But how? Through its lusts—its strong cravings for evil, its submission to the desires of the fleshly mind. We either become degenerate or regenerate!

*God's Children* are those who have fled from and *escaped* the corruption of this world. They are no longer dominated by the flesh. Some, however, have *claimed* to be partakers of the *divine* nature, but have never escaped the lusts of their *human* nature. The strong desires for admiration, prestige, excessive food, strong drink, fornication, and material possessions are still within their hearts and minds. They have not yet escaped; they are still in bondage!

**1:5-7 Yea, and for this very cause adding on your part all diligence, in your faith supply virtue; and in your virtue knowledge; and in your knowledge self-control; and in your self-control patience; and in your patience godliness; and in your godliness brotherly kindness; and in your brotherly kindness love.**

### Expanded Translation

And, indeed, for this very reason (that is, that you might be partakers of the divine nature) having added to your life all diligence and earnest application, you must in your faith and trust supply (furnish, present) moral goodness; and in your moral goodness knowledge (intelligence, understanding); and in your knowledge self-control; and in your self-control enduring fortitude, and in your enduring fortitude godliness (piety, devotion); and in your godliness brotherly-kindness; and in your brotherly-kindness love.

---

**Yea, and for this very cause**

We have been granted great promises and escaped from the corruption of the world (v. 4), that we might be sharers in God's divine nature. *For this same reason*, we must make the virtues listed here our own.

### adding on your part all diligence

"Adding on your part" being one word in the original (*pareis-phero*). The King James Version's "giving" does not provide an adequate meaning. It means, literally, to bring in besides (*para*, beside; *eis*, in; and *phero*, bring), hence to superinduce, add, exhibit in addition. In addition to what? To what God has *already* done (vs. 3-4). As Woods well remarks, the term indicates the comparative unimportance of man's participation in his salvation, by showing that his part is only *contributory* to God's work. Yet our part is very essential, for God's part is not fulfilled in our lives *if we do not do ours.*

DILIGENCE—*spoude*, literally, haste; hence earnestness, zeal, earnest application. It is used of one's earnestness in accomplishing, promoting, or striving after anything. Here it is prefaced with "all."* We are to *bend every effort* to do our best for our Master! If we would be diligent, then the virtues here mentioned will be inculcated into our lives.

### in your faith supply virtue

Or, "supplement your faith with virtue," and so on with each of these phrases. The word "supply" (*epichoregeo*) has been the subject of much discussion. It is an emphatic form of the word *choregeo*, which originally meant to be a chorus-leader, lead a chorus, and secondly to furnish a chorus at one's own expense; procure and supply all the things necessary to fit out a chorus. This "chorus," from the Greek *choros*, is not to be interpreted as equivalent to our word "choir." It was a band of dancers, who, in the process of their dancing performance also sang.** Both *choregeo* and *epichoregeo* later means to supply, furnish abundantly (*choregeo*, "supplieth" I Pet. 4:11), the latter word being more emphatic and expressive than the former. Just as this chorus had to have several items of dress and make-up to be completely furnished, so the Christian must *supply* these various attributes if he is to be equipped properly for the spiritual life.

---

*Jude so uses it in verse 3 of his epistle: "Beloved, while I was giving *all diligence* to write unto you . . ."
**The word *choros* is used only once in the N.T.! Luke 15:25 where it merely refers to *dancing.*

FAITH—*pistis*, here referring to their trust, confidence, and belief in God and His Son. Such a precious faith had resulted in their salvation (1:1); now they were to build upon this foundation. So they are told to supplement their faith with

VIRTUE—*arete* (see also v. 3). Thayer says the word means "a virtuous course of thought, feeling, and action; virtue, moral goodness." But as the word was commonly used, it referred to manliness, courage, vigor, and energy, particularly in overcoming or enduring anything. "True virtue is not a tame and passive thing. It requires great energy and boldness, for its very essence is firmness, manliness, and independence."—Barnes. Many modern translators have decided "courage" most accurately expresses the idea of the original. This must be supplemented with

KNOWLEDGE—*gnosis*, the acquisition of information (concerning spiritual truth) and the understanding and discrimination which results from having such information. However, knowledge by itself is ruinous. It must be coupled with

SELF-CONTROL—*egkrateia*, the virtue of one who masters his desires and passions, especially his sensual appetites (Thayer); countenance, temperance. It is from the root *egkrates*, meaning strong, stout, possessed of mastery. The Christian must be a master of himself!

### and in your self-control patience

PATIENCE—*hupomone*, literally an abiding under or after, hence, to remain behind (when others have departed); to remain, not to flee. "Patience" is not a *passive* virtue, it is a very *active* one! It is the characteristic of a man who is unswerved from his deliberate purpose to serve God, and his loyalty to faith and piety, *by even the greatest trials and sufferings*. It is that temper which does not easily succumb under suffering, as opposed to cowardice or despondence. See I Pet. 2:19-20. To this quality we must add

GODLINESS—*eusebeia*, from *eu*, well, good, and *sebomai*, to be devout. It denotes that piety which, characterized by a Godward attitude, does that which is well-pleasing to Him. This person is conscious and mindful of God and His will! Oh that their number might increase! With such an attitude, the next virtue should not be difficult. For true religion involves

BROTHERLY-KINDNESS—*philadelphia*. (See comments under I Pet. 1:22). But loving our brothers and sisters in Christ is not enough! To this specific type of love, we must add the general.

**and in your brotherly kindness love.**

LOVE—*agape*. (See comments, 1:22). The man possessing this quality seeks the good and welfare of all—whether deserved or not. In this way he becomes like God (Jn. 3:16). It is that outgoing, self-forgetful love that a person has within himself for God and others—*all* others! We are to love our enemies (Matt. 5:44). We are to "walk in love" (Eph. 5:2). Ours is to be a "labor of love" (I Thes. 1:3). We are to speak the truth in love (Eph. 4: 15); and be rooted and grounded in love (Eph. 3:17).

It is interesting to note that Peter, like Paul, places love in a preëminent position. "And the greatest of these is love" (I Cor. 13:13). "And above all these things put on love, which is the bond of perfectness" (Col. 3:14).

**1:8-9 For if these things are yours and abound, they make you to be not idle or unfruitful unto the knowledge of our Lord Jesus Christ. For he that lacketh these things is blind, seeing only what is near, having forgotten the cleansing from his old sins.**

### Expanded Translation

For if these things are your possessions and superabound, you are not caused to be lazy (idle, at leisure) or unfruitful (not developing good works or personal virtues) as you direct your minds toward a full and accurate knowledge of our Lord Jesus Christ. But he who does not possess these things (mentioned above) is blind (to the truly good life) being near-sighted; having taken on a short memory (i.e., being forgetful) concerning the cleansing from his old (former) sins.

---

**For if these things are yours**

That is, the things spoken of in verses 5-7. The verb "are yours" (*huparcho*) here refers to one's goods, possessions, or property—that which *he himself* possesses.

**and abound**

To superabound, be "more than enough," to have in abundance. The word is *pleonazo*, which is from the root verb *pleo*, to fill. We must strive to *fill* our cup up and let it *run over* with these graces!

**they make you to be not idle**

*Argos*, according to Thayer, is compounded from the *alpha* negative plus *ergon*, work. Hence, literally, one without work or one who does not work—an inactive, idle person. His definition here is, "lazy, shunning the labor which one ought to perform."

**or unfruitful**

*Akarpos*, bearing no fruit. A fruitful person is one who, as he grows older in the faith, *produces* in his life those Christian virtues that are a blessing to himself, God, and man.* He leads other souls to Christ, reproducing "after his own kind," and dispenses to others such fruits as are edifying and nourishing.

**unto the knowledge of our Lord Jesus Christ**

That is, as we direct our minds toward the acquisition of the knowledge of Christ. Here again we have the significant word *epignosis* for "knowledge" (see v. 2). We noticed the normal word for knowledge (*gnosis*) appeared in verse 6 as one of those virtues to be added *as we obtain the full, rich, and intimate* knowledge (*epignosis*) of Christ for which we are striving. *All* of the qualities of verses 5-7 are necessary as abounding possessions if we would have the *epignosis* of Christ.

**for he that lacketh these things is blind, seeing only what is near**

The last five words are only one in the original—*muopazon*, a present participle which might be rendered "being near-sighted," or "being dim-sighted." It specifies the particular kind of blindness that afflicts this man—purblindness. Heaven, and the things that pertain to the spiritual life are pictured here as off in the distance—perceptible only to those with good eyesight (spiritual eyes); for some, having eyes, see not (Mk. 8:18). The Laodicean church was so blinded (Rev. 3:17). Spiritual truths, to such a one, are covered with a blanket of smoke,** and he does not perceive their true significance.

---

*See Jn. 15:1-8, Heb. 13:15, Tit. 3:14, Matt. 7:15-23, Phil. 1:11, and Col. 1:10 on the subject of fruitbearing.
**The verb *tuphloo*, "to blind," is from the root *tupho*, to raise a smoke, to darken by smoke. Now, when the air is filled with smoke, one's vision is limited—the more smoke, the less vision. Discernment is difficult, except for things near. So it is with one's spiritual discernment, when his mind is beclouded with the "affairs of this life." He sees only the nearby things—the things of this corrupt world!

Do not fail to notice *who* the blind one is in this passage. It is the man who fails to see his need of adding these traits (vs. 5-7) to his life, and therefore does not possess them. The immediate, convenient, and lustful things attract him — but they lead to damnation!

**having forgotten the cleansing from his old sins**

His eyesight is short and so is his *memory!* Isaiah reminded the righteous of Israel, "look unto the rock whence ye were hewn, and the hole of the pit whence ye were digged," (Isa. 51:1). To become forgetful and unmindful of what a blessing it is to have our sins removed is disastrous to our souls! "Blessed is he" David said, "whose transgression is forgiven, whose sin is covered" (Psa. 32:1. See also 103:1-4). If we do not frequently recall to our minds the great blessing of being clean through the blood of Jesus, we will soon go back to the dogvomit and the sow-wallow (2:22).

**1:10-11 Wherefore, brethren, give the more diligence to make your calling and election sure: for if ye do these things, ye shall never stumble: for thus shall be richly supplied unto you the entrance into the eternal kingdom of our Lord and Saviour Jesus Christ.**

## Expanded Translation

On which account, brothers, you must exert yourself more to make your calling (the invitation of the gospel which you accepted) and election (your place among God's chosen ones) sure, certain, and stedfast. For if you practice these things (mentioned in vs. 5-7) you will never stumble and fall (i.e., be lost eternally); for by following this course it shall be richly and abundantly supplied unto you the entrance into the eternal kingdom (heaven) of our Lord and Saviour Jesus Christ.

---

### Wherefore, brethren, give the more diligence

Christians are in constant need of earnest effort in maintaining and confirming their salvation. (See "diligence" defined under v. 5, where we have the noun form of this verb.)

### To make your calling and election sure

CALLING—*klesis*, a calling, is always used in the New Testament of that calling the origin, nature, and destiny of which are heavenly (the idea of invitation being implied). It is used especially of God's invitation to man to accept the benefits of salvation, when they are presented through the Gospel message

(I Thes. 2:13-15). Here it refers to the *accepted* call, for these are "brethren."

ELECTION—*ekloge*, denotes the act of picking out, choosing. (See also I Thes. 1:4.) It refers to God's choice to bless a certain group with salvation. What group? Those who *obey* him—who comply with his plan for redeeming man (Heb. 5:9, Matt. 7:21-23). Concerning the "elect" and the free will of man, see comments under I Pet. 1:2-3.

SURE—*bebaios*, stable, firm, steadfast, established. If it is impossible, as some maintain, to lose one's salvation, what need is there here for such an exhortation? The very fact that these "brethren" were told to *make it firm*, presupposes that at least some of them were in danger of letting it slip from them.

### for if ye do these things, ye shall never stumble

If you add to your lives the graces mentioned in vs. 5-7.

The apostle is not teaching here that his readers could expect to be without moral fault or shortcoming. If they would practice these things they would never "stumble" (*ptaio*), a word basically meaning to cause one to stumble or fall. But Thayer says it often signified in Greek writings *to fall into misery, become wretched*. The reference here, then, is to the *loss of our salvation*. If we practice the virtues here mentioned, we shall not fail to *stand up* and keep on progressing for Christ.

### for thus shall be richly supplied unto you the entrance into the eternal kingdom of our Lord and Saviour Jesus Christ

See "supplied" (*epichoregeo*) defined under v. 5. This entrance would be "richly" (*plousios*) supplied; that is, it will be abundant and rich in glory, dignity, and bliss.

The "eternal kingdom," in this passage, has reference to heaven, for *Christians* are to *enter into* it. Admittedly, there is a sense in which heaven is only the church (the usual meaning of "kingdom" in the New Testament) in a different role, for Daniel prophesied that the kingdom (church) would stand forever (Dan. 2:44) and the church is to be delivered up to the Father (I Cor. 15:23-24) at Christ's return. But I think *heaven* was definitely in the mind's eye of the apostle here, for these saints were to have an entrance (*eisodos*) into (*eis*) it. The word "entrance" (literally, a way into) may either refer to the act of entering, as it seems to here, or to a doorway or admission for getting into a place. We do not "enter into" a kingdom in which we are presently dwelling. Jesus used the term "kingdom" in a similar manner as he spoke of the Judgment Day. "Then shall the King say unto them on his right hand, Come, ye blessed of my Father, inherit the kingdom prepared for you from the foundation of the world" (Matt. 25:34). Paul, in one of his last written statements, said, "The Lord will deliver me from every evil work, and will save me unto (*eis*) his heavenly kingdom . . ." (II Tim. 4:18).

**1:12 Wherefore I shall be ready always to put you in remembrance of these things, though ye know them, and are established in the truth which is with you.**

## Expanded Translation

On this account (the truths of verses 10-11) I shall be ready always (in the future, as I have been in the past) to remind you of these matters, although you know them and have been (and still are) established, fixed, and made fast in the truth which you possess.

---

### Wherefore

Beginning a new thought based on the previous context. as he did in v. 10.

### I shall be ready always to put you in remembrance of these things

The future verb *melleso* ("shall be ready") indicates that the apostle will be prepared. as he was in the past and the present, to remind his readers of the truth they know.

But the better manuscripts have here *ouk ameleso*, "I shall not neglect" or "I shall not disregard." He would never be careless about fulfilling his responsibility toward them in keeping the truth before their minds.

The term "put you in remembrance" (*hupomimnesko*) signifies to cause to remember, remind, admonish of something. It is not meant by this that the readers had *totally forgotten* the truths which had established them. Rather, he continues

### Though ye know them, and are established in the truth which is with you

Here is an ever-present need in the church: to exhort, admonish, and teach Christians to be conscientious in keeping what they have learned in mind, and act rightly upon that knowledge. Paul said, "only, whereunto we have attained, by that same rule let us walk" (Phil. 3:16).

147

We need to be reminded and exhorted even though we may presently be established in the truth. (See "established," *sterizo*, defined under I Pet. 5:10.) "Wherefore let him that thinketh he standeth take heed lest he fall" (I Cor. 10:12).

**1:13-14 And I think it right, as long as I am in this tabernacle, to stir you up by putting you in remembrance; knowing that the putting off of my tabernacle cometh swiftly, even as our Lord Jesus Christ signified unto me.**

## Expanded Translation

Yet I think (deem), it right, proper, and correct, as long as I am in this tent (as long as my spirit dwells in my body), to arouse your mind (literally, wake you up) by putting you in remembrance; realizing that the laying aside of my tent (that is, my *body*) will be abrupt, sudden, and swift, even as our Lord Jesus Christ made known unto me.

---

**And I think it right, as long as I am in this tabernacle**

Our bodies are the tabernacles or tents housing our spirits. ("Tabernacle," (*skenoma*) is translated "habitation" in Acts 7:46.) By calling it a tent, the apostle emphasized the temporary and perishable nature of our outward beings.

Peter did not plan to put himself "on the shelf" in his older years. "As long as I am alive and able," he says, "I will stir you up." What a wondrous attitude to have toward the work of the Gospel! Let us serve our Master *to our fullest capacity until our dying day!*

**to stir you up by putting you in remembrance**

(See also 3:1).

*Diegeiro*, "stir (you) up" means to wake up, awaken, arouse from sleep. It is here used as a metaphor meaning to arouse or activate the mind, animate.

The word rendered "putting . . . in remembrance" (*hupomnesis*) is the noun form of the verb defined in v. 12. One means every faithful Gospel preacher must use to challenge and activate God's people, is to *remind* them of their responsibilities and privileges as Christians.

**knowing that the putting off of my tabernacle cometh swiftly**

Peter was now getting along in years, for he was an older man when he wrote his first epistle (I Pet. 5:1). Now he speaks of the laying aside of his earthly tabernacle and the time of his decease

(v. 15). When the spirit returned to God who gave. it (Eccl
12:7), it would leave its earthly abode or tabernacle, his body.
The adverb *tachinos* (the poetic and later form of *tachus*)
means literally swift, speedy, and has reference to the *manner* of
his death, not the time.* His life was to be taken abruptly and
suddenly in his old age.

**even as our Lord Jesus Christ signified unto me**
Where? In Jn. 21:18-19 are these words: "Verily, verily I say
unto thee, When thou wast young, thou girdest thyself and walk-
est whither thou wouldest: but when thou shalt be old, thou shalt
stretch forth thy hands, and another shall gird thee, and carry
thee whither thou wouldest not. Now this he spake, signifying
by what manner of death he should glorify God. And when he
had spoken this, he saith unto him, Follow me." The significant
part of the prophecy was *not* the fact that Peter would die during
his older years—most people do that. The historian plainly tells
us Christ was signifying by what *manner* of death he should
glorify God in his old age. It was to be an abrupt, sudden, force-
ful death.

Now that Peter *was* an older man, he knew he was completely
qualified to fulfill this prophecy at any moment. Some day in the
near future, his life would be suddenly snuffed out.
**1:15 Yea, I will give diligence that at every time ye may be able
after my decease to call these things to remembrance.**

## Expanded Translation

But I will give forth earnest effort so that after my exodus
(death), you shall always be able to bring these things back to
mind.

**Yea, I will give diligence**
See v. 5, where the noun form of the verb *spoudazo* (which
also occurs in v. 10), is defined.
**that at every time ye may be able after my decease to call
these things to remembrance**
Peter wanted his work for the Master to be a lasting one. He
wanted the effects of his labors to live on after his "decease." The

*However, some lexicons have "near at hand," or "impending" as a proper
definition for the word here, agreeing with the King James Version's "shortly." And Thayer *does* cite several secular sources to show that the word may
refer to an event soon to come.

word *exodos* indicates literally a way out; then, a going out, departure. See Heb. 11:22, "departure." It is used here of one's departure from this earth, as in Luke 9:31.

By his instructions and exhortations, including the writings of his two epistles, he hoped they would keep the true teachings in mind and live by them.

## 2. The certain and trustworthy sources of saving knowledge, 1:16-21

**1:16 For we did not follow cunningly devised fables, when we made known unto you the power and coming of our Lord Jesus Christ, but we were eyewitnesses of his majesty.**

### Expanded Translation

For we did not follow (use as our guide) cleverly or cunningly invented fiction stories (lying fables, myths), when we disclosed to you the power (might) and arrival (literally, presence) of our Lord Jesus Christ, but we were eye-witnesses and lookers-on of his magnificence, splendor, and excellence.

---

Beginning from v. 12, Peter discussed the message and attitude of a true preacher of the Gospel. Now he begins a discussion of the *false* teachers—and the validity of his own teachings in contrast to theirs. His warnings concerning these deceivers continue throughout chapter three (3:3-5, 16, 17). We will note their doctrines as we proceed.

**For we did not follow cunningly devised fables**

That is, we apostles (see below). The word "follow" (*exakolutheo*) is a rather emphatic word, and Peter is the only New Testament writer to use it. It means literally to follow out; hence, imitate, observe another (person or thing) and follow it as a guide. See also 2:2, 15.

The "fable" (*muthos*, hence our word myth), has an interesting history. It primarily signified speech or conversation. The first syllable *mu-*, meant to close, keep secret, be dumb, (thus our word *mute*). So Trench says our word must have originally signified the word (speech) shut up in the mind, or muttered within the lips. "At first there is nothing of the fabulous, still less of the false, involved in it." At the second stage of its history *muthos* is the mentally conceived, as set over against the actually true. These were stories that were intended for good, involving a higher teaching or a moral. Some of these ancient "fables" are still widely read, as Aesop's.

". . . at its third stage *muthos* is the fable, but not any more the fable undertaking to be, and often being, the vehicle of some lofty truth; it is now the *lying* fable with all its falsehoods and all its pretences to be what it is not . . ." It is a word which belongs to the kingdom of darkness and lies.

The apostle calls them *cunningly* devised (*sophizo*) fables, i.e., skillfully invented, devised cleverly and artfully.*

**when we made known unto you the power and coming of**

**our Lord Jesus Christ**

Which coming? The word *parousia* (presence) when referring to the Saviour, has consistent reference to the second advent in the epistles of Paul, and is certainly so used in 3:4 and 12 in *this* epistle. Unless this passage be the sole instance, there is no New Testament passage in which it is used of his *first* coming or his life, ministry, and death while on earth.

The word here rendered "and," (*kai*) is *sometimes* better translated "even." If such is the case here, we have "power, even the coming," both words referring to the return of our Lord to earth. Surely at that time his might will be displayed as never before!

The second coming of Christ was the very doctrine the mockers were denying (3:3-4). But neither this, nor any of his other teachings, could be disputed by Peter and the apostles (particularly here, James and John), for they were

**eyewitnesses of his majesty**

And, therefore, had every reason to *believe* him. To be an eyewitness (*epoptes*)** affords the highest kind of evidence—evidence that is not easily set aside. The author was frequently an actual "on-looker' of the great events in the life of Christ. (See the *Biographical Sketch* of Peter's life.) The transfiguration affords an excellent example, and is therefore cited in vs. 17 and 18.

The true preacher and teacher of the Gospel message is not a trickster, deceiver, or magician, *nor does he attempt to follow such!* His business is to acquire and reach, insofar as it is possible to do so, the true teachings of Christ and the apostles. *These* teachings, and no others, make up his doctrinal menu. Peter did not follow the myths of men—let us learn from his example!

---

*This word also had a good sense at *first*, meaning to make wise, enlighten (II Tim. 3:15, "make . . . wise").
**Notice our discussion of the verb form (*epopteuo*) under I Pet. 2:12, 3:2.

**1:17-18 For he received from God the Father honor and glory, when there was borne such a voice to him by the Majestic Glory, This is my beloved Son, in whom I am well pleased: and this voice we ourselves heard borne out of heaven, when we were with him in the holy mount.**

### Expanded Translation

For he (Christ) was the one who received from God the Father honor (respect, valuing as one of worth) and glory (credit and glorification arising from the good opinion of another) when a voice such as this was conveyed (borne, carried) by the Majestic Glory: This is my beloved (dear, loved) Son, in whom I am well pleased (approve, think well of). And this voice we ourselves heard conveyed (borne, carried) out of heaven, being, as we were, with him in the holy (sacred) mountain.

---

**For he received from God the Father honor and glory, when there wos borne such a voice to him by the Majestic Glory, This is my beloved Son, in whom I am well pleased**

The term "Majestic Glory" is not indicated as a title of God in the King James Version's "excellent glory," but should be so considered. (It is one word in the original, meaning, by itself, magnificence, splendid, becoming or befitting a great man.)

In Verse 16 we are given the testimony of their *eyes*—they actually saw the majesty of Christ when he was transformed before them. In *these* verses we have their "earwitness" — what they themselves *heard* concerning Christ from the very mouth of God!

Both honor and glory were conferred upon the Saviour in the statement, "This is my beloved Son, in whom I am well pleased." The Father also added, "hear ye him"—this Son of mine must be listened to and obeyed!

**and this voice we ourselves heard borne out of heaven, when we were with him in the holy mount**

The mountain is labeled "holy" simply because Christ's transfiguration took place there. (Most geographers believe it was Mount Tabor.) Similarly, Zion is often called the "holy mount" by the prophets because the temple and Jerusalem, the "holy city" were located there. (Isa. 27:13, 66:20, etc.)

The "we ourselves" of this verse is deliberately emphatic in the Greek. We saw it with our own eyes, heard God's voice with our own ears—we were actually there *with* him! Peter, James and John had the most personal and iron-clad evidence of Christ's deity. Therefore, when they preached His *message*, they could do so with certainty, boldness and authority.

See Matt. 17:1-9, Mark 9:2-10, Luke 9:28-36 concerning the transfiguration of Christ. The reading of *all* these accounts is necessary for a complete picture.

**1:19 And we have the word of prophecy made more sure; whereunto ye do well that ye take heed, as unto a lamp shining in a dark place, until the day dawn, and the day-star arise in your hearts:**

## Expanded Translation

So we have the word (i.e., the statements) uttered by the prophets more fully established (by this event that James, John and I witnessed). You will do well to continually pay close attention to it as unto a lamp (torch) shining (and thus *providing light*) in a dark (squalid, murky) place, until the time when the daylight breaks through the darkness of the night and the Morning Star arises (comes into being) in your hearts.

---

### And we have the word of prophecy made more sure

That is, the discourses and utterances of the prophets are *made more certain* because of the things these apostles witnessed on that great day of the transfiguration. The event supplied *additional confirmation* of the deity of Jesus.

The meaning is *not* that the prophetic word of the Old Testament was "more trustworthy" or "more certain" (that is, *superior*) evidence concerning the majesty and greatness of Christ *than the personal testimony the three apostles had received on the mount.* Rather, the thought is that the prophecies concerning Jesus were *confirmed* in that wondrous event. A literal rendering of this phrase is, "and we have the prophetic word more firm"— *not* more firm than the transfiguration evidence, but more firm ITSELF *because of* the transfiguration. Peter includes himself in the "we have . . ." It is difficult to believe that Peter himself considered *any* evidence more iron-clad than that which he had seen with his own eyes and heard with his own ears. A careful reading of the account in the Gospel will reveal that Peter was *especially* impressed at the occasion.

The prophecies of the Old Testament (v. 21) which foretold of Christ's coming, deity, and greatness, are rendered more sure and unimpeachable now that he *had* come and the transfiguration had taken place. Therefore, the American Standard Version's "And we have the word of prophecy *made more sure*" is to be preferred above the King James Version's "We have also a more sure word of prophecy," for it appears that the translators of the former version were only trying to say that the transfiguration made the prophecies more *certain* and, therefore, more *believable*. This, I believe, was the intention of the Holy Spirit.

But what was there about the transfiguration of Christ that would solidify and confirm the prophecies? Notice these points:

1. The miracle of the transforming of Christ was itself an act of God.
2. The miraculous presence of Moses and Elijah, and their talking with Him. Also, their miraculous disappearance.
3. The bright cloud overshadowing them—probably the same as the *shekinah* of the Old Testament — indicating God's presence.
4. God's own voice proclaiming, "This is my beloved Son, in whom I am well pleased, hear ye him" (Matt. 17:5)—not Moses, not Elijah, but *MY BELOVED SON!*
5. The closest friends of Jesus (Peter. James and John) were deeply moved by this miracle, and *believed*. Peter himself wanted to build three tabernacles on the spot as a memorial.

### whereunto ye do well that ye take heed

Literally, "unto which [word] you do well taking heed." Both "do" and "take heed" are in the present tense—indicating continuous or regular action. The latter (*prosecho*) is defined, literally, to bring to or near; hence, to turn the mind to, be attentive to, devote thought and effort to. The prophetic utterances, being as they are very trustworthy and reliable (as the apostle has just shown) are deserving of our most careful consideration and study!

### as unto a lamp shining in a dark place

If a man doesn't have a lamp in a dark place (the original indicates a *very* dark place), he will soon be *lost*. He is dependent upon the light for guidance. Here *prophecy* is spoken of as such a lamp.

Of John the baptizer, Jesus said, "He was the lamp that burneth and shineth; and ye were willing to rejoice for a season in his light" (Jn. 5:35). David could say of God, "Thy word is a lamp unto my feet, And light unto my path" (Psa. 119:105).

What a passage this is! How we should ever regard the prophecies of the Old Testament with value, prizing them as greatly as a lamp on a dark and dangerous night, and heeding the light they provide.

**until the day dawn, and the day-star arise in your hearts**

This speaks of the duration of the lamp. It shined until the Gospel sunlight of Jesus Christ arrived and fulfilled its prophecies, that is, until the Gospel Age (See Luke 1:78-79.) The "day star" in Greek, *phosphoros* (literally, light bringing star), had technical reference to the planet Venus in the world of astronomy. The day fully "dawned" at Pentecost, but the day star (which signifies the approach of day) does not arise IN OUR HEARTS until we accept and obey Christ individually (Acts 3:19-20).

**1:20-21 knowing this first, that no prophecy of scripture is of private interpretation. For no phophecy ever came by the will of man: but men spake from God, being moved by the Holy Spirit.**

### Expanded Translation

Knowing this first (keeping this foremost in your minds): that no prophecy of Scripture exists (or, is created; or, occurs) of the prophet's own invention (the prophet did not put his personal slants on the message he spoke). For no prophecy ever came (was brought) by the will (purpose, design) of man; rather, men spoke from God, being moved (borne, carried) by the Holy Spirit.

---

These verses tell us *why* the prophecies are worthy of our time and attention; because, when they were given, the *Holy Spirit* was speaking!

**knowing this first, that no prophecy of scripture is of private interpretation**

There are at least three basic views concerning the meaning of this phrase.

1. The view of the Roman Catholic Church: Because every part of Scripture was written by men inspired by the Holy Spirit and declared as such by the Church (note the capital "C"), *the Church is also to interpret it.* God has promised to guide the

Church into all the truth to the end of the world; therefore, we must submit to the judgment of the Church and not depend upon our own fallible and erroneous judgment.*

Thus we are not to trust the meaning *we* would place on Scripture, for the divine task of "rightly dividing the word of truth" is in the hands of the Roman Catholic hierarchy, and, finally, in the hands of its head, the pope.

2. That no one can explain prophecy by his own mental power, as it is not a matter of subjective interpretation. To explain it, one needs the same illumination of the Holy Spirit in which it originated. The idea is that Divine assistance is needed. Thus several translators have renderings such as, "that no prophecy of Scripture can be understood through one's own (unaided) powers."

That there is a degree of truth to this explanation I would not question, though it seems to present several difficulties. Consider a third possibility:

3. That no prophecy of Scripture exists as a result of one's private or personal views. The reference in the phrase under consideration is not primarily to the *receivers* of prophecy, but the *writers* or *speakers* of it, the prophets.

The word *epilusis* ("interpretation") is from the verb *epiluo*, which, as Macknight points out, primarily signified to untie a knot, to unloose a bundle so as to disclose what it contains. The prophets only released the "burden" God had given them, *only untied the bundle and revealed its contents to mankind for all ages to view.* So Young's literal translation reads, "No prophecy of the Writing doth come of private exposition . . ." The writers of Scripture did not put their own construction on the God-breathed words they wrote.

". . . the apostle teaches that the truths which the prophets communicated were not originated by themselves; were not their own suggestion or invention; were not their own opinions, but were of higher origin, and were imparted by God; and according to this passage may be explained '. . . that it is a great principle

---

*A summary of the footnote in the Duay-Rheims (Catholic) Version of the Bible. The word "Church," in Roman Catholic terminology, does not here have reference to the members of that organization, or even to the Priests and Bishops (as a full reading of the quote will show). It refers to "The Most Holy See"—the Pope himself!

in regard to the prophets, that what they communicated was not of their own disclosure; that it was not revealed or originated by them.' "—Barnes.

**for no prophecy ever came by the will of man: but men spake from God, being moved by the Holy Spirit**

This verse seems to confirm the rightness of our interpretation of verse 20. No true prophecy *ever* came because some man willed it or decided to manufacture it. Rather, men spoke as though they were the very mouth of God.

How strongly were the prophets influenced by the Holy Spirit as they spoke? The apostle specifies that they "were moved" (*phero*) by its power. (The same word is rendered "came" earlier in the verse.) They were "borne along," or "impelled" by the Holy Spirit in their speech—not expressing their own thoughts, but expressing the mind of God in words provided and ministered by Him.*

## QUESTIONS OVER CHAPTER I

1. How does Peter's description of himself in the salutation differ from that found in the first letter?
2. To whom is this epistle addressed (using the terminology of verse 1)?
3. Look at v. 1. Who does the "us" refer to?
4. Do you remember another possible translation of the phrase "in the righteousness of our God and the Saviour Jesus Christ"?
5. The word "knowledge" (*epignosis*) appears in verses 2, 3, 8. Do you remember its significance? How does it differ from the "knowledge" (*gnosis*) of verses 5 and 6?
6. What has God's power granted unto us?
7. Through what do we become partakers of the divine nature?
8. In *what way* do we become partakers in the divine nature? (i.e., how should we be like God?)
9. From what must we *escape* if we are to be partakers of the divine nature?
10. The various attributes of vs. 5-7 are to be added "for this very cause." For *what* very cause?
11. What is the meaning of "virtue" (v. 5)?
   (Note: In a sense, *all* of these graces may be thought of as "virtues" in *our* terminology. But the apostle obviously has

---

*W. E. Vine, *An Expository Dictionary of New Testament Words*.

a particular one in mind, as he lists it separately.)
12. What is meant by "patience" (v. 6)?
13. Carefully distinguish between the graces of "brotherly kindness" and "love."
14. Why do you suppose love is placed at the end of the list? Does any other New Testament writer do this?
15. These traits are not simply to be ours, but also must_____(?)
16. If so, then we will not be _____ or _____ unto the knowledge of our Lord Jesus Christ.
17. The man that lacks these things is spiritually _____ (?)
18. Does he see *anything*?
19. What has he forgotten?
20. What is our "calling" and "election"?
21. What is "the eternal kingdom of our Lord and Saviour Jesus Christ"?
22. Is it ever necessary to *remind* someone of that which they already know?
23. In what city was Peter's "tabernacle" located?
24. Did Peter ever intend to stop working in God's vineyard?
25. He was going to stir them up by _____(?)
26. Where did Jesus signify that Peter's death would be swift?
27. He wanted them to remember these things even after his _____(?)
28. What great event is being described in vs. 16-18?
29. To whom, then, does the "we" refer in v. 16?
30. Through what two basic avenues had testimony concerning the deity of Christ been brought to their minds?
31. Explain, in the context, the phrase, "and we have the word of prophecy made more sure" (v. 19).
32. How is Bible prophecy to be heeded?
33. When did "the day dawn"?
34. Who or what is the day-star?
35. How does it arise *in our hearts*?
36. What is the Roman Catholic view of the phrase "no prophecy of Scripture is of private interpretation"?
37. Carefully define the word "interpretation."
38. Give a satisfactory explanation of the meaning of verses 20 and 21, keeping the *whole context* in mind.

## III. THE FALSE TEACHER: HIS DOCTRINES, CHARACTERISTICS, INFLUENCES, AND DOOM
### 2:1-22
### CHAPTER II

**2:1 But there arose false prophets also among the people, as among you also there shall be false teachers, who shall privily bring in destructive heresies, denying even the Master that bought them, bringing upon themselves swift destruction.**

*Expanded Translation*

But (in contrast to these prophets who spoke from God) there arose false prophets among the people, as among you also there shall be false teachers, who shall stealthily, secretly, and craftily introduce destructive (ruinous, devastating) heresies, denying (disclaiming, disowning) the very Master who redeemed them, bringing upon themselves swift destruction, ruin, devastation, (hence) misery.

---

**But there arose false prophets also among the people**

With reference to the Old Testament times of which he had just spoken (1:19-21). Besides those who were moved by the Holy Spirit, there were those who were moved by Satan and the demons. One of these, Balaam, is mentioned later in the chapter. Just what group of false teachers is referred to here, is a pertinent question. It is difficult in this epistle to settle with *certainty* on the exact class of false teachers which is meant. Some are libertines like those described by Jude, and others are mockers and deniers of the second advent. Do they all belong to one large group? It is generally supposed that they all form some part of the Gnostic belief (so frequently denounced in I John).

**as among you also there shall be false teachers**

History, the apostle says, is going to repeat itself. Just as the Mosaic dispensation had its false *prophets*, you will have your false *teachers* — those who inculcate false doctrines. See Matt. 7:15-23; 24:5; Acts 20:29, 30; I Tim. 4:1-3; II Tim. 4:3-4; I Jn. 4:1.

**who shall privily bring in destructive heresies**

The word "heresy" (*hairesis*) basically means a choosing or choice (of the mind) hence, opinion. But its meaning here is a *wrong opinion*, an opinion varying from the true exposition of the faith.

God's people bring his word in freedom, boldness, and without deceit. Not so with this falsifier—he must be secretive and subtle!

The teachings of such a one are labeled "destructive" by the apostle. A good synonym for this word is *ruinous*. Moulton and Milligan say the word *apoleia*, indicates "the loss of all that gives worth of existence." A *destructive* heresy is false teaching, the endorsement of which causes ruin and devastation—such ruin as makes one worthless to God and Man. It ruins character, moral concepts, virtue, friendships, and, above all, the salvation and spiritual safety of the one who is led astray.*

### denying even the Master that bought them

That is, the Lord Jesus Christ, I Pet. 1:17-19.** It should not be *necessarily* supposed here, that these men claimed to be true Christians *while* they were denying the Saviour, though I suppose this is a possibility. (They may have used the term "Christian" just as loosely as some of our acquaintances do today.) Before *reaching* the point of denial, they may have been true and faithful. (See 2:20-22.) Yet Christ has, in a sense, "bought" them also, for he died for *all*, including those who presently disown him.

How were they denying him? Evidently in their *teachings*, for this rejection of Christ formulated the core of their "destructive heresies." The false teachers held doctrines that were, in fact, a *denial* of Jesus. Peter does not specify what doctrine(s) constituted such a denial, but any teaching which represents Christ, his work, or his person as essentially and basically different from the *truth*, amounts to such a denial.

### bringing upon themselves swift destruction

See "swift," (*tachinos*) defined under 1:14. The Greek word *apoleia* ("destruction") is the same here as that in the former part of the verse rendered "destructive." Their *heresies of destruction* bring upon themselves what their false teachings are bringing to others—*eternal* destruction.

When a wicked man is "destroyed" in Biblical terminology, it does not mean that he is annihilated (see notes, 3:6, 16).

---

*Peter uses *apoleia* ("destruction") several times in this book. See also v. 2, 3:7, 16.
**See "master" (*despotes*) defined under I Pet. 2:18. The term emphasizes Christ's *absolute authority*.

**2:2 And many shall follow their lascivious doings; by reason of whom the way of truth shall be evil spoken of.**

## Expanded Translation

And many shall follow (imitate, observe and use as a guide for their own lives) their unbridled, unrestrained, and shameless ways; because of whom the way of truth shall be reviled, railed at, and spoken of with contempt.

---

### And many shall follow their lascivious doings

See the word "follow" (*exakoloutheo*) defined under 1:16. Following close at their heels, imitating and copying their ways, the weak, simple-minded, and ignorant would be led astray! How great will be the damnation of those who so lead others! (Note Jas. 3:1.) And into what are their followers led? Into "lascivious doings" (*aselgeia*). Be sure to see our definition of this term under I Pet. 4:3. Instead of teaching them to *restrain* their immoral and sinful ways, these prevaricators help their dupes throw off their restraints and lose their self-control. How God shall hold them accountable in the day of judgment!

### by reason of whom the way of truth shall be evil spoken of

The irreligious and the worldling often lump all "religion" together. These false teachers were instructors in *religion*. But their *doctrines* denied Christ and their *lives* were unrestrained, lawless, and immoral. How easy it was, then, for many to speak reproachfully of the *right* way.*

**2:3 And in covetousness shall they with feigned words make merchandise of you: whose sentence now from of old lingereth not, and their destruction slumbereth not.**

## Expanded Translation

And with a greedy desire to have more (of this world's goods, riches, etc.) shall they with feigned, fabricated, and counterfeit words use you for gain; whose (condemnatory) sentence of old (that is, of long standing) lingers not, (literally, is not inactive) and their destruction, devastation, ruin, (and consequent misery) slumbers (sleeps, naps) not.

---

*blasphemeo* (hence our word blaspheme), literally meant to speak against; to calumniate, rail at, revile.

**And in covetousness**

Here is what motivates these men. They are not truly concerned for the souls of men. They are interested in their *own* enrichment. The word *pleonexia* refers to a grasping, greedy individual—one who has an inordinate desire for riches. Because of this desire, he will often, as here, stoop to low and unethical means, such as extortion.

**shall they with feigned words make merchandise of you**

The word translated "feigned" is *plastos*, from which our word *plastic* is derived. It properly signifies moulded, formed (as from clay, wax, or stone). From this came the idea of what was formed (in the mind) and related as if true; hence, invented, fabricated, counterfeited, delusive. *Feigned* words, then, are words which are manufactured by the speaker (or writer) to *deceive*. They are *seemingly* useful and profitable (to the unenlightened mind) but they are hollow and useless.

By such words the false teacher turns his listeners into so much chattel from which money can be derived. The word rendered "make merchandise," *emporeuomai* (from the same root as our word *emporium*), meant first of all to go trading, to travel for business purposes (Jas. 4:13, "trade"). But Thayer shows that it also meant to import for sale, to use a person or thing for gain. These fabricators of the truth simply used their followers as a means to their own profit—under the guise of religion!*

**whose sentence now from of old lingereth not,**
**and their destruction slumbereth not**

Both of these phrases depicting the inevitability and certainty of their eternal doom.

The word "sentence" (*krima*), means literally, the sentence of (God as) a judge, judgment. Here, the obvious reference is to the *condemnatory* sentence or *penal* judgment of God upon the wicked. Peter says it does not "linger (*argeo*), literally, is not idle or inactive. God is not "loafing on the job." Their punishment has long been impending, and he will not fail to carry out his sentence against them.

Their destruction (*apoleia*, see discussion under 3:6-7 "perished," "destruction," and 3:16) is here pictured as a person. This person is not *nustazo*—taking a nap.** (Literally, to nod in sleep, to sink into a sleep.) We again get back to God, who decreed their destruction. He is neither loafing nor napping concerning their doom—*they shall not escape!*

---

*Compare Christ's description of the hireling in Jn. 10:12-13.
**Note Matt. 25:5, where this word ("slumbered") is carefully distinguished from *katheudo*, to be fast asleep.

**2:4 For if God spared not angels when they sinned, but cast them down to hell, and committed them to pits\* of darkness, to be reserved unto judgment;**

## Expanded Translation

For if God did not spare (keep back his wrath from) the angels when they sinned, but gave them over to pits (dens, caves) of darkness (blackness, gloom) when he thrusted them down to Tartarus, being reserved unto (for) judgment (at which time they will be condemned);

---

*Some manuscripts have "chains."

---

The apostle begins a trend of thought here that does not culminate until verses 9-12; namely, that the wicked shall not go unpunished. But intertwined with this objective seems also to be another: to show how God protects and *preserves* the righteous.
**For if God spared not the angels when they sinned**

Here is the first case in point concerning the inevitable punishment of the wicked—the very *angels of heaven* were punished for sinning!

Angels are created moral beings. Paul says they are "sent forth to do service for the sake of them that shall inherit salvation" (Heb. 1:14). (See comments, I Pet. 1:12.) As moral beings, they may sin, and those here referred to *did* sin. We are not told of the nature of their sin. But Jude says in verse 6, "And angels that kept not their own principality, but left their proper habitation, he hath kept in everlasting bonds under darkness unto the judgment of the great day." If the same angels are depicted here as in Jude, their sin was in abandoning their proper place of abode.

Heb. 2:16 indicates that angels are outside the redeeming provisions of God's grace. When they sinned there was no possibility of salvation. In spite of their former rank, glory and holiness,

163

*they were not spared.* If God punished *them* so severely, the false teachers could not hope to escape.*

### but cast them down to hell

That is, "consigned them to Tartarus" for so the verb *tartaroo* signifies. This is its only occurrence in the New Testament. It is not properly *hell,* for that comes after the judgment— *a time still in the future* for these occupants.

The word *Tartarus* is taken from Greek mythology and used here as a descriptive term for a place that *really* exists. Homer represents Tartarus as a deep place under the earth,** and Hesiod speaks of it as a place far under the ground, where the Titans are bound with chains in thick darkness.*** It was anciently used, then, as a place of restraint and punishment for the souls of wicked men after death.

As used here, it is evidently the same place, or, rather, a *section* of the same place, as Hades, described in Luke 16:23-26.

### committed them to pits of darkness

A phrase descriptive of Tartarus. In that place are "pits" (*seiros*, a pitfall, den, cave) a word used by ancient profane writers of underground graneries. They are full of gloom and thick darkness—"a darkness darker still, that, namely, of the sunless underworld . . . being ever used to signify the darkness of that

---

*The devil himself was *evidently* an angel, or, more specifically, an Archangel. Macknight paraphrases I Tim. 3:6, "A bishop must be one newly converted, lest being puffed up with pride on account of his promotion, he fall into the punishment inflicted upon the Devil." *His* particular sin was evidently pride.

Other Scriptures cited in this relation are Rev. 12:7-8 (discounted by many), and Isa. 14:12ff (which does not refer to Satan at all, but the king of Babylon, as v. 4 plainly shows). John 8:44(b) states of Satan, "He was a murdered from the beginning, and standeth not in the truth, because there is no truth in him." The word "standeth" (*histemi*) is here in the perfect tense, indicative mode. So Thayer comments, "Satan *continued not* in the truth . . ."

I Jn. 3:8 adds "the devil sinneth from the beginning." If we take the statements of Jn. 1:3 and Col. 1:16-17 without reserve, it seems to me we must assume that Satan was also created by Christ (God). God would not create anything sinful, hence he must have been holy *at first*, sinning "*from* the beginning," i.e., soon after his creation.

**Iliad, line 13 under the Greek letter theta.

***Theogen, line 119, 718.

shadowy land where light is not, but only darkness visible" (Trench, on *zophos*, "darkness").

It appears from what is said here that Tartarus has a number of these pits—perhaps individual ones for each person abandoned to that horrible place.

**to be reserved unto judgment**

The word "reserve" (*tereo*, meaning to guard, keep, preserve), as we saw under I Pet. 1:4, may have a very happy issue. But here (as in 2:9, 17; 3:7; Jude 6, 13) it is a very *unhappy* issue. They are kept under guard (as if they were in prison) until the day of judgment. Note the similarity of Jude 13 especially: ". . . for whom the blackness of darkness *hath been reserved* for ever."

They were held in this place "unto" (*eis*) judgment—either *until* the time of, or *for* the time of judgment. The word *krisis* ("judgment") means properly a distinction or discrimination. Here it evidently refers to the judgment *day*—the time of trial and the administration of justice.**

**2:5 and spared not the ancient world, but preserved Noah with seven others, a preacher of righteousness, when he brought a flood upon the world of the ungodly;**

### Expanded Translation

and did not spare (forbear, restrain his wrath from) the ancient (literally, original) world, but guarded and protected (kept in safe custody) Noah along with seven others, a preacher who summoned others to righteous living, when he (God) brought a flood upon the ungodly, impious, and irreverent.

---

**and spared not the ancient world**

Here is Peter's *second* proof that God punishes the wicked. The wicked antediluvians did not escape! (Compare comments, I Pet. 3:19-21. See also Matt. 24:37-39.)

**but preserved Noah with seven others**

His wife, his three sons (Shem, Ham and Japheth) and their wives.

**a preacher of righteousness**

*Kerux* ("preacher") originally signified a herald or messenger, vested with public authority, who conveyed the official messages of kings, magistrates, military commanders, etc., or who gave public summons or demands on their behalf. Noah was *God's* ambassador—a proclaimer of the *divine* word. He was a "preacher

---

**Bagster would refer it to the time of their *impeachment*; Thayer to their *sentence of condemnation* or *damnatory judgment*.

of righteousness"—a preacher whose message, when adhered to, caused people to *be righteous*. Thayer defines "righteous" (*dikaiosune*), "The state of him who is such as he ought to be . . . the condition acceptable to God . . . virtue, purity of life, uprightness, correctness in thinking, feeling, and acting."

**when he brought a flood upon the world of the ungodly**

This act shows that God *spared not*. "Ungodly" (*asebes*, which occurs also in I Pet. 4:18) refers not to one who is merely irreligious, but who acts, thinks, and lives in contravention of God's commands—a downright sinner. He is destitute of reverential awe toward God, and because of such an attitude he rebels at the attempt of others who would help him out of his sinful state.

**2:6 and turning the cities of Sodom and Gomorrah into ashes condemned them with an overthrow, having made them an example unto those that should live ungodly;**

### Expanded Translation

and he reduced the cities of Sodom and Gomorrah to ashes with a destructive overthrow, having condemned them; by this act having set them forth as an example (sign) to those living ungodly, irreligious and irreverent lives.

---

**and turning the cities of Sodom and Gomorrah into ashes condemned them with an overthrow**

Either of the above translations of this phrase are possible in the original. For this account, see Gen. 19, where one notices the historian also terms it "the overthrow."

**having made them an example unto those that should live ungodly**

Here is a third instance where God "spared not." (Or, one may regard it as a part of the second, including it along with the pre-flood people of the "ancient world.") An example (*hupodeigma*) is a sign suggestive of anything, delineation, figure, or copy. Here, their example was *bad* and, therefore, should serve as a *warning* to the ungodly. How our *whole* nation, so filled with vices as vile as sodomy (which sin derives its name from Sodom) could well take heed to what befell these cities!

**2:7-8 and delivered righteous Lot, sore distressed by the lascivious life of the wicked (for that righteous man dwelling among them, in seeing and hearing, vexed his righteous soul from day to day with their lawless deeds);**

## Expanded Translation

and delivered (saved, rescued) righteous (upright, just) Lot, who was worn out (because of the pain of mind and distress caused) by the unrestrained, insolent, immoral way of living of those without law or rule. For that righteous man in seeing and hearing (their deeds and words) while living among them, was tormenting, torturing, and afflicting his righteous soul from day to day with their lawless deeds.

---

### and delivered righteous Lot

See Genesis, Chap. 19. Because the contrast with Abraham is ever present in the reader's mind, so that the most lasting impressions are made by Lot's selfishness, worldliness, vacillation, cowardice, and finally his drunkenness and incest, our tendency is to label him "*un*-righteous." Peter, though, is fair-minded, and gives credit where credit is due. His life *taken as a whole*, was righteous, especially when compared to those around him.

### sore distressed by the lascivious life of the wicked

The word *kataponeo* ("sore distressed") means to exhaust by labor or suffering, to be, as it were, "beat" from the distress, pain, or agony of a thing. It is to Lot's credit that his conscience was not seared and his heart was not hardened by his surroundings. It seems, however, that his daughters and wife *were not* "distressed" by their surroundings. Rather, they were influenced *toward wrong* by those wicked inhabitants. See "lascivious" (*aselgeia*) discussed under I Pet. 4:3.

### vexed his righteous soul from day to day with their lawless deeds

That is, *because* of what he saw and heard of their actions he vexed his soul. The word "vexed" is *basanizo*, and means properly to apply the lapis Lydis or touchstone. This was a species of stone from Lydia, dark in color, which, being applied to metals was thought to indicate any alloy which might be mixed with them and, therefore, used in the *trial* of metals. Used here metaphorically, *basanizo* means to torture, torment, distress.

### 2:9 the Lord knoweth how to deliver the godly out of temptation, and to keep the unrighteous under punishment unto the day of judgment;

## Expanded Translation

(From the preservation of Noah and Lot with their families, remember that) the Lord knows how to rescue (save, deliver. Literally, draw, drag) the pious, godly, and devout out of temptation, and (or, but) keep the unrighteous under guard while being punished, unto the Judgment Day.

---

### the Lord knoweth how to deliver the godly out of temptation

As one may see from the previous examples cited. A key question here is, in what sense is the word "temptation" (*peirasmos*) to be taken? Evidently in the broad sense of trials, afflictions, or trouble—*including* the idea of direct inducement to sin, but not limited to it. It is the same word that is translated "trial" in I Pet. 4:12, but certainly refers to a direct temptation to sin in Luke 4:13, I Cor. 10:13.*

Here again we see the apostle *encouraging* the Christians to steadfastness, even as he so often does in the first epistle.

### and to keep the unrighteous under punishment unto the day of judgment

The word "keep," (*tereo*) meant properly to guard a prisoner or one who was in a prison, Acts 12:5 ("kept") 16:23-24, etc. These unrighteous ones would be confined in Tartarus (as the angels who sinned, v. 4) a place of punishment, *unto* (*eis*, literally, into, that is, *until*) the Judgment Day when they would receive God's sentence of doom and be abandoned to the fires of hell.

"Punishment" (*kolazo*) means properly, to prune or lop, as trees or wings. Thus it began to assume the meaning of checking, curbing, or restraining, and eventually to *chastise* or *punish*. In what way is Tartarus or Hades a place of *punishment?*

1. It is a place of torments (Lk. 16:28).
2. It is a place of anguish (Lk. 16:24).
3. It is a place of extreme thirst (Lk. 16:24).
4. It is a place of flame (Lk. 16:24).
5. It is a place of complete separation from God and his people (Lk. 16:26).
6. It is a place of blackness, darkness, and gloom (2:4, 17).

**2:10-11 but chiefly them that walk after the flesh in the lust of defilement, and despise dominion. Daring, self-willed, they tremble not to rail at dignities: whereas angels, though greater in might and power, bring not a railing judgment against them before the Lord.**

---

*See notes under I Pet. 1:6-7 where the same word is again rendered "trials." It has a number of meanings; in each of its occurrences the *context* must be carefully considered.

## Expanded Translation

But the unrighteous ones I have particular reference to are those that pursue after and are devoted to the flesh, and indulge in passion (strong craving) which stains, pollutes, and defiles them, who disdain and slight constituted authority. Being bold (audacious, presumptuous) and self-pleasers (hence, willful, obstinate), they do not tremble (i.e., are not fearful) to revile, reproach, and blaspheme dignitaries (i.e., those in places of glory or preëminence): whereas angels, though greater in ability and power, do not bring a blasphemous, railing, or reproachful judgment against *them* (i.e., the revilers) before the Lord.

---

**but chiefly them that walk after the flesh in the lust of defilement**

The apostle is evidently still speaking of the false teachers. He again mentions here, as in 2:1, a phase of their lives that is shockingly true of many promoters of falsehood today, namely, immorality and the perversion of sexual appetites.

These men "walk" after the flesh, i.e., they pursue after or are devoted to their fleshly lusts *as a way of life.** But more than this, we are told they are "in the lust of defilement" (*en epithumia miasmou,* "in cravings which stain"); i.e., in such lusts as defile, corrupt, and pollute the soul. In Jude 7 two immoral practices of Sodom and Gomorrah are specified: (1) They "gave themselves over to fornication," and (2) they had "gone after strange flesh," referring to their practice of sodomy. The *sins* these false teachers fell into are in the same basic category as those of the ancients— and their doom was just as certain!

**and despise dominion. Daring, self-willed, they tremble not to rail at dignities**

(See also Jude 8.) Both the words "dominion" (*kuriotes,* literally, lordship) and "dignities" (*doxia,* literally, glory; hence, one who is in a *place* of glory, a dignitary), refer to whatever authorities might be binding upon a person, whether civil or religious. They had nothing but *contempt* for such authority.

Two reasons are given for this: (1) They were "daring" (*tolmetes*), literally, "one who is bold." But *this* boldness has a *bad* sense, and describes one who is presumptuous and contemptuous. Where he should be sensitive, polite, and respectful, he is brazen

---

*So *poreuomai* ("walk") is frequently used, as, for example, in Eph. 2:2.

and rude. He is the fool that rushes in where angels fear to tread! (2) They were "self-willed" (*authedes*). This is quite a word. It is composed of two parts: *autos*, self, and *hedomai*, which means to enjoy oneself. Putting the two together, we literally have, "one who pleases *himself*." Thus it came to describe an obstinate, arrogant individual. "One so far overvaluing any determination at which he has himself arrived, that he will not be removed from it" (Trench). With such attitudes, they did not fear to rail at the "powers that be."

It seems very probable that Peter, in the phrase under consideration, is pointing the finger of guilt toward that class of false teachers that preached that religious freedom and license to sin were synonymous. Taught along with this was freedom from *civil* authority. Their great cry was liberty, but they themselves were bondservants (2:19). That the repudiating of *civil* or *human* authority is meant *here* seems most likely, for there are many *warnings* concerning this sin in the first epistle (2:13-18, 4:15-16).

**whereas angels, though greater in might and power**

i.e., greater than the wicked men just spoken of. "Might" (*ischus*) and "power" (*dunamis*) are very similar in meaning. Thayer says, "*dunamis*, power, natural ability, general and inherent . . . *ischus*, strength, power [especially physical] as an endowment."

**bring not a railing judgment against them before the Lord**

That is, the angels do not treat these *wicked* men like *they* were treating the dignitaries.

The verse teaches us a significant lesson about our speech. Concerning the most vile persons it is not our place to bring railing judgments! The term "railing" (*blasphemos*) means abusive (report), false or malicious (accusation), reproachful, blasphemous. Though it may be necessary to tell others they are hypocrites and backsliders, liars and adulterers, it must never be done from a *malicious motive* on our part. The angels, though superior in every way than these men, did not speak of them abusively! Take a lesson from the angels! "Let your speech be *always* with grace, seasoned with salt, that ye may know how ye ought to answer each one" (Col. 4:6).

**2:12 But these, as creatures without reason, born mere animals to be taken and destroyed, railing in matters whereof they are ignorant, shall in their destroying surely be destroyed,**

## Expanded Translation

But these deceivers are like (irrational or) brute beasts (creatures) who are born and exist in accordance with mere natural instincts unto (for) the capture (taking, catching) and slaughter, (in that in both cases their doom is certain). Railing and speaking reproachfully in matters of which they are ignorant and do not understand, they shall because of* their (spiritually and morally) corrupting influence certainly be destroyed themselves (i.e., perish eternally).

---

### But these, as creatures without reason, born mere animals to be taken and destroyed

The second comma in this phrase could be ommitted. The false teacher was *as* (*hos*, like as, similar to) the brute beast in that his doom was certain and unavoidable. Compare the similar picture drawn in Jas. 5:5. As brute beasts are born and raised for the inevitable day of slaughter, so the *everlasting* misery of these men awaited them, and would just as certainly befall them. The word "destroyed" (*phthora*) here means "killing, slaughter" (Bagster).

### railing in matters whereof they are ignorant

"Railing" (*blasphemeo*) also appears in 2:10. They use their slanderous and profane speech in regard to areas of knowledge of which they are ignorant—where they do not know the *facts* of the case. Paul speaks of a similar group in I Tim. 1:6-7.

### shall in their destroying surely be destroyed

The words in this verse translated "destroyed . . . destroying . . . destroyed" all come from the same basic Greek verb (*phtheiro*). In the first case it appeared as a noun (*phthora*) in regard to the animals that were "killed." Its *root* idea is *corruption, decay, destruction*, or *ruin*. So the body which is subject to decay ("corruption") "shall not inherit incorruption" (I Cor. 15:50). But Peter uses the word more often of *moral* and *spiritual* corruption, the depravity and decay of the *soul* (see 1:4, 2:19 "corruption"). In the phrase before us he is showing how the condemnation and eternal misery of these men was as certain as the capture

---

*Literally, "in their corrupting . . ." But Dana and Mantey (in *A Manual-Grammar of the Greek New Testament*) show that *en* ("in") may have the resultant meaning "because of," as in Rom. 1:24, Col. 1:21.

and slaughter of beasts. They shall "in their *destroying* (*phthora*, the noun) also be *destroyed* (*phtheiro*, the verb). *Who* were they destroying, corrupting, or "bringing into a worse condition"? Their followers! Their disciples were becoming inferior, lower, and "rotten" spiritually and morally BECAUSE OF THE FALSE TEACHERS' CORRUPTING INFLUENCE! And what would be the "reward" for their services? THEY THEMSELVES would be "brought into a worse condition"—a *much* worse condition! They will be consigned to the black pits of Tartarus and reserved for the fires of hell!

**2:13 suffering wrong as the hire of wrong-doing; men that count it pleasure to revel in the day-time, spots and blemishes, reveling in their deceivings while they feast with you;**

### Expanded Translation

Being wronged and treated unjustly as the wages (pay, reward) of their unrighteousness [or, as other manuscripts have, bringing upon themselves (receiving) the wages of unrighteousness]; persons considering it enjoyable and gratifying to live soft, luxurious, effeminent lives during the day-time, spots (morally stained) and blemishes (*disgraces* to society), living luxuriously, delicately, and in revelry, by their deception as they are feasting (banqueting) together with you.

---

#### suffering wrong as the hire of wrong-doing

If this reading is correct, the idea is that these men *themselves* were being injured, wronged, or treated unjustly *as punishment* (wages) *for their own unrighteous deeds.* But the marginal reading, "receiving the hire of wrong-doing" is preferred by many. This would simply mean they will be paid (i.e., *punished*) for their wickedness. Compare v. 12. The King James Version reads, "And shall receive the reward of unrighteousness . . ."

#### men that count it pleasure to revel in the day-time

"Pleasure" (*hedone*, compare our word *hedonism*) or "gratification," has no wicked connotation by itself and in modest and legitimate surroundings. But as used in the *New Testament*, it is descriptive of those who are *slaves* to pleasure, especially sensual pleasure (Luke 8:14, Tit. 3:3, Jas. 4:1-3). These place a high premium on the pleasurable or delightful effects of something— to the damnation of their own souls! How many Christian people have gone back to the ways of the world because of "the pleasures of sin for a season" (Heb. 11:25).

172

And what did these men regard with such delight? To "revel in the day-time." The word *truphe* ("revel"), a noun, is from the root *thrupto*, to break small, enfeeble, enervate. The noun came to refer to a *way of living* that enervates—delicate, soft, luxurious living, which included many evils—parties, drinking bouts, dancing, and festivities of various sorts. Many people wait until evening to carry on in such sin, but not these—they reveled "in the day-time."

**spots and blemishes**

These are picture words which show defects of character. The first (*spilos*, a spot or stain) would picture a *moral blemish*. Instead of wearing clean and pure garments, his are splattered with sin. The second word (*momos*, a blemish or blot) was used by the classical Greek poets and later prose writers in the sense of *blame, insult,* or *disgrace*. These men, because of their licentious behavior, were disgraces to society, and certainly to true religion.

**reveling**

This verb is an emphatic form of the noun "revel" already discussed. It means to live luxuriously or delicately, to revel in, riot.

**in their deceivings while they feast with you**

Describing at least in part *how* these wicked men were able to "live luxuriously"; in (or *through*) their deceit (*apate*). With deception, they could somehow horn their way into the Christian's *agapae* (love feasts) and eat (like gluttons, no doubt) with the Christians for whom the feast was originally designed.

Thayer says that the word "deceivings" as it occurs here (*apatai*) was "by a paragram [or verbal play] applied to the *agapae* or love-feasts . . . because these were transformed by base men into seducive revels." But in some manuscripts the reference to the love-feasts is more direct (as in Jude 12), actually including the word *agapais* in the text instead of *apatais*.* These were "feasts expressing and fostering mutual love which used to be held by Christians before [or after] the celebration of the Lord's supper, and at which the poorer Christians mingled with the wealthier and partook in common with the rest of food provided at the expense of the wealthy" (Thayer). Reference is apparently made to these social-religious gatherings in Acts 20:11, I Cor. 11:20-22, 33, 34, and some think Acts 2:46.

---

*Though the reference here *does* seem to be to the love-feasts, the text of the American Standard Version is considered more accurate. The International Bible Encyclopedia calls the insertion of *agapais* "a very doubtful reading." The only *actual* use of *agape* in the New Testament with reference to these common meals is in Jude 12.

## 2. Concluding Exhortations and Doxology, 3:14-18

**2:14 having eyes full of adultery, and that cannot cease from sin; enticing unstedfast souls; having a heart exercised in covetousness; children of cursing;**

### Expanded Translation

having eyes that are filled with adultery (adulterous looks) who cannot stop and are unceasing in this sin; baiting, alluring, and deceiving unsettled and unstable souls, having a heart that covetousness (or the love of gain) has trained in its crafty ways; children (i.e., persons, men) worthy of a curse or execration.

___

**having eyes full of adultery, and that cannot cease from sin**

These two clauses should be taken together. This man's eyes, in the presence of women, are continually and unceasingly sinning because they are filled with lust. His heart is so filled with adulterous and immoral thoughts that his eyes express the desire. It might be added, however, that the basic sin here mentioned is not limited to men. In addition to casting a lustful look, a woman may, by her dress, walk, and conduct, strive to charm the eyes of men and so influence them to sin. The fellow here described cannot "cease from sin"; that is, he cannot *as long as he is ruled and dominated by such passion.* The immoral stares would cease if his heart was clean and pure.

Jesus explicitly condemns this sin in Matt. 5:27-29. Let every man make the covenant of Job with his eyes (Job 31:1).

**enticing unstedfast souls**

The word "enticing" (*deleazo*) means properly to bait, catch by bait; thus, metaphorically, to beguile by blandishments, flattery, allurements, etc. It is used again in v. 18, and in both instances with reference to immoral practices.

Whom do these lewd men seek out and entice? The steadfast, strong and virtuous? No. It is the *un*steadfast—those who have no *fixed and unmovable convictions* in regard to their conduct; especially, "those who are just escaping from them that live in error" (v. 18). Those Christian women whose principles are firm, settled, and stable will not be drawn away by the "bait" of pleasure, promises, flattery, or possessions offered by sensual men. Nor are such men long attracted to a woman of virtue. Let every Christian lady be a steadfast soul!

**having a heart exercised in covetousness**

Besides being lewd, they are excessively covetous. The word

"exercised," (*gumnazo*, from the same root as our word *gymnasium*) meant properly to train in gymnastic discipline; then, to exercise vigorously *in any thing*, whether the body or mind was being used, or both. The hearts and lives of these men were *trained*—in covetousness and its methods!

**children of cursing**

An expression taken from Hebrew terminology. Their condition was so vile and wicked that they were only worthy and *deserving* of God's curse, that is, his sentence of condemnation and doom.*

**2:15-16 forsaking the right way, they went astray, having followed the way of Balaam the son of Beor, who loved the hire of wrongdoing; but he was rebuked for his own transgression: a dumb ass spake with man's voice and stayed the madness of the prophet.**

### Expanded Translation

Abandoning the straight, true, and right course of conduct, they (the evil men just spoken of) were caused to wander away from it, having followed and imitated the conduct of Balaam the son of Beor, who loved the wages (pay, reward) of unrighteousness (promised to him by Balak, so that he resolved to curse the Israelites whether God gave him permission to do so or not). But he received a rebuke for his own transgression (literally, violation of [God's] law); an ass on which he rode, destitute of the power of speech, spoke in a man's (human) voice and restrained the prophet's madness, insanity, and folly.

---

**forsaking the right way, they went astray**

The right (literally, *straight*) way is that which adheres to the true teachings of Christ. This was left behind, and therefore they were caused to wander and fall away by Satan. Christ is "the way" (Jn. 14:6); therefore, the church, his body, is "the Way" (Acts 24:14). Let us not forsake it!

**having followed the way of Balaam the son of Beor**

See also Jude 11. As was pointed out in 1:16 and 2:2, the word *exakoloutheo* ("having followed"), may mean to *imitate* another's conduct or behavior. The prophet Balaam was influenced and motivated by covetousness, and these men were treading in his steps.

---

*katara ("cursing") is similarly used in Gal. 3:10,13. But others understand the phrase differently. If "children of obedience" (I Pet. 1:14) means "those who are pre-eminently obedient," then why could *this* phrase not mean "those who are pre-eminently cursers"—"people who are always cursing"?

But it is well to point out that in *fact* these wicked men resembled Balaam in *other ways:* (1) Both professed to be servants of God, or religious teachers. (2) Both induced others to commit sin—the *same kind* of sin. Balaam counselled the Moabites to entice the children of Israel to illicit practices with their women, thus introducing licentiousness into the camp of the Hebrews. See Num. 25:1-9 where this sin is recorded, and 31:13-16 for Balaam's part in causing it.

### who loved the hire of wrong-doing

That is, he loved the wages or pay he received for disobeying God. Balaam was continually sent gifts from Balak, the king of Moab, that he might curse Israel. At first the prophet refused, saying, "If Balak would give me his house full of silver and gold, I cannot go beyond the word of Jehovah my God, to do less or more" (Num. 22:18). But soon afterward he began to seek God's permission to go with Balak. He was allowed to go, *but only on the condition he speak God's words.*

### but he was rebuked for his own transgression

In a most unusual way!

### a dumb ass spake with man's voice and stayed the madness of the prophet

Num. 22:21-35. After the rebuke from his ass (and also the angel of Jehovah), Balaam confessed, "I have sinned; for I knew not that thou [the angel] stoodest in the way against me: now therefore, if it displease thee, I will get me back again" (v. 34). Evidently, the prophet *was* truly sorrowful and penitent, for he *does* speak precisely what God tells him to, to the utter consternation of Balak.

It might be fairly asked, how was the prophet's madness stayed, *when he proceeded on with Balak?* It appears from comparing Num. 22:20 with v. 35 that the wrath of God was not kindled against him for *going* (for Jehovah had told him to go). But we are nowhere told when he *first* left that he *intended* to speak just what God told him to. He was evidently going with the *wrong motive* — to curse God's people. He would have his expensive gifts, and Israel would be cursed! This was "madness." (Love of money often makes one act insanely!) God then talked to him through two mouthpieces: an ass and an angel. Afterward, his *intentions* changed and he was allowed to proceed—himself a mouthpiece of God. The "transgression" and "madness" was more in his *reason* or *motive* for going, than in the going itself.

The complete Scriptural account of Balaam and his deeds may be found by reading Numbers, Chap. 22—25, 31:1-20. After his *cursing* was stayed, he later gave sinful *counsel*, causing thousands of Israelites to be slain by the plague. Thus the "staying" of his madness was not permanent.

**2:17 These are springs without water, and mists driven by a storm; for whom the blackness of darkness hath been reserved.**

### Expanded Translation

These men are like springs without water (dry), and like clouds driven by a violent attack of wind which comes in furious gusts; for whom the blackest and gloomiest darkness has been reserved, kept, and preserved.

---

**These are springs without water**

Jude adds, "*clouds* without water" as well as "autumn trees without fruit" (Jude 12). In each case the *appearance* provided an expectation which was not fulfilled. From a spring (or a well fed by one, as the word is used in Jn. 4:6, 14, where it is rendered "well") we expect *water*. The *unexpected benefits* are not received from these false teachers. They may build up hope by "uttering great swelling words of vanity" (v. 18) and "promising them liberty" (v. 19), but the thirst of the soul will never be quenched at their fountain. *Jesus* and his righteous teachings provide us with the real water of life. See Matt. 5:6, Jn. 4:10-14.

**and mists driven by a storm**

The word "mists" (*homichle*) may signify a *cloud* as well as a mist. And many manuscripts have the word *nephele* here, which *only* means "a cloud." These clouds (men) are urged forward by a *storm* (*lailaps*). This is not *any* storm, but one involving strong and erratic winds. It is "never a single gust, nor a steadily blowing wind, however violent; but a storm breaking forth from black thunder-clouds in furious gusts, with floods of rain, and throwing everything topsy-turvy (Schmidt, quoted by Thayer).

Now the "clouds" in the figure are *people* — false teachers! These unstable and unsettled souls were not solidly grounded or rooted in the true teachings of Christ (Col. 2:6-7). They themselves were "tossed to and fro and carried about with every wind of doctrine" (Eph. 4:14), and yet were posing as the spiritual leaders of *others!* The reference here to their unsettled and unsteadfast condition seems to point to their whole way of living— moral, spiritual and doctrinal.

**for whom the blackness of darkness hath been reserved**

Again referring to Tartarus, as in vs. 4, 9, Jude 6. It will be a place of absolute and total darkness!

Hell also shall be a place of darkness (Matt. 8:12, 22:13, 25:30).

**2:18 For, uttering great swelling words of vanity, they entice in the lusts of the flesh, by lasciviousness, those who are just escaping from them that live in error;**

### Expanded Translation

For these deceivers, by uttering big, overswollen, immoderate words expressive of vanity, emptiness, and folly; allure, beguile, and entice in (into) the lusts and strong cravings of the fleshly or sensuous nature, through lasciviousness (abandonment of moral restraint), those who are just escaping* from (unchristian people) who are living in error and perverseness.

---

**For, uttering great swelling words of vanity, they entice in the lusts of the flesh**

See also v. 14 and Jude 16. The "great swelling words of vanity" are evidently *flattering* and *seductive* words, for with these they "entice" their listeners into the lusts of the flesh. The word "entice" (*deleazo*) means literally, "to catch by bait," and thus came to signify to beguile by blandishments or flattery. Part of their "bait" was their ability to use big, vain words. But in addition to this, they enticed

**by lasciviousness**

(*aselgeia*). See notes under I Pet. 4:3, II Pet. 2:2. It is unbridled lust, excess, wantonness, shamelessness. The one who has this trait shows little or no restraint or self-control in his moral behavior—gives free vent to his sensual and lustful appetites. And *who* do they entice by such means?

**those who are just escaping from them that live in error**

In many cases the same as the "unsteadfast souls" mentioned in v. 14. These sinister men were striving to lead others back to the ungodly *life* and the ungodly *people* from which they had escaped. It is much easier to bring about the death of a baby than a strong and full-grown man. Knowing this, the false teacher tried to snuff out the spark of spiritual life which had been ig-

---

*Other MSS, have "who have just escaped . . ."

nited in the souls of these Christians, but had not long been burning.

It is hard to *imagine* such immoral and unprincipled men as those here described, claiming to be teachers of the *truth.* But upon a close scrutiny of some of our modern-day sects *right here in America,* one will find men (and women) carrying on in a similar fashion. And it all justified under the cloak of "true religion"!

**2:19 promising them liberty, while they themselves are bond-servants of corruption; for of whom a man is overcome, of the same is he also brought into bondage.**

## Expanded Translation

promising those whom they deceive liberty and freedom, while they themselves live as bondservants (slaves) of corruption, decay, and ruin; for by whatever (thing or person) anyone is conquered or vanquished (and thus brought into a worse condition), by the same (thing or person) he is also brought into bondage and slavery.

---

**promising them liberty, while they themselves are bondservants of corruption**

The young or "short-time" Christians were being promised *freedom* by those in a far worse condition! *From what* would such persons offer them freedom? Probably from those elements of the Christian religion that the unregenerate regard as *rigorous* and restraining. Perhaps they taught their followers that the Apostles' teaching was *too severe* to be the *truth* and, therefore, should be abandoned. Peter warned against such abuse in his first epistle (2:16, where see notes). The "liberty" these men offered was not real liberty at all, but *license to sin!* Lawlessness is not *true* liberty. *True* freedom always involves an element of law and restraint, even in the government of countries. Our country would be in chaos if *freedom* meant license to break the law at will.

The truth of the matter was that they themselves did not have what was promised, being slaves to "corruption" (*phthora*)—that which brings moral and spiritual decay, and ruins the soul. Christians have escaped from this corruption (1:4), but they may certainly return to it, as this and the following verses show.

**for of whom a man is overcome, of the same is he also brought into bondage**

Further proof that these liberty-promisers did not themselves possess what they offered to others. The word translated "over-come" (*hettao*), which appears again in v. 20, meant primarily to be inferior (II Cor. 12:13 "were made inferior"). It carries here, then, not only the thought of being subdued by a thing, but of being in a worse or inferior condition because *of* being conquered. The term was anciently employed when an army was "worsted" or vanquished in a war: II Maccabees 10:24.

When a man *serves* sin (whether it be pride, sensuality, jealousy, anger or *whatever* might get the mastery of him) he is certainly in no condition to proclaim *freedom* to others! He is in bondage—"*cruel* bondage!"

All people are servants—either of sin or righteousness. See Jn. 8:34, Rom. 7:15-23. Paul said, concerning indifferent things, "I will not be brought under the power of any" (or, more fully, "I will not be brought under the authority, rule, or dominion of any"). Let us volunteer ourselves as bondservants of Christ—happy and joyous that in this position we are free from both the curse and the dominion of sin.

**2:20 For if, after they have escaped the defilements of the world through the knowledge of the Lord and Saviour Jesus Christ, they are again entangled therein and overcome, the last state is become worse with them than the first.**

### Expanded Translation

For if, after having fled away from and escaped the pollutions, contaminations, and defilements of the world (i.e., the ungodly mass of mankind) through an exact and full knowledge of the Lord and Saviour Jesus Christ, they are again intertwined, entangled, and involved, being conquered (and thus brought into a worse condition), the last state of things has become worse with them than the first.

---

**For if, after they have escaped the defilements of the world**

Compare 1:4. The persons described *had been* Christians. They had fled from and were free from the world's defilements. Thayer defines "defilements" (*miasma*) here, as "vices the foulness of which contaminates one in his intercourse with the ungodly mass of mankind" (*miasmos*, "defilement is defined in v. 10). The verb form, *miaino*, means literally to dye with another color, stain. Sin discolors the soul! The garments of these men, once made white in the blood of the Lamb, were now, once again, being spotted and stained by this world's corruption.

**through the knowledge of the Lord and Saviour Jesus Christ**

On the word "knowledge" (*epignosis*) see 1:2. It appears again in 1:3, 8, and the verb (*epignosko*) in 2:21 (twice). In each case it refers to a *Christian's* knowledge of God, Christ, or holy things. But here this "precise and correct knowledge" is of the Lord and Saviour Jesus Christ. They had a true knowledge of Christ's nature, dignity, and benefits. Oh, that they would have retained it!

How difficult it is to explain with logic the doctrine of "eternal security" or "once in grace always in grace" in the light of what is stated here!

**they are again entangled therein and overcome**

On the word "overcome" (*hettao*), see v. 19. The "again" signifies they were once *out* of sin's entangling mesh. Foolishly, they went back into Satan's net.

**the last state is become worse with them than the first**

Their *first* entrance into sin was soon after the age of accountability. Then they transgressed God's law and were in need of his saving grace. At some time during the course of their lives they had seen this need and escaped the world's filth by accepting Christ. But then they decided to return! Having once been untangled from the ropes of Satan, they are now "entangled again"! Now their condition is much worse, for they know the truth concerning salvation and righteousness, and shall therefore have "many stripes" (Luke 12:47-48).

It is also true, we might add, that the apostate frequently goes deeper into sin, and with less restraint, than he did formerly. His conscience often becomes branded and seared into insensibility (I Tim. 4:2)—far harder and more calloused than before he was a Christian. As a rule, his ears are closed and his eyes are shut to any further help.

**2:21-22 For it were better for them not to have known the way of righteousness, than, after knowing it, to turn back from the holy commandment delivered unto them. It has happened unto them according to the true proverb, The dog turning to his own vomit again, and the sow that had washed to wallowing in the mire.**

### Expanded Translation

Concerning these who have again become entangled in the lusts of this world, it would have been better for them not to have

fully, accurately, and personally known the way of righteousness,
rather than, having fully, accurately, and personally known it,
to turn back (return) from (literally, out of) the holy and sacred
commandment (that is, the whole body of Christian precepts)
given over and entrusted to them. It has come to pass in their
case in accordance with the true proverb; a dog who has returned
to his own vomit, and (another true saying is) the sow that had
bathed her body returned to the wallowing-place of mud, filth
and dung.

---

**For it were better for them not to have known the way of
righteousness, than, after knowing it, to turn back from the
holy commandment delivered unto them**

The verbs rendered "have known" and "having known" are
both forms of the verb *epiginosko* (see v. 20). The noun form is
defined in 1:2. This "full and accurate" knowledge can only describe persons who were *Christians*, and is never used in this book
with reference to one who only *professes* or *claims* to be a follower of Christ. Nor could it be construed to refer to those who only
"knew" the way of Christ *mentally*, as one "knows" of a historical character. Peter never uses the term *epignosis* ("knowledge")
in this loose sense.

To the candid mind it must be admitted that Peter is saying
that a man *may* at one time be a Christian—a *real* one—and then
turn back into the ways of the world. The very *reason* for giving
this exhortation was so that the presently *faithful* ones might
take heed *and not fall away themselves!*

The holy "commandment" (*entole*, order, charge, injunction)
given to them is here used in a collective sense of the whole body
of the moral or spiritual precepts of Christianity, as in 2:2.

**it has happened unto them according to the true proverb,
the dog turning to his own vomit again**

See Prov. 26:11. This is not a pretty picture, but God did not
intend that it should be. Sin is repugnant to the Almighty—and
*should* be to *us!* Let us not more think of taking sin into our
*spiritual* beings than we would of sharing this dog's meal with
him!

But the *particular* kind of sin here indicated by returning to the vomit, is sin which one has at one time been *coughed up* or cast off. After ridding himself of it, this man goes back and again takes it into his life. The dog, once having cleansed his inward parts by getting the poisonous and upsetting materials *out of* his body, is far healthier *if he keeps away from it!* God help us to despise and hate all our former ways of rottenness and filth!

**and the sow that had washed to wallowing in the mire**

This proverb is not found in the Old Testament. However, it was common in the Rabbinical writings, and is found in the Greek classics. Peter does not maintain that it was a part of *Scripture* (much less of the Book of Proverbs), but only that it was expressive of *truth.* The old sow, once washed (literally, "bathed"), would be far better off to *stay away* from the mire and dung from which she was just cleansed. Here again, the terribleness of sin—particularly sin returned to—is emphasized. We should no more think of returning to our former worldly ways than we would of joining this sow after we had just taken a bath.

The Calvinists make much of the fact that Peter here likens men to dogs and pigs. Now *pigs* and *dogs,* they tell us, could never have their natures changed—they will only act, in the end, according to their *true nature.* This passage is cited as proof that their real character *never was changed,* and when they apostatized from their outward profession, they only acted out their nature—only showed that in fact there had never been any real change.

To make such an assertion concerning this passage is certainly to miss the very point of the inspired writer. Peter has just spoken of those who *in fact* had *"escaped* the defilements of the world" (v. 20) and this "through the knowledge (*epignosis*) of the Lord and Saviour Jesus Christ. This "full and careful knowledge" of Christ is referred to every time the word "know" or "knowledge" is used in verses 20 and 21. Who then, is the person that is willing to affirm that the apostle is only speaking of those who *seemed* to be Christians, but were only hypocrites? The basic and main reason for citing the case of the *dog* and the *sow* was to show their foolishness and harm in *returning* to something *filthy.* We are not told here to contemplate long and hard on the unchangeable nature of animals. Admittedly, many of us did have dog-like and pig-like characters before conversion. But "if any man is in

183

Christ, he is a *new* creature: the old things are passed away; behold, they are become new" (II Cor. 5:17). Let all new creatures
STAY NEW CREATURES!

## QUESTIONS OVER CHAPTER TWO

1. What does the author discuss in the last part of Chapter 1?
2. How does *this* chapter begin, in contrast?
3. What kind of heresies would the false teacher bring in?
4. What (or whom) would they deny?
5. And therefore they would bring themselves _____
   _____(?)
6. What does "destruction" mean, when referring to a living soul?
7. The apostle said those who would follow their lascivious doings would be (a) few (b) multitudes (c) thousands (d) many (e) some.
8. Because of this, what shall happen to the way of *truth*?
9. What are "lascivious doings"?
10. What motivates these evil men? (v. 3.)
11. What are "feigned" words?
12. In what way are *people* here spoken of as *merchandise*?
13. The false teacher's "_____ now from old lingereth not, and their _____ slumbereth not."
14. T. or F. God did not spare angels when they sinned.
15. Why is the case of the angels cited?
16. Specifically, they were cast into: (a) hell (b) sheol (c) hades (d) the "great gulf" (e) abandon (f) Tartarus.
17. Give several descriptive characteristics of this place.
18. Are souls committed there *before* or *after* the judgment day?
19. *Why* do you suppose Peter spent time showing how God "spared not the ancient world"?
20. What persons did he "preserve" from that world?
21. Noah was "a preacher of _____(?)
22. Into what material were the cities of Sodom and Gomorrah converted?
23. What happened to these two cities should serve as a reminder to all, but particularly "those that should live _____
    _____(?)
24. Would you call Lot righteous or unrighteous? (Explain answer.)
25. What did he do to himself because of the sin about him?

26. What does the Lord know how to do? (Two things, v. 9.)
27. *Where* is the unrighteous "under punishment unto the day of judgment"?
28. How does one "walk after the flesh"?
29. What does one do who despises dominion?
30. At whom do these wicked men rail?
31. How do angels treat *them,* in contrast?
32. Note v. 12. What *picture* is drawn here?
33. What do they receive as their "hire of wrong-doing"?
34. When do they revel?
35. At what occasions would they particularly come in contact with the Christians?
36. What were their eyes full of?
37. What particular people were they enticing?
38. Explain the phrase, "children of cursing."
39. What man's ways did they follow (imitate)?
40. What did he love?
41. Who rebuked him (as recorded here)?
42. Was the "madness" of the prophet stayed *permanently* by this rebuke?
43. What kind of springs are these false teachers?
44. What kind of mists (clouds)?
45. Their vain words may be described as: (a) small (b) medium (c) large (d) very large.
46. How do they entice in the lusts of the flesh?
47. What particular class of Christians is especially in danger? (v. 18, cp. v. 14.)
48. What are these Christians *promised?*
49. Why is the *promiser* unqualified to make such a promise?
50. What do they really mean by "liberty"?
51. According to the apostle, how may the last state of one become worse than the first?
52. Do the words "knowledge" and "know" have any particular bearing on the interpretation of verses 20-22?
53. Are both of the proverbs (v. 22) found in the Bible?
54. What, exactly, does "vomit" and "mire" represent here?
55. Do verses 20-22 apply to one who was a true Christian and who became a backslider? (Give reason(s) for your answer.)

## IV. THE CHRISTIAN'S HOPE, 3:1-18
### 1. Christ's Second Coming and the End of the World, 3:1-13

## CHAPTER III

**3:1-2 This is now, beloved, the second epistle that I write unto you; and in both of them I stir up your sincere mind by putting you in remembrance; that ye should remember the words which were spoken before by the holy prophets, and the commandment of the Lord and Saviour through your apostles:**

### Expanded Translation

This, loved ones, is the second epistle (letter) that I now write to you. In both of these, I thoroughly arouse (literally, wake up) your honest, candid, and sincere minds by putting you in remembrance (reminding you of your duties and privileges in the Gospel); in order to call back to your mind the words which have previously been spoken by the holy (reverent, upright) prophets, and the commandment (charge) of the Lord and Saviour by (from) your apostles.

---

One immediately notices the striking similarity of 1:12, 13 to this passage.

**This is now, beloved, the second epistle that I write unto you**

Unless we assume the writer to be an utter imposter and deceiver, we must accept the fact that the Apostle Peter is the author of *both* New Testament books which bear his name. Throughout the book he speaks of himself as an *apostle of Christ:* 1:1, 14, 16-18, etc. The claim of the writer and the historical evidence are in favor of Peter as the inspired author. It remains for the "higher critics" to *disprove* this claim and evidence. See the *Introduction.*

**and in both of them I stir up your sincere mind by putting you in remembrance**

Showing he had a common objective in writing both letters. Notice what Peter could stir up—a *sincere* mind. This word (*eilikrines*, from the root words *heile*, sunshine, and *krino*, to judge) means properly, that which being viewed in the sunshine is found clear and pure. It is used here (as in Phil. 1:10) metaphorically, and means pure, unsullied, undefiled, sincere, especially in the sense of being *candid.* When one's mind is not filled with deceit, sinister motives, hate, or evil thoughts, *it can be aroused to love and good works!* May each of us strive to keep our minds pure, and may they be found as such even when viewed in the sunlight of God's Word!

**that ye should remember the words which were spoken before by the holy prophets, and the commandment of the Lord and Saviour through your apostles**

This statement provides somewhat of a summary of Peter's writings—the words of the prophets and apostles. Chap. 1:16-21 especially showed that the teachings of the prophets and apostles coincided with and corroborated each other concerning the person of Christ.

In the parallel statement of Jude 17, 18 is added: "that they [the apostles] said to you, In the last time there shall be mockers . . ." Similarly is verse 4 connected to the words of *both* the prophets and the apostles in *this* passage. Their words must be remembered and heeded unless we want to imbibe false doctrines!

*The words which were spoken before by the holy prophets* here has particular reference to the prophecies of the Old Testament concerning the character and work of the Gospel Age. In view of the fact that the New Testament was not yet completed, an appeal to these prophetic utterances was very appropriate. Passages such as those found in Dan. 2, Isa. 2, 11, 53, Micah 4, Jer. 31, Joel 2—all of which speak of the coming Messiah or the days following his advent—should often be brought to our memory. Especially is this necessary when *false doctrine* is about to creep into the church—a very evident danger here.

The *"commandment (entole)* of the Lord and Saviour through your apostles" refers to the *whole scope* of teachings we accepted when we came to Christ. Christians have had "the holy commandments delivered unto them" (v. 21, where see notes) from which they must not turn back.

**3:3-4 knowing this first, that in the last days mockers shall come with mockery, walking after their own lusts, and saying, Where is the promise of his coming? for, from the day that the fathers fell asleep, all things continue as they were from the beginning of the creation.**

## Expanded Translation

Realizing this first (and keeping it uppermost in your minds), that at the time of the last days mockers (deriders, scoffers) shall come with (or, in) mockery (scoffing, derision), walking according to (dominated by) their own personal cravings and strong desires (not what God desires), while they are saying, Where is the (fulfillment of the) promise of his (Christ's second) coming? For from the time that the fathers fell asleep (i.e., died), all things are remaining as they are (fixed and permanent in their pattern, course, or place) as they were at (and from) the beginning of creation.

------

### knowing this first, that in the last days mockers shall come with mockery

Jesus prophesied of mockery concerning Himself (Matt. 20; 19, fulfilled in 27:29-31, 41). If we live the Christ-like life, we may expect similar treatment. See Jn. 15:18-20.

"The last days" is a term used sometimes in the New Testament with reference to the last days of Judah (and Jerusalem) as a nation (Acts 2:17, Jas. 5:3). This *could* be true here, but it seems likely that the term is more general in its meaning and indicates *the last days of the world*, the final dispensation of history. *The Christian Age*, then, is evidently meant here, as in II Tim. 3:1, Heb. 1:2, I Pet. 1:5, 20. The word *eschatos* ("last") used here, occurs in all these verses.

### walking after their own lusts

Both the words "their" and "own" are emphatic in the Greek. These men are quick to scoff, mimic, and ridicule the Christian, but their own personal lives are rotten to the core! Why? They live for *themselves*, utterly indifferent to the laws of God.

### and saying, where is the promise of his coming

That is, Christ's return to earth. It is significant that the *very same doctrine* is frequently the subject of mockery today among worldlings. "You're as slow as the second coming of Christ," or "You'll never get that done until Christ returns" and similar statements are to be heard from their foul mouths. Others, while not deriding the doctrine verbally, do so *inwardly*, for they make no preparation to meet the Saviour. This shows their *unbelief*, for the Master said, "Watch therefore, for ye know not the day nor the hour" (Matt. 25:13).

### for, from the days that the fathers fell asleep, all things continue as they were from the beginning of the creation

Their statement simply was not true, for they willfully forgot the facts of history (v. 5). Many today placate their consciences by the same means—purposely forgetting (and many times *disbelieving*) what took place in the days of Noah.

It seems best to take the term "fathers" here as meaning *their* fathers, or the *previous generation*. Between that time and the creation, they asserted, summer and winter, springtime and harvest, had come and gone in regular sequence. "Why should we worry *now*? Will it not be the same in the future?"

The second coming of Christ was an oft-discussed subject in the early church, and many of the Thessalonians, particularly, were of the belief that the Lord's coming was "just at hand" (II Thes. 2:2). It may be that some of these mockers were acquainted with those who continued to believe this erroneous doctrine. If so, it doubtless added fuel to the fire of their already insulting remarks. Today, "date setting" has cheapened the *true* doctrine of the return of Christ in the minds of the world.* But we may still expect our belief in this glorious event to be ridiculed and mocked, even when the worldlings about us are not acquainted with the false teachings of men on the subject.

**3:5-6 For this day they wilfully forget, that there were heavens from of old, and an earth compacted out of water and amidst water, by the word of God; by which means the world that then was, being overflowed with water, perished:**

### Expanded Translation

For they, because of their desire to do so, purposely and wilfully ignore and let go unnoticed the fact that by (through) the word of God the heavens of long ago were brought into being, and an earth was put together—part of it sticking up out of water and part of it in the midst of water—through which means (words and actions of God) the world which existed at that time perished and was brought to ruin, being (as it was) flooded over with water.

---

**For this they wilfully forget**

Literally, "For this goes wilfully unnoticed to them . . .";  that is, the facts of history as recorded by Moses (Gen. 6-8). The

---

*William Miller, the actual founder of the Seventh-Day Adventists, said Christ would come in 1843. The prophecy failed, so he fixed a day in October of 1844. That failed also. Other Adventists have set 1847, 1850, 1852, 1854, 1855, 1863, 1866, 1867, 1877, etc., etc., etc. Because of such foolish predicting, the *true doctrine* of Christ's return has suffered ridicule, and is "evil spoken of."

word "wilfully" (*thelo*) includes the thought of desire, along with volition or exercising the will.* What had previously happened to the world had escaped the attention of their minds, *not* because they had never been *told* or were *uninformed* upon the subject, but because the thought of it was painful to them! It is a well-known axiom that "history repeats." Of this truth they were aware. The thought of God again bringing woe and destruction upon the earth grated upon their minds. They found a simple "solution"—ignore it and refuse to let the mind dwell upon it! How Satan has succeeded in keeping many people from responding *as they should* to the truth of God's word, BY TELLING THEM TO "FORGET IT." God asks a man to *reason* concerning divine things (Isa. 1:18). If he stubbornly refuses to *consider the facts,* salvation is impossible. Sinners wilfully forget many things *to their own damnation:* the brevity and uncertainty of life, the knowledge that all men must die and give an account for their deeds, etc. These very truths, if kept in mind and thought upon, would cause them to look upon life more *seriously,* and prepare for the life to come as they should. The thoughts they avoid and neglect *are the very thoughts that would be of everlasting benefit to them!*

**that there were heavens from of old, and an earth compacted out of water and amidst water, by the word of God**

The word "compacted" (*sunistemi*) is from *sun,* together, with, and *histemi,* to make it stand, set, place. The world was "put together," i.e., "put together by way of composition or combination" (Thayer). But a key question concerning this passage has been, Is Peter telling of the *materials used* when the earth (land)

was made, or simply the *manner* of its creation? In the original, either idea is possible, *kai ge ex hudatos kai di' hudatos* may be

rendered "and the land out of water and by means of water," or "and the land (stood) out of water and in the midst (or between) water." In view of the fact that we have no record of God using water in the composition of land (that is, that God composed the earth *from* water), the last idea is preferred. It also accords with the Genesis record: "And God said, "Let the waters under the heavens be gathered together unto one place, and let the dry land

---

*See Thayer's extensive note under *thelo.* Also see comments under v. 9, "wishing" (*boulomai*).

appear: and it was so. And God called the dry land Earth; and the gathering together of the waters called he Seas: and God saw that it was good" (Gen. 1:9-10). The earth was compacted "out of" water only in the sense that it *rose up above the water.*

**by which means the world that then was, being overflowed with water, perished**

The pronoun "which" here is in the plural (*hon,* from *hos*) and may not only refer to the flood itself, but to the edict of God to cleanse the world by such a means. Or perhaps the Apostle is referring to *"waters"* here, for in the historical account both the waters from *above and below* combined to bring about the deluge (Gen. 7:11).

PERISHED—This verb (*apollumi*) is quite common to Peter: I Pet. 1:7, II Pet. 3:9; as in the noun form (*apoleia,* "destruction"): II Pet. 2:1 (twice); 2:3, 3:7, 16.

The thought of annihilation is not inherent within this word. The idea is not extinction, but *ruin.* It is the loss "not of being but of well-being" (Vine). Gold that "perishes" (I Pet. 1:7) is gold that is so utterly worn or ruined that it can no longer be of usefulness to society. When the sheep was "lost" (*apollumi*) in the parable of Jesus (Lk. 15:3-6) he surely did not fade into nothingness. Neither did the "lost" (*apollumi*) son (see Lk. 15:24, 32). Jesus said if a man would put new wine in old skins they would "perish" (*apollumi*). Disappear? Disolve into non-existence? Go up in a puff of blue smoke leaving no trace behind? No. They were made totally useless for their intended purpose— "ruined." The same was true of the ancient world. The flood did not cause either the globe itself or the sinful people who dwelt thereon to be *annihilated.* The people of that age *perished*—died prematurely and were lost eternally—unable to enter their *intended* home with God.*

**3:7 but the heavens that now are, and the earth, by the same word have been stored up for fire, being reserved against the day of judgment and destruction of ungodly men.**

*The force of Peter's argument is not particularly lost if we only take the word "perished" in the sense of "died," as in Matt. 8:25. But the word's normal sense in the middle voice (here) is to perish *eternally,* lose one's salvation, and suffer the agonies of hell, as in 3:9.

## Expanded Translation

but when God decides to destroy the earth a second time, the case will be different. The heavens that exist now and the earth (land), by means of the same word (which word caused the antediluvians to perish by water), have been kept in store (preserved) for fire, being kept, guarded and reserved unto the day of judgment and (the day of the) destruction (perishing) of ungodly and irreverent men.

---

**but the heavens that now are, and the earth, by the same word have been stored up for fire**

The "earth" (*ge*) in this passage can only refer to this globe. The word literally means land or ground—*terra firma* (comp. v. 5) and is frequently used to refer to our *planet as a whole*, as opposed to *the heavens* (Matt. 5:18, 35, 6:10, etc.). But how limited is the term "heavens" here (or in verses 10, 12, 13)?

The Jews divided the heaven into three parts, viz., (1) The air or atmosphere, where clouds gather and birds fly; (2) The firmament, in which the sun, moon, and stars are fixed; and (3) the upper heaven, the abode of God and his angels, the presently invisible realm of holiness and happiness, the home of the children of God.

It is this classification which is needed to explain Paul's "third heaven" of II Cor. 12:2. But which of these three is meant by *Peter* in *this* chapter? Surely not the third, so we must either choose between the first and second, or combine them.

It is a debated question as to whether there is *any* real Biblical evidence that the second coming of Christ and the destruction of the world will involve any planets or heavenly bodies outside of our own. The references in Matt. 24:29, Mk. 13:24, 25; Lk. 21:25-26, so commonly taken to refer to the second coming of Christ, speak of stars falling from heaven and the powers of the heavens being shaken. But many would *limit* these passages to the destruction of Jerusalem, making the stars, sun, etc., *figurative*, representing the rulers of Jerusalem and Judea. The "coming of the Son of man," while referring to Christ, does *not* (according to these interpreters) refer to his *second* coming, but the *presence* and *manifestation* of his *wrath* upon the rebellious Jews.* Similarly, the sun, moon, and stars of the sixth seal (Rev. 6:12-17)

---

*Compare our notes on the term "day of visitation" (I Pet. 2:12). See also I Pet. 4:7 under the phrase, "The end of all things is at hand."

are now thought by many exegetes to be symbolic of rulers and others of high political rank. If the student would take the time to carefully examine each of the above passages contextually, I believe you will agree that in each case the evidence is weighty *against* attaching a literal significance to the various celestial bodies mentioned.

In verse 10 the marginal reading, "heavenly bodies" for "elements" has caused others to believe that even *Peter* taught that planets and stars will be involved in the destruction of the world. But see notes on that passage. The marginal reading is not preferred.

It is my conclusion, based on the evidence of this chapter and the *apparent* teachings of Scripture elsewhere, that the "heavens" mentioned here have only to do with the atmosphere which surrounds our own globe. The evidence that other planets (or even the moon) will be involved in that great catastrophe seems, at best, to be shaky and uncertain.

### by the same word have been stored up for fire

Just as God's Word brought the world into *existence* (v. 5), and caused it to perish by the flood (v. 6, compare Gen. 6:7), so he has, by that same infallible and unchangeable word, proclaimed that the world would be destroyed by fire. In that day long ago, God said "yet shall his days be a hundred and twenty years" (Gen. 6:3). But *we do not know* what day God has set aside for the great conflagration spoken of in this passage. We *do* know *its coming is certain!*

### being reserved against the day of judgment and destruction of ungodly men

*All* will appear at the Judgment Day (II Cor. 5:10). For the righteous it will be a day of *acquittal.* But for the unrighteous it will be the day their doom is pronounced. The word "destruction" (*apoleia*) is discussed in the previous verse.

**3:8-9 But forget not this one thing, beloved, that one day is with the Lord as a thousand years, and a thousand years as one day. The Lord is not slack concerning his promise, as some count slackness; but is longsuffering to you-ward, not wishing that any should perish, but that all should come to repentance.**

## Expanded Translation

But, loved ones, instead of being like those around you (who wilfully forget, v. 5), *you* must not ignore, let go unnoticed, or forget this one thing: that one day is as a thousand years as far as the Lord is concerned, and a thousand years is as one day (therefore, the elapse of time does not hinder his purposes). The Lord is not slow or delaying concerning (the fulfillment of) his promise (to destroy the world by fire) in the manner that some men think of slowness or delay, but rather is long-suffering and patient, (withholding His wrath) toward you, not purposing, determining, or wishing that any person perish and be lost, but rather that all should come to repentance (a radical change of mind for the better, which influences the whole life).

---

**But forget not this one thing beloved**

The word "forget" (*lanthano*) occurs in v. 5 (where see definition). The idea here is, "These false teachers wilfully let the true facts of religion, especially concerning the world's destruction, go unnoticed. You Christians must *not* let this of which I am now about to speak escape your memories . . ."

**that one day is with the Lord as a thousand years,
and a thousand years as one day**

That is, time means *nothing* to God, particularly here as it concerns the fulfillment of his promises and purposes (see verse 4). As far as God is concerned, he might just as well have decreed the end of the world *a couple of days ago!* The lapse of time between His decree and its fulfillment is no weighty argument against the *certainty* and *truthfulness* of the prophecy.

This statement again refutes the mockers' idea that the Lord had not appeared as yet, and "all things continue unchanged from the beginning . . ." (v. 4). In verse 6 the apostle shows that things have not continued unchanged. And here he points out that the passing of centuries means nothing to *God*. Yet such a delay may seem *long* to *man*.

Thus two basic arguments stand out against those who made light of the coming destruction of the world.

1. True history (verses 5-7).
2. God's view of time (verses 8-9).

**the Lord is not slack concerning his promise, as some
count slackness**

That is, the Lord is not *slow* or behindhand in fulfilling His promise, though some *men* may *think* so who do not understand His timeless nature. The verb "slack" (*braduno*) and the noun "slackness" (*bradutes*) may be simply defined "slow" and "slowness" respectively, or "tardy" and "tardiness." As most *men* reckon time, God is certainly "slack." But that is *man's* idea of slackness, *not God's*.

#### but is longsuffering to you-ward

He is patient, forbearing, and slow in avenging wrongs, for so *makrothumia* signifies. The word generally describes "the self-restraint which does not hastily retaliate a wrong" (Thayer), and stands opposed to the quick or impulsive manifestation of wrath or revenge. (God has this trait, and we are to be holy as he is holy—I Pet. 1:16.)

It is because of this characteristic of God that he may appear "slack" concerning his promise. When he decreed that the ancient world would be destroyed, His longsuffering caused him to spare that world for a hundred and twenty years (Gen. 6:3). How much longer will his patience hold out with the present world? With crime, lust, war, and rebellion everywhere, it is surely difficult to believe that the awful event described in these verses is very far distant.

#### not wishing that any should perish, but that all should come to repentance

Giving a *reason* for his longsuffering. God has nothing but the good of his creatures at heart! He "would have all men to be saved, and come to the knowledge of the truth" (I Tim. 2:4).* It is not "a few" or "some" that he desires to be saved, but "all"! "And he that is athirst, let him come: he that will, let him take of the water of life freely" (Rev. 22:17b).

> (See notes on the word "perish" (*apollumi*) under v. 6. Concerning the foreknowledge of God as it pertains to salvation, see notes under I Pet. 1:2.)

---

*In I Tim. 2:4 the verb "would have" is *thelo*, while the verb "wishing" (*boulomai*) is used here. The distinction between these words is not always clear-cut, but Abbot-Smith expresses the consensus when he says *boulomai* implies more strongly than *thelo* the deliberate exercise of volition. Thus it is neither God's purpose or intention *nor* his wish or desire that any person be lost. When a man opposes the desire and purpose of God to save him, God, being both merciful and righteous, must exercise justice. But let no man blame God for being in a state of condemnation! See further notes on *thelo* ("willfully"), v. 5.

**3:10 But the day of the Lord will come as a thief; in the which the heavens shall pass away with a great noise, and the elements shall be dissolved with fervent heat, and the earth and the works that are therein shall be burned up.**

## Expanded Translation

However long it may seem to be delayed, be assured, the day of the Lord *will* come. It will come as a thief (that is, suddenly and unexpectedly). At that time the heavens shall pass away, (pass by, disappear, vanish) with a loud, rushing, crashing noise, and the elements or basic components of the earth (atoms?)* shall be disengaged, unbound, and broken apart while they are burning intensely. and the earth and the works (accomplishments of man) that are in it shall be burned up (consumed by fire).**

### But the day of the Lord will come as a thief

The expression, "the day of the Lord" is frequent in the Scripture. and generally points to some great calamity (Isa. 2:12, 13:6, Jer. 46:10). The idea of the phrase seems to be: "You've had *your* day (in living according to your own lusts), now I'll have *mine!*" However, the expression here may point to the second coming of Christ, as it certainly does in I Thes. 5:2. But whether "Lord" here refers to Christ or God, the *event* spoken of by the expression is still the same: the second coming of the Master and the destruction of the world. In *this* passage they may be thought of as the same event. That day will come as a *thief,* that comes quickly, stealthily, and without warning. Suddenly and abruptly, it will be upon us. Compare the teaching of Christ, Matt. 24:42-44.***

### in the which the heavens shall pass away with a great noise

See comments, v. 7. The word *hroizedon* ("great noise") was used anciently of various rushing or roaring noises, as the rushing of wings. the sound of mighty winds, the roaring of mighty waters, the roaring of flames, or the sound of thunder. It is difficult to say with certainty just *what kind* of noise is meant in this

---

*or, possibly, "heavenly bodies." But see notes.
**or, according to other MSS, including the Vatican and Sinaitic, "discovered" or "found out" (*heurisko*). Cp. Eccl. 12:14.
***Many doubt that the Matthew passage refers to Christ's *second* coming. But the same lesson of *preparedness* is taught.

passage, other than it will be *loud* and *roaring.*

With such a sound the earth will "pass away" (*parerchomai,* to go past, pass by, etc.). This expression, to my mind, precludes the idea that the "new heavens" will be the old heavens re-made or "fixed up." The atmosphere surrounding the world, we are told by scientists, has potentially combustible materials. So Peter says, "the heavens *being on fire* shall be dissolved" (v. 12). Two age-old fears of man will be present in the skies on that day: (1) A loud noise or blast. (2) A great fire.

It would not be my place to here make a prophecy that God will somehow employ atomic energy or nuclear weapons to destroy the world. But the reader can certainly see in these words of Peter that such is *possible.*

**and the elements shall be dissolved with fervent heat**

Considerable controversy is waged among the critics here as to the proper meaning of the word "elements" (*stoicheion*). Two meanings are given as possibilities in this passage: (1) heavenly bodies—planets, stars, etc., and (2) the basic components or constituent parts of the earth. The first *is* a possibility, for the word is so used by ancient writers: Diogenes Laertius, Justin, Tryphidorus, and Theophilus. But in other ancient writings (such as Plato's works and the Septuagint Version), it carries the idea of the material elements or components of the universe—the primary material of which anything is made. The word is several times in the New Testament used of those things which are primary or fundamental (that is, the "A-B-C's" of something). In this sense it applies to knowledge: Heb. 5:12 ("rudiments") or to the "basics" of any way of thinking or living (Gal. 4:3, 9; Col. 2:8, 20—"rudiments"). As far as I can see, this word, as it stands in *this context*, is approximately equivalent to our word "atom"— the smallest unitary constituent of a chemical element.

I would take, then, the present passage to teach that the very elements which make up all matter shall disintegrate within the mighty furnace of fire that shall envelop the earth in that day.

The verb "shall be dissolved," is from *luo,* literally, to loosen, unbind, unfasten, disengage. In v. 5 we saw that God, by his mighty power, "compacted" or "put together" the earth. *Now* we find that he is also going to pull it apart—at its very seams! Precisely *what* will happen to this globe when its elements break apart is a moot question—nor is it necessary for us to know.

Peter's main point here is to show the *terribleness* of that great cataclysmic day. Let us be warned! Let us be found faithful to our God! Let us be *ready!* For,

**the earth and the works that are therein shall be burned up**

The word *katakaio* means to consume with fire, burn completely (Matt. 13:30, Acts 19:19), but does not *necessarily* carry with it the thought of obliteration or annihilation. If something is "burned up," its chemical relation is changed and much of it goes up in smoke. Whether this globe will look like a ball of charcoal, or whether it will *exist at all*, after this event, is not answered with certainty in this chapter. (See notes under v. 13.)

Paul also speaks of fire in relationship to Christ's second coming: ". . . at the revelation of the Lord Jesus from heaven with the angels of his power in flaming fire" (II Thes. 1:7).

**3:11-12 Seeing that these things are thus all to be dissolved, what manner of persons ought ye to be in all holy living and godliness, looking for and earnestly desiring the coming of the day of God, by reason of which the heavens being on fire shall be dissolved, and the elements shall melt with fervent heat?**

### Expanded Translation

Realizing that these things [the earth, v. 10; and the skies, v. 12] are all to be broken apart, unfastened, and dissolved in the manner of which I speak, what kind of persons it is necessary and proper for you to be in all things which are manifesations of holy (pure, sanctified, dedicated) living and godliness (devotion, reverence toward God)? looking for (anticipating) and earnestly desiring (eagerly expecting) the coming (appearance, presence) of the day of God. On account of this manifestation of his presence, the heavens, being set on fire and burning shall be caused to disintegrate (break apart, dissolve) and the elements (basic) or primary components of matter, as in v. 10) burning intensely and with great heat, shall be liquified and melted.

---

**Seeing that these things are thus all to be dissolved**

See v. 10. Everything burnable and capable of being dissolved *shall be dissolved* on that day! How this ought to sober every thoughtful mind! The fine estates, the beautiful homes, the lovely gardens, the expensive clothes, the chrome-laden automobiles— ALL shall be dissolved at the command of God. How foolish it is, then, for us to make *material* things the object of primary interest and concern in life.

198

In view of the certainty of this world's doom, the apostle argues
**what manner of persons ought ye to be in all holy living
and godliness (?)**

The word "all" is in the plural number in the Greek, as is
shown in the Expanded Translation. See "godliness" (*eusebeia*)
defined under 1:6.*

### looking for and earnestly desiring the coming of the day of God

That is, the day I am now describing to you. "The day of God"
and "the day of the Lord" (v. 10) are synonymous in these verses.

The worldly man, after reading this account, has every right
to fear and tremble! But the man *who is living as he should*, looks
into the future with the hope that that day is not far distant. He
is "looking for" it (*prosdokao*): to expect, wait for, anticipate.
And he is "earnestly desiring" it (*speudo*): literally, to hasten;
hence to be eager for, etc. (But some, preferring to hold to the
more primary meaning, believe something like "urge on" or "ac-
celerate" to be the proper definition here.)

### by reason of which the heavens being on fire shall be dissolved, and the elements shall melt with fervent heat?

Compare v. 10 and note the difference in wording. Whereas in
that passage we are told the heavens shall "pass away with a
great noise," here we are also told they shall *be on fire* and *dissolved* (the latter word, *luo*, is discussed under v. 10). And whereas in that passage we are told the elements shall be dissolved, here
we are told they shall *melt* (*teko*, to melt, melt down, liquefy;
hence, "to perish or be destroyed by melting"—Thayer).

The only possible picture one can draw from these words is
that of a mighty, flaming, searing holocaust, enveloping the earth
itself and all the atmosphere about it. A day of anticipation and
expectation? Yes, indeed, *for those who are ready to live with
Christ!* When the last trump shall sound, it shall strike terror
into the heart of many. But to the righteous that day shall be a
day of joy, and we may "comfort one another with these words"!
(I Thes. 4:18).

**3:13 But, according to his promise, we look for new heavens and
a new earth, wherein dwelleth righteousness.**

---

*The impersonal verb *dei* ("ought") generally implies *necessity*, and is frequently rendered "must." See, for example, Lk. 2:49, Jn. 3:7, Acts 4:12, 5:29,
9:6, 16:30; Heb. 11:6.

## Expanded Translation

But (though this world shall surely be destroyed as I have described), in accordance with his promise to grant us such, we look with anticipation and expectation for new, fresh, unused heavens and a new, fresh, unused earth.

---

### But, according to his promise,

We are again reminded of our promises, as in 1:4. See also v. 9. The promise of a heavenly home for the righteous is repeated several times in Scripture: Jn. 14:1-3, Lk. 20:34-36 ("that world"), etc. But see especially Isa. 65:17, 22; Rev. 21:1, where the new heavens and new earth are promised. Note our discussion of "the eternal kingdom of our Lord and Saviour Jesus Christ" (1:11). In that new world, righteousness and justice shall "dwell," that is, shall prevail and be practiced everywhere. "And there shall in no wise enter into it anything unclean, or he that maketh an abomination and a lie: but only they that are written in the Lamb's book of life" (Rev. 21:27).

### we look for new heavens and a new earth,

But precisely what is meant by *new* heavens and a *new* earth? The word *kainos*, according to the lexicons, is used with respect to *form* or *quality*, and means fresh, unused, novel. W. E. Vine tells us that it does not necessarily mean new in *time*, but new as to *form* or *quality*, of a different nature from what is contrasted as old. The *"new"* (*kainos*) tomb in which Joseph of Arimathea laid the body of the Lord (Matt. 27:60, Jn. 19:41), was not a tomb recently hewn from the rock, but one that had never yet been used or occupied, in which no dead person had lain (which would have made it ceremonially unclean). It might have been hewn out a hundred years before, but in view of the fact that it had not been *used*, it is termed *kainon* (from *kainos*). So heaven may be ready and waiting for us *now*, and perhaps will wait for another thousand years, but it will still be *kainos* as long as it is unused and unoccupied.

Had Peter wanted to say that the new heavens and earth were only the old remade or cleansed, he would *probably* have chosen another Greek word—*neos*, which also means "new." Thayer says "*neos* denotes the new primarily in reference to *time*, the young, recent; *kainos* denotes the new primarily in reference to quality, the fresh, unworn." This distinction is confirmed by Vine, for in

200

speaking of *neos* he says it "may be a reproduction of the old in quality and character . . ." but no such statement is made of *kainos*, used here.*

Because of the above distinction, along with what is said elsewhere in Scripture, it is difficult to believe that our eternal home will be on *this* globe, for it is very "used," yea, "worn out"! Jesus said, "I *go* to prepare a place for you" (Jn. 14:2). Did Christ *go to some place on earth?***

John saw "a *new* heaven and *new* earth [*kainos* in both instances]: for the first heaven and the first earth are *passed away;* and the sea is no more" (Rev. 21:1). No, the heavens and earth that shall *then be* are *not* the heavens and earth *we have at present*. It shall not be a renovated earth, but "brand new"!

**3:14 Wherefore, beloved, seeing that ye look for these things, give diligence that ye may be found in peace, without spot and blameless in his sight.**

### Expanded Translation

Wherefore (in conclusion) loved ones, in view of the fact that you are looking for and anticipating these things, you must be diligent, exert yourself, and put forth earnest effort to be found in peace, without spot (moral or spiritual blotch) and blameless (without censure) before him (or *in* him).

#### Wherefore, beloved, seeing that ye look for these things

The events just spoken of, and especially the new heavens and new earth (v. 13).
#### give diligence
*spoudazo.* See 1:5, notes.

#### that ye may be found in peace

With whom? The reference could be to peaceful relations

---

*The careful Greek student will want to read Trench, *Synonyms of the New Testament*, pp. 219-225, where *neos* and *kainos* are distinguished.
**The "Jehovah's Witnesses" have made *hamburger* out of this verse! They affirm that the world to be destroyed is only Satan's system of human society. The earthly globe, they say, will remain *forever* and will never be burned up or desolated. (*Make Sure of All Things*, 1053 ed., p. 108). Others have made all kinds of speculations concerning this changed earth and how it shall be used after "cleansing." See *Bornes' Notes* on this verse. Also, *The International Standard Bible Encyclopaedia*, Vol. IV, pp. 2357-2358.

among brethren and within the church (Eph. 4:2). But in view of the *context*, peace *with God* seems primarily to be meant. "Whosoever therefore would be a friend of the world maketh himself an enemy of God" (Jas. 4:4b). See Rom. 5:1-2. Peter speaks of God's peace in its various aspects; I Pet. 1:2, 3:10-11, 5:14; II Pet. 1:2.

### without spot and blameless in his sight

The false teachers were "spots and blemishes" (2:13). Christians are to be "spotless," (*aspilos*). They must be free from the vices whice soil and stain their garments—garments made white in the blood of the Lamb.

To be "blameless" (*amometos*) is to live a life that cannot truthfully be censured—that is irreprehensible (Phil. 2:15).

### 3:15 And account that the longsuffering of our Lord is salvation; even as our beloved brother Paul also, according to the wisdom given him, wrote unto you;

### Expanded Translation

And, instead of considering his delaying to come as a proof that he will never come, you must account (deem, consider) that the patience, forbearance, and longsuffering of our Lord provides a means and opportunity for the salvation of sinners (giving them time to repent); even as (just as) our beloved and cherished brother Paul, in accordance with the wisdom (skill and discretion in imparting Christian truth*) which was imparted to him by God, wrote unto you;

---

### And account that the longsuffering of our Lord is salvation

See v. 9, and notes there. We must look upon the longsuffering of God for what it *is*—a staying of his wrath to give men more time to repent and turn to Him—not for what it may *appear* to the world to be. The ungodly make a mockery of God's promise because they have not seen its fulfillment (vs. 3-4), and because it seems *to them* he is "slack" (slow, behind) in bringing about the destruction of the world. The *truth* is that God is *longsuffering*, and *this* is why the earth continues as it has. Christians must consider the longsuffering of God *in this light*, knowing that every day God is only allowing the world to survive so that a few more souls may come to know Christ as their Saviour.

---

*Thayer, citing this verse under *sophia*.

202

The word "salvation" (*soteria*) is sometimes used contextually to refer to the *means* or *opportunity* for salvation: Acts 13:26. Rom. 11:11, Heb. 2:3. It may be so considered here. *Because of* God's longsuffering, many will see heaven who would *not* otherwise. His longsuffering provides a means of attaining, an opportunity to accept, and results in, the SALVATION of sinners.

**even as our beloved brother Paul also, according to the wisdom given to him, wrote unto you**

A remarkable example of Christian love is revealed here. Peter was sharply rebuked by this apostle in Antioch some years before (Gal. 2:11ff.). But he is now "our" (not just "your") "beloved brother." True Christians grow to love those who, *out of love for them*, have rebuked them for their evil ways.

"Wisdom" (*sophia*) properly signifies broad and full intelligence, knowledge, ability, or skill. Its *precise* meaning is determined by the context. "The wisdom given him" here refers to God-given wisdom, that is, the *Divine* wisdom which he had as an inspired apostle. Paul not only had skill and discretion in imparting Christian truth, but the very *source* of his wisdom was Christ (Gal. 1:15-17), "in whom are all the treasures of wisdom and knowledge hidden" (Col. 2:3). Paul appealed to his own statements as the words of God. "If any man thinketh himself to be a prophet, or spiritual, let him take knowledge of the things that I write unto you, that they are the *commandments of the Lord*" (I Cor. 14:37).

With such wisdom Paul wrote all his epistles, but he is here said to have written *to these people* concerning "these things" (v. 16), that is, the events pertaining to the end of the world. In 3:1 it is seen that the same persons are addressed in this epistle as in the first—i.e., "the elect who are sojourners of the Dispersion in Pontus, Galatia, Cappadocia, Asia, and Bithynia" (I Pet. 1:1. See notes there for the meaning of "sojourners" and "Dispersion").

One immediately recognizes these countries as areas where Paul's letters circulated. He wrote to the "churches" of Galatia (Gal. 1:2), to the Ephesians in the province of Asia, to the Colossians (including the Laodiceans, Col. 4:16) in the same country (and not far from Lycia and Pamphylia). His letters to Timothy were written while that young man was in Ephesus (I Tim. 1:3). These epistles, circulating in the area (and also perverted, v. 16), spoke of these events, as did "all his epistles."

But the *particular* similarity of Paul's writings cited in *this* verse is the *longsuffering of God* as it pertains to the salvation of man. This general theme is treated by Paul in various places in the epistles he sent to the Christians of Asia Minor.

**3:16 as also in all his epistles, speaking in them of these things; wherein are some things hard to be understood, which the ignorant and unstedfast wrest, as they do also the other scriptures, unto their own destruction.**

### Expanded Translation

as also is true in all his epistles (letters), speaking in them concerning these very things (of which I have just spoken). In these epistles certain things (statements) are hard to understand, which the unlearned, (uninstructed, ignorant) and unstedfast (unsettled, unstable) wrench, distort, and pervert, as they do also the other scriptures, unto their own destruction, ruin, and damnation.

---

**as also in all his epistles, speaking in them of these things**

The letters of Paul, particularly those addressed to the Thessalonians, say much concerning the very subjects treated in this epistle (and especially of matters pertaining to the end of the world, which seems primarily to be meant by "these things").

It is well to note here that many of Paul's writings were now in circulation—and so well-known that Peter assumes his readers are acquainted with them. As was mentioned in the *Introduction*, this fact, of necessity, points to a relatively late date for this epistle. Notice, also, that *Peter* believed Paul's writings to be inspired, for he placed them alongside "the other scriptures." Therefore to deny that Paul's writings deserve to be classified as "scripture," is also to impeach the truthfulness and inspiration of Peter.

**wherein are some things hard to be understood**

That is, some of the subjects and statements treated in Paul's epistles. Any careful student of his writings will not find it hard to admit this truth! But notice that Peter does *not* say, "for this reason cast them aside and do not study them"! The book of Revelation certainly is not easily understood, but the Holy Spirit says, "Blessed is he that readeth, and they that hear the words of the prophecy, and keep the things which are written therein . . ." (Rev. 1:3).

**which the ignorant and unstedfast wrest, as they do also the other scriptures, unto their own destruction**

The word rendered "wrest" (*strebloo*) is akin to *streble*, a windlass, wrench, instrument of torture, rack. Thus the word properly means "to distort (or stretch) the limbs on a rack." Used here metaphorically, the reference is to "one who wrests or tortures language" (Thayer), i.e., the language and words of scripture.

And who does this? The ignorant and unstedfast—often members of the same class. If they would admit their ignorance, seek out the truth, and *abide* by it, all would be well for them. But persisting in such ways, their only end is destruction. See notes, 2:1. (On "destruction," *apoleia*, see under v. 6, "perished.")

**3:17 Ye therefore, beloved, knowing these things beforehand, beware lest, being carried away with the error of the wicked, ye fall from your own stedfastness.**

## Expanded Translation

You therefore, loved ones, knowing ahead of time that these men treat the scripture in this manner, be on the watch! Keep guard! Lest, having been carried away (led astray) by the error (wrong opinion, misleading doctrines) of the wicked, lawless and unrestrained, you fall from (and thus *lose*) your own stedfastness and firmness.

---

### Ye therefore, beloved, knowing these things beforehand

"To be forewarned is to be forearmed," and so should it be with Christians today. False teachers are still "torturing" the truth, and such torturing ought to be painful to the heart of all who have a love for genuine, saving knowledge. But more than that, Peter exhorts us to

### beware lest, being carried away with the error of the wicked, ye fall from your own stedfastness

The word rendered "beware" (*phulasso*) means to be on watch, keep guard, protect. But it appears here in the middle voice, and means specifically to be on one's guard (against), keep oneself from. And being in the aorist tense and imperative mode, we have here a very pointed *command* to be heeded at once! How it is needed in this day when false teachings (and the conveyors of such) are everywhere! They may fairly *carry us away* (*sunapago*). See also Gal. 2:13.

Their teachings are clearly labelled by the apostle, who terms them "error" (*plane*), literally, a wandering, straying about. The word here signifies teachings that *cause one* to wander or stray from the right way, i.e., those doctrines which mislead one. Christian, *keep your guard up!* Be on the watch! (Compare I Pet. 5:8.)

We again find here (as in 2:1-3, 19) that the *false teacher himself* is living in sin. The word "wicked" (*athesmos*) is made up of the alpha negative plus *thesmos*, law custom. It therefore describes one who breaks through the restraints of law and conscience and gratifies his lusts—a lawless, unrestrained, licentious individual. Its only other New Testament occurrence is in 2:7, where the above definition is also borne out by the context.

The next step is only natural if we begin to cater to these men.

**lest ye fall from your own stedfastness**

In verse 16 the "unstedfast" (*asteriktos*) were those headed for destruction. Here *Christians* are warned to be on guard lest *they* fall from *their* stedfastness and be found in the same plight as the false teacher. We are reminded of the exhortation of our Lord, "Let them alone: they are blind guides. And if the blind guide the blind, both shall fall into a pit" (Matt. 15:14).

To be in a state of stedfastness (*sterigmos*) is to be in a settled or firm state of mind; therefore fixed and stable in fulfilling spiritual responsibilities. From this condition we may *fall* (*ekpipto*, fall out of, fall from, fall off). This very same word appears in I Peter 1:24, "the flower falleth . . ." It takes time to become a truly stedfast Christian, and the false teachers were successful in enticing "unstedfast souls" (2:14) and "those who are just escaping from them that live in error" (2:18). But those *here* described are now stedfast. Are they therefore out of danger? No! "Wherefore let him that thinketh he standeth take heed lest he fall" (I Cor. 10:12).

**3:18 But grow in the grace and knowledge of our Lord and Saviour Jesus Christ. To him be the glory both now and forever. Amen.**

### Expanded Translation

But rather than falling from your own stedfastness, you must keep on growing (increasing, enlarging) in that way of living which gains the grace (favor, acceptance) and knowledge (understanding) of our Lord and Saviour Jesus Christ. To him be the glory (praise, honor) both now and forever (literally, unto the day of eternity).

---

**But grow in the grace and knowledge of our Lord and Saviour Jesus Christ**

The word "grow" (*auxano*) is in the present imperative—"continue growing!" Peter wished God's grace upon them at the beginning (1:2), but he wants it to be increased. He also wants them to grow in *knowledge* (*gnosis*), one of those virtues mentioned in the cluster found in 1:5-7, which was to be "yours and abound" (1:8). Thus Peter is not saying his readers had no grace or knowledge, but that these should and must cause them to increase!

**to him be the glory both now and forever**

Literally, "unto (or *for*) the day of eternity," i.e., "for all time, forever" (Thayer). That day shall be a "day" indeed—a day that shall never end!

## QUESTIONS OVER CHAPTER THREE

1. What direct statement in this chapter causes us to believe Peter was the author of both books bearing his name?
2. What was his common objective for both books?
3. Whose *words* were the Christians to remember?
4. Whose *commandment*?
5. In what days were the mockers to come?
6. The mockers were saying, "Where is the promise of _____ _____(?)"
7. How had the world continued since creation, according to these fellows?
8. Was their history accurate?
9. Were they sincerely trying to remember the facts?
10. What part of history was forgotten?
11. Explain: "an earth compacted out of water and amidst water" (v. 5).
12. Give a brief but accurate definition of the word "perish" (*apollumi*), v. 6.
13. With what other word (which occurs several times in this chapter) is it closely related?
14. What are the three "heavens" of the Bible?
15. Which of the three is meant when the word is used in *this chapter*?

16. In v. 7 we are told the earth has been "stored up for fire," and v. 10 also speaks of the effects of fire on the earth. In what *other* New Testament passage is fire connected with the second coming of Christ?
17. Finish v. 8: "But forget not this one thing, beloved, one day . . ."
18. How does this statement fit into the *context*?
19. Explain: "The Lord is not *slack* concerning his promise . . ." (v. 9).
20. Does God hope some people never repent?
21. What two basic arguments of the mockers (both false) has Peter now refuted?
22. In *what way* will "the day of the Lord" come as a *thief*?
23. At that time the heavens shall _____ _____ with a _____ _____ (?)
24. What are the "elements" which shall be dissolved with fervent heat? (Give two possible answers.)
25. "Seeing that these things are thus all to be dissolved," what should the effect be upon our daily lives?
26. How should Christians regard "the coming of the day of God"?
27. What is probably true of your life if you cannot think upon Christ's coming with eagerness and joy?
28. Will just the *earth* be dissolved at that time?
29. How could the *sky* be on fire?
30. The elements shall both _____ and _____ with fervent heat (vs. 10, 12).
31. We look for new heavens and a new earth "according to his promise." What promise? Where is it found?
32. In what sense will the future heavens and earth be "new"?
33. Do you believe heaven will be on this globe? Why, or why not?
34. What will dwell there? (one word.)
35. Do you believe any of our recent inventions pertaining to the use (or misuse) of atomic energy and nuclear weapons could play a part in the world's destruction?
36. How should we be found in the day of Christ's coming?
37. "And account that the longsuffering of our Lord is _____ _____" (?) Now explain this statement.
38. Peter terms Paul "our _____ _____" (?)

39. By what power or influence did Paul write (using Peter's words).
40. Did Paul ever write to the same people as Peter?
41. Did Peter say his own writings were hard to understand?
42. Should we only study Scriptures that are easily understood? (Prove answer.)
43. How does one "wrest" scripture?
44. What class of persons do this? (According to Peter.)
45. How do you *know* Peter regarded Paul's writings as inspired?
46. Is it possible to fall from a state of steadfastness?
47. What is Peter's final exhortation to the Christians?

# BIBLIOGRAPHY

Here is a partial list of the works used:

## I. LEXICONS

1. *A Greek-English Lexicon of the New Testament*, by C. L. W. Grimm. Translated from the German, revised and enlarged by J. H. Thayer. American Book Co., New York.

2. *A Manual Greek Lexicon of the New Testament*, by G. Abbott Smith. Charles Scribner's Sons, New York. 1953.

3. *A Greek-English Lexicon to the New Testament*, by Thomas Sheldon Green. 24th Edition. Samuel Bagster & Sons Limited, 80 Wigmore St., London.

4. *The Analytical Greek Lexicon*. Harper and Brothers, New York.

5. *The Vocabulary of the Greek New Testament*, illustrated from the Papyri and other non-literary sources, by J. H. Moulton and G. M. Milligan. Wm. B. Eerdmans Publishing Co., Grand Rapids, Michigan. 1959.

6. *A Greek-English Lexicon*, by Henry G. Lidell and Robert Scott. A New Edition, revised and augmented throughout, by Henry Stuart Jones and Roderick Mckenzie. Unabridged edition of 1940, reprinted, 1958. OXFORD, at the Clarendon Press.

7. *A Greek-English Lexicon of the New Testament* and Other Early Christian Literature. A translation and adaptation of Walter Bauer's Greek-German *Worterbuch*. Fourth Revised and Augmented Edition. By Wm. G. Arndt and F. Wilbur Gingrich. The University of Chicago Press, Chicago, Illinois. 1952.

8. *An Expository Dictionary of New Testament Words*, with their Precise Meanings for English Readers. By W. E. Vine. Oliphants Ltd., London, Edinburgh. 1953 Ed.

9. *Word Studies in the New Testament*. By Marvin R. Vincent. Volume I. Wm. B. Eerdmans Publishing Co., Grand Rapids, Michigan.

10. *The Interlinear Translation of The Greek New Testament* (Greek-English New Testament Lexicon section). George-Ricker Berry. Wilcox and Follett Co., Chicago. 1954.

11. *A Pocket Lexicon to the Greek New Testament*, by A. Souter. OXFORD at the Clarendon Press, London. 1918 Ed. Reprinted, 1953.

# PREFACE

The objective of *The Bible Study Textbook Series* is to improve the average Christian's knowledge and understanding of the Scriptures. I have tried to keep this objective in mind in the process of compiling this material. References are frequently made to Greek words (normally in their lexicon form), but these words are all anglicized and no knowledge of that language is necessary to understand these notes.

The *Expanded Translation* is as original as I could make it with my present knowledge and resources. It is best to consider this part of the work as an expression of the whole scope and meaning of the passage translated. For this reason, the Greek studnt will frequently notice words (and even phrases) not actually present in the original text. In those instances, the context and setting seemed to justify the insertion of such words or phrases. By this method of translation, it is hoped that misunderstandings and false ideas concerning the meaning of a passage will be kept to a minimum. But I have tried to be discreet and conservative in using words not found in the original, so that it may still be referred to as a translation and not a commentary. As a rule, words that fall within a parentheses indicate that the meaning of the previous word is being amplified; but this is not always true, and the reader may consider the decision of the translator to insert or omit these marks as purely arbitrary.

A Biographical list will be found in the closing pages. Authors and their works not mentioned in the footnotes are found there.

So many persons have assisted me in the compilation and arrangement of this volume that two or three pages would be necessary to record their names. However, a few acknowledgments are in order. To sister Eileen Crist, who has typed this entire work at least twice in the process of eliminating obscurities and errors, goes my heartfelt thanks. She has not only assisted me in this project, but in numerous others, and has never received a cent for her labors. Like Phoebe, "she hath been a helper of many, and of mine own self" (Rom. 16:2).

The encouragement of my wife has been a constant source of inspiration. She has gone out of her way to see to it that I had sufficient time to study and write. J. Charles Dailey has also provided much encouragement, with his appreciative remarks concerning the value of the book's contents. In addition, he gave many valuable suggestions concerning sentence structure and wording.

The original Scriptures were written by God through men

"moved by the Holy Spirit" (II Pet. 1:21). All other books were written by fallible man. This book is no exception. The author would sincerely appreciate letters pointing out ways in which the material might be improved, or his understanding of any passage made more accurate. Meanwhile, if these pages shall help some soul "grow in the grace and knowledge of Christ" (II Pet. 3:18). I shall feel genuinely rewarded.

—BRUCE OBERST

Suggested memory verses:

      1:3-5; 13-20.
      2:1-2; 10-11; 17.
      3:16 (women); 7-9 (men); 15-16; 21.
      4:15-16.
      5:5-9.

## II. COMMENTARIES

1. *The Pulpit Commentary*. Edited by H. D. M. Spence and Joseph S. Excell. Vol. 50. Funk & Wagnalls Co., New York.

2. *A Commentary on the Holy Scriptures*: Critical, Doctrinal and Homiletical, with Special Reference to Ministers and Students. By John Peter Lange. Translated from the German and edited by Philip Schaff. New York: Charles Scribner's Sons, 1915.

3. *The New Bible Commentary*, Davidson, Stibbs, and Kevan. Wm. B. Eerdmans Publishing Co., Grand Rapids, Michigan, 1953.

4. *Bible Commentary*, by E. M. Zerr. Vol. Six. Mission Messenger, 7505 Trenton Ave., St. Louis 14, Missouri. 1954.

5. *Ellicott's Commentary on the Whole Bible*, Vol. VIII. Edited by Charles John Ellicott. Zondervan Publishing House, Grand Rapids, Michigan. 1954.

6. *Barnes' Notes on the New Testament*, James-Jude. Edited by Robert Frew. Baker Book House, Grand Rapids 6, Mich., 1951.

7. *A Critical, Experimental and Practical Commentary on the Old and New Testaments*, by Jamieson, Fausset, and Brown. Vol. VI. Wm. B. Eerdmans Publishing Co., Grand Rapids, Mich. 1948.

8. *The Interpretation of The Epistles of St. Peter, St. John and St. Jude*, by R. C. H. Lenski. The Wartburg Press, Columbus, Ohio. 1945.

9. *A Commentary on the New Testament Epistles of Peter, John, and Jude*. Gospel Advocate Co., Nashville, Tenn. 1958. By Guy N. Wood.

10. *A Commentary and Exposition of the Epistles of James, Peter, John and Jude*, by N. T. Caton. Gospel Light Publishing Co., Delight, Arkansas.

11. *The People's New Testament with Explanatory Notes*, by B. W. Johnson. Vol. II.

12. *The Apostolical Epistles*, by James Macknight. A New Edition. Baker Book House, Grand Rapids, Michigan. 1949.

## III. OTHER BOOKS USED (partial list)

1. *Illustrations of Holy Scripture*, by George Bush. J. B. Lippincott & Co., 1865.

2. *A Manual of Church History*, by Albert Henry Newman. Vol. I. The American Baptist Publication Society, Philadelphia. 1953.

3. *The Life and Works of Flavius Josephus*. Translated from the Greek by William Whiston. Standard Edition. The John C. Winston Co., Philadelphia.

Also the following: The Encyclopaedia Americana, The Encyclopaedia Brittanica, several atlases, The International Standard Bible Encyclopaedia, The Schaff-Herzofi Encylopaedia of Religious Knowledge, Chamber's Encyclopaedia, and six or seven different translations of the New Testament.

While Peter thought on the vision, the Spirit said unto him, Behold three men seek thee, Arise therefore, and get thee down, and go with them, doubting nothing: for I have sent them. Acts 10: 19-20.